“Labor is not a Commodity!”

North American Studies

Edited by the The John F. Kennedy Institute for North American Studies of Freie Universität Berlin, the Center for North American Studies (ZENAF) of Goethe-Universität Frankfurt am Main and the Department of English and American Studies of Humboldt-Universität zu Berlin.

Volume 37

Philipp Reick is a Martin Buber postdoctoral fellow at the Hebrew University of Jerusalem.

Philipp Reick

"Labor is not a Commodity!"

The Movement to Shorten the Workday in Late Nineteenth-Century Berlin and New York

Campus Verlag
Frankfurt/New York

The publication of this book was made possible through generous grants from the Ernst Reuter Society, the FAZIT-STIFTUNG Gemeinnützige Verlagsgesellschaft mbH and the Graduate School of North American Studies, Freie Universität Berlin.

ISBN 978-3-593-50627-2 Print
ISBN 978-3-593-43506-0 E-Book (PDF)

Werderstr. 10, 69469 Weinheim, info@campus.de.
Cover design: Beltz Verlagsgruppe GmbH & Co. KG
Cover illustration: Parade of working men on strike for an eight hour work day in New York City by Matthew Somerville Morgan, Frank Leslie's Illustrated Newspaper, June 29, 1872
Printing office and bookbinder: Libri Plureos GmbH, Friedensallee 273, 22763 Hamburg
Printed in Germany

www.campus.de
www.press.uchicago.edu

Contents

Acknowledgements

Over the past three years, I have spent an enormous amount of time in front of microfilm readers in the basements and backrooms of libraries and archives. I am grateful to all the people who made this experience nevertheless a pleasant one. I thank the staff at Tamiment Library & Robert F. Wagner Labor Archives at New York University for providing an excellent atmosphere for archival research. I also would like to extend my gratitude to the archival staff at the International Institute of Social History in Amsterdam, the New York Public Library, the Center for Berlin Studies at the Berlin Central and Regional Library, the Library of the German Federal Archive in Berlin-Lichterfelde, and the Prussian Privy State Archives. I wish to thank Gabi Bodmeier, Katja Mertin, and David Bosold at the Graduate School of North American Studies, as well the entire team at the Library of the John F. Kennedy Institute at FU Berlin and Julia Mayer in particular, who is sadly missed. I also thank Daniel Moure García for his excellent copy-editing service. Research for this book has been funded by the Excellence Initiative of the German Research Foundation. The publication has been made possible by generous funding from the Ernst-Reuter-Stiftung, the FAZIT-Stiftung, and the Graduate School of North American Studies. Parts of Chapter 6 have been previously published in Vol. 6, No. 1 (2015) of "Interdisciplines: Journal of History and Sociolgy."

Many people have offered helpful criticisms and suggestions. In particular, I wish to thank M. Michaela Hampf, Thomas Welskopp, and Nancy Fraser, who supervised my dissertation project. In addition, I would like to express my gratitude to Andreas Etges, Gudrun Löhrer, and Victoria Tafferner, as well as the GSNAS class of 2011, for feedback during an early phase of this project. Many thanks go to Joshua B. Freeman for his support during my visiting scholarship at the CUNY Graduate Center. Finally, I am very grateful to John Connelly at UC Berkeley, who convinced me to become a historian in the first place. Important comments and criticism also came from friends who read parts of the manuscript. In particular, I wish to thank Nils Utermöhlen and Matthias Martin Becker, who first introduced me to Karl Polanyi's *Great Transformation* in a highly appreciated reading group. I also thank my brother Robert for his comments at a time when he was wrapping up his own dissertation in philosophy. Likewise, I thank my uncle Michael for his support. A very special thanks goes to Franziska Nadler for her healthy distrust of office chairs. To more than anyone else, I am grateful to my parents, who always supported my interest in what Germans call the "breadless arts." I dedicate this study to their memory.

Jerusalem,
September 2016

Preface

The past three decades have witnessed an astonishing rebirth of market liberalism. Although it is hardly conceivable for present-day observers, the demand to deregulate markets revolutionized established notions of economic stability and social progress. After all, markets had been anything but free for decades. During Keynesian postwar prosperity, European and North American markets were embedded in a complex system of democratically legitimized control. Labor markets were regulated by protective legislation and strong welfare states; real-estate markets were restricted by public-housing programs; currency markets were governed by an international system of fixed exchange rates. Yet the paradigm of regulated markets dissolved quickly in the late 1970s due to its apparent inability to address the era's major challenge of *stagflation*. Heavily indebted to the liberal legacy of the nineteenth century, the neoliberal turn of the 1980s thus ended the intermezzo of market regulation. While this free-market renaissance was largely conceived of in the centers of political power across Western Europe and the US, its message was never confined to these regions. From Latin America in the 1980s to the disintegrating Soviet Union in the early 1990s to South East Asia at the turn of the century, the demand to free markets from extra-economic control defined the structural adjustments that transformed the various local, national, and inter-regional economies. Promoted by Western governments and administered as well as sanctioned by powerful international institutions, the free-market creed quickly developed into a global reality. In so doing, it gained center stage in political discourse. Following the transformation of the US subprime mortgage crisis into global financial turmoil, the free-market paradigm tightened its already firm grip as severe budget cuts were implemented in order to restore the confidence of markets. According to then Prime Minister David Cameron, the 2010s thus heralded a new "Decade of Austerity" in the international political economy. And the lesson this decade had to teach was clear: The trust of markets would not be won easily.[1]

Given what Thomas Piketty termed the "sacralization of the market" in today's politics and economics, it is hardly surprising that current social opposition focuses on the notion of self-regulating markets as well.[2] When on May 15, 2011, hundreds of thousands of protesters took to the streets across Spain in what has become known the *Movimiento 15 de Mayo*, they did so under the unifying and programmatic slogan: "We are not commodities in the hands of politicians and bankers!"[3] What unites much of present-day protest is the conviction that humans differ essentially from market commodities, and therefore should not be exposed defenselessly to unregulated labor, housing, or currency markets. Rather, societies are expected to provide some means of protection against the intrusion of powerful markets. What the protesters call for is a de-commodification of social relations, which would in turn foster the well-being of all—or at least "the 99%"—instead of promote the interests of the few. From Occupy Wall Street in New York to the *Geração à Rasca* in Lisbon and the *Indignados* in Madrid and Athens, these movements embrace the idea that the unregulated commodification of natural entities (such as land or genes) and human interaction (such as public

---

1 Hannah Kuchler, "Cameron Warns of Decade of Austerity," *Financial Times online*, 19 July 2012, http://on.ft.com/Malp18. From Ireland to Spain, from Greece to the US, cuts are regularly sold as "painful" but "necessary" means for economic recovery and market reassurance; see "Herrera cree que el nuevo ajuste 'produce dolor' pero lo ve necesario," *ABC online*, 11 July 2012, http://www.abc.es/20120711/local-castilla-leon/abci-herrera-cree-necesario-tratamiento-201207111416.html; "EU Austerity Drive Country by Country," *BBC online*, 21 May 2012, http://www.bbc.co.uk/news/10162176; Alan Silverleib and Tom Cohen, "Democrats, Republicans Agree on a Budget Deal," *CNN online*, 9 April 2011, http://edition.cnn.com/2011/POLITICS/04/08/congress.budget; "Zinsen steigen stark: Spanien sieht sich in äußerst heiklen Phase," *FOCUS Online*, 24 April 2012, http://www.focus.de/finanzen/news/staatsverschuldung/zinsen-steigen-stark-spanien-sieht-sich-in-aeusserst-heiklen-phase_aid_742303.html; David McKittrick, "Ireland's Austerity D-Day: How much Pain Can It Take?" *The Independent online*, 30 May 2012, http://www.independent.co.uk/news/world/europe/irelands-austerity-d-day-how-much-pain-can-it-take-7800898.html; "Remarks with Greek Foreign Minister Stavros Lambrinidis before Their Meeting," *US Department of State*, 27 October 2011, http://www.state.gov/secretary/20092013clinton/rm/2011/10/176305.htm (all accessed 7 August 2016).

2 Piketty, "Das Ende des Kapitalismus," 48.

3 This is the official slogan of "Real Democracy Now," one of the most visible groups in the mobilization of protests in 2011; see "¡Democracia Real YA! ¡No Somos Mercancía en Manos de Políticos y Banqueros!" http://www.democraciarealya.es/ (accessed 7 August 2016).

health or higher education) threatens the democratic constitution and very existence of their respective communities.

Yet the phenomenon of commodification not only constitutes a central element in present-day economics and social-movement rhetoric, it also provides an important analytical category for the social sciences that study these movements.[4] Social historiography, in contrast, has all but neglected the impact of commodification on the emergence of past social movements. This disregard is especially puzzling for a period that gave birth to the first generation of laborers whose life and work were fully determined by market relations. While the rise of organized labor in the nineteenth century has produced an enormous wealth of historical scholarship, the role that the phenomenon of commodification played in this process has been largely ignored by Marxist and non-Marxist historiography alike. In the first chapters of *Das Kapital*, Marx created a captivating tension that seemingly had to erupt in the complex relation between sellers and buyers. Yet, Marx argued with evident delight, surplus value could not be generated through the exchange of equivalents. He thus took the reader by the hand and led her into the dark halls of capitalist production, away from the apparently meaningless sphere of circulation.[5] Largely following this logic, Marxist historiography has concentrated on the sphere of production as the intrinsic site of exploitation. As much as Marx's notion of commodity fetishism has influenced politico-philosophical ideas about the reification of social relations, it has hardly affected the historiography of organized labor and working-class movements.[6]

But Marxist historians have not been alone in neglecting this question. Specializing in the history of particular sectors and individual corporations or focusing on questions of political participation and social mobility, non-Marxist historiography of nineteenth-century market relations has largely

4 Commodification (and de-commodification) occupy a prominent place in different fields of social-movement research. For housing movements, see Holm and Kühberger (eds.), *Wohnraum ist keine Ware*; Pattillo, "Housing: Commodity versus Right;" Marcuse, "The Housing Change We Need." For environmental movements, see Halbert, "Resistance Is Fertile." For discussions about the ambiguity of female labor commodification and de-commodification, see Fraser, "Feminism, Capitalism and the Cunning of History;" Federici, *Revolution at Point Zero*. For a discussion about the impact of commodification on the discipline of sociology in general, see Burawoy, "Public Sociology vs. the Market."

5 Marx, *Das Kapital* I, 190–191.

6 Cf. Welskopp, "Markt und Klasse." For the philosophical classic on the concept of commodification and consciousness, see Lukács, *Geschichte und Klassenbewusstsein*, 170–355. For a more recent discussion, see Honneth, *Reification*.

focused on consumption, finance, or services.[7] The labor market has primarily attracted the interest of economic historians studying large-scale developments, such as wage or employment levels, or of political-institutional historians concentrating on the emergence of welfare states and social security. As much as scholarly interest in the exchange of consumer goods, services, and ideas has thus grown over the past two decades, it has utterly neglected the impact that the commodification of labor had on the mindset of working people and their constitution as a social class.[8] In fact, it is surprising how little influence the concept of commodification has had on the generation of social historians who came of intellectual age witnessing the fierce resistance of movements protesting the marketization of social relations and resources since the late 1980s. While these movements continue to oppose the global commodification of water, land, seeds, and emissions; while urban movements keep resisting the commodification of housing and infrastructure; while, in short, ideas about the *commoning* of public life experience a powerful revival, Social History still lacks an understanding of the role that the phenomenon of commodification played in the making of modern working classes.

Against this backdrop, Thomas Welskopp argues that social historiography has accepted too easily the notion that, from the early to mid-nineteenth century onwards, an increasingly homogenizing workforce resisted the spread of wage labor primarily because it opposed the expropriation of abstract labor power. In his comprehensive study of early German social-democracy, Welskopp shows that well into the 1870s, socialist workers, craftsmen, and intellectuals continued to reject the commodification of labor because it defied the prevalent equation of producerist independence and political participation. According to this interpretation, the commodification of labor and the spread of the free market jeopardized the worker's quest for political rights.[9] Welskopp's contribution indicates that an analy-

---

7 Cf. Abelshauser, *Die BASF;* Baumann, *Von der Stahlhütte zum Verarbeitungskonzern*; Bodenhorn, *A History of Banking in Antebellum America*; Davis and Cull, *International Capital Markets*; Eichengreen, *Globalizing Capital*; Feldenkirchen, *Siemens*; Mizen (ed.), *Monetary History*.

8 Cf. Nolte, "Der Durchbruch der amerikanischen Marktgesellschaft;" Wilentz, "Society, Politics, and the Market Revolution."

9 Welskopp, *Das Banner der Brüderlichkeit*, 60–97; Welskopp, "Diktatur der Einsicht: Die SPD begeht ihren 140. Geburtstag," *Berliner Zeitung*, 23 May 2003. Paul Nolte highlights the fruitfulness of the concept of commodification for the historical study of nature and ecology; see Nolte, "Amerikanische Sozialgeschichte in der Erweiterung," 373.

sis of past struggles for de-commodification promises to reveal the diversity of social opposition in the past. On the other side of the Atlantic, New Labor Historians likewise draw attention to the nexus of the free-market paradigm and nineteenth-century labor opposition. In his celebrated book *Citizen Worker*, David Montgomery argues that the further the democratization of the American polity progressed, the more the economy was stripped of democratic control. In the second half of the century, organized labor succeeded in influencing local, state, and federal decision-making processes, yet workers also learned that the conditions under which they worked were increasingly exempt from democratic control and subjected to the supposedly immutable law of supply and demand. Thus the very egalitarian promises that American workers had been fighting for were increasingly jeopardized "by an emerging economic system propelled by the quest for private profits within the parameters set by market forces."[10]

Inspired by these approaches, this study argues that resistance against commodification at the dawn of the Second Industrial Revolution was a central feature of working-class discourse that has nonetheless been widely ignored. Rather than investigating the notion of commodification from a purely theoretical perspective, this book asks what role the concept played in the formulation of workers' demands. One of the key demands of organized labor in the second half of the nineteenth century was the introduction of a shorter working day. The following pages thus explore the ideas that shorter-hour activists in two centers of mid- to late nineteenth-century organized labor expressed vis à-vis the commodification of work and the logic of markets. In so doing, this study reveals that the historical rhetoric and reality of free labor markets profoundly influenced protective struggles on both sides of the Atlantic. Assuming that such struggles did not necessarily promote the equal protection of all members of society, the book examines what the demand for protection from unregulated commodification meant for working women in Berlin and New York. In the 1860s and early 1870s, women were being drawn in large numbers to the labor markets of the two urban economies. Due to their peculiar political and social position, the protective notion of de-commodification could be both promising for and menacing to women's struggles for participation and equality.

10 Montgomery, *Citizen Worker*, 2.

The book is divided into thematically distinct chapters. This arrangement caters to the respective wants of readers. Those less attracted by theoretical and methodological questions, for instance, may skip the Introduction; those particularly interested in the historical application of contemporary feminist theory may fast forward to Chapter 6; etc. The following provides a brief overview of each chapter. As indicated above, the Introduction provides a detailed discussion of theory and methods. Given its length and centrality, the Introduction is considered the first chapter of the study. Here, I define what exactly I mean by commodification, how I understand the relationship between commodification and the free market, why I assume that the historical shorter-hour struggle of the 1860s and early 1870s in fact qualifies as a de-commodifying movement, why I think that a comparison is helpful for analyzing the movement, why Berlin and New York City are appropriate places for comparative study, and, finally, why I focus on the few years between the end of the Civil War and the beginning of the Long Depression. The Introduction (or Chapter 1) is topped off with an overview of the current state of research and the primary sources used in this study.

Chapter 2 then provides the historical context out of which the shorter-hour struggle emerged. Portraying the rise of the free market as both an intellectual paradigm and an everyday reality, this chapter concentrates on the legislation that governed wage labor in mid-nineteenth-century Berlin and New York. In addition, Chapter 2 introduces the state of organized labor in the two cities at the end of the Civil War. In this chapter, the reader will find a comprehensive socio-economic comparison of the two cities, including their expanding worlds of working-class life and the organizations these worlds gave birth to.

Having provided the historical background, the following three chapters explore the rationale that fueled the shorter-hour movements of Berlin and New York. Rather than presenting a chronological account of the local movements, these chapters are organized along the different political, social, and economic spheres from which the respective movements derived legitimacy. Echoing Clifford Geertz, Ira Katznelson suggests that if we are prepared to see culture as "webs of significance," then we might see that "these webs were spun by working people suspended between very hard and jagged economic, social, and political rocks."[11] This study provides an interpretation of the webs that working people in Berlin and New York spun

11 Katznelson, "Working-Class Formation," 22.

between those rocks. With a clear focus on the polity, Chapter 3 analyzes how the early workers' movement assessed the commodification of labor vis-à-vis claims to political participation. In so doing, this chapter reveals that shorter-hour activists feared the free market as a threat to civic rights and democratic sovereignty. Moving from polity to society, Chapter 4 explores how commodification jeopardized working-class notions of dignity, morality, and the historical evolution of social rights. This chapter thus studies the impact of commodification on what I call the social rationale of the shorter-hour demand. Investigating the economic arguments that were made in defense of this demand, Chapter 5 then discusses hopes for full employment, higher wages, and increased productivity. Concentrating on a dominant trade in the urban economy of the 1860s and early 1870s, this chapter is particularly interested in how the material work realities of construction workers influenced their analysis and forms of collective action. The construction workers' experience at the same time testifies to a striking departure from the anti-commodification rhetoric established so far.

In sum, Chapters 3 to 5 portray working-class claims towards their respective *polity*, *society*, and *economy*. Obviously any such categorization remains somewhat artificial. After all, economic demands clearly have a political meaning, just as political ideas are shaped by social convention. However, the separate focus on polity, society, and economy reveals that the discursive rationale differed profoundly depending on the respective sphere that workers addressed. As a consequence of this distinction, the three chapters give voice to different actors. Chapter 3 is dominated by skilled artisans and the respective political associations they established. In Chapter 4, we primarily meet socio-political protagonists such as the labor reformers and intellectuals who led the nascent socialist parties. Chapter 5 finally explores the local trade-union movement. The comparative analysis thereby shows that the same working-class activist could express very different ideas depending on whether he spoke as a representative of a political association or a local trade.

Having discussed the diversity of arguments by shorter-hour activists in Berlin and New York, Chapter 6 finally contrasts male perceptions with the experience of working women in the two cities. This chapter is particularly interested in working-class (male) opposition to the commodification of women's work and struggles for the protection of female labor. Rather than analyzing an independent proletarian women's movement—which, in any case, did not (re)emerge in Berlin and New York before the end of the century—Chapter 6 focuses on the distinct argumentation for shorter male and female workdays.[12]

Each of the chapters is followed by a short chapter conclusion that, for reasons to be discussed in the Introduction, illustrates how the chapter's findings add to discussions in contemporary social theory. The Conclusion provides an evaluation of the reasons that workers, activists, and reformers in Berlin's and New York's shorter-hour movements articulated with respect to the free market and the alleged special need for the protection of working women. In so doing, the Conclusion articulates the book's historical-empirical contribution to contemporary debates on commodification and social protection.

As David Montgomery stated, *Citizen Worker* was heavily influenced by the international political developments of the early 1990s and the hegemonic equation of democracy with the free market. Montgomery wanted to understand how it came to be that the unregulated exchange of goods, labor, and land was identified with democratic sovereignty and how the state, despite being formally democratic, implemented what Ray Gunn has called the insulation of the economy from democratic control.[13] Against the backdrop of neoliberal transformation, *Citizen Worker* revisited the birth of American labor in the mid-nineteenth century and asked how the free market managed to win the sole prerogative to determine production and the distribution of wealth. This book is likewise a child of its time. Indebted to the transnational expressions of opposition to the commodification of life that have erupted over the past two decades, the following pages explore how working people in two centers of nineteenth-century capitalism reacted to the commodification of their labor power and the paradigm of free markets. But rather than studying dominant liberal rhetoric or the evolution of discourse into policy, this book directs its attention to the ideas that evolved in opposition to the

12 By the late 1850s, working women had largely been driven out of New York City's organized labor movement. According to Burrows and Wallace, it took decades for working women to rebuild a movement of their own; see Burrows and Wallace, *Gotham*, 802. Although working women in Berlin had made first attempts to organize in the early 1870s, it was not until the 1880s that a proletarian women's movement gathered pace in the German capital. The lifting of the Anti-Socialist Law in 1890 further accelerated the growth of female working-class associations in Berlin. For the analysis of an eyewitness, see Berger, *Die zwanzigjährige Arbeiterinnen-Bewegung Berlins*. See also Evans, *The Feminists*, 159–160; Losseff-Tillmanns, *Frauenemanzipation und Gewerkschaften*, 66–87; Twellmann, *Die deutsche Frauenbewegung*, 166–172.

13 Montgomery, *Citizen Worker*, 2.

commodification of labor and the unregulated exchange of human labor power. In the nineteenth century, people brought forward a wide array of arguments against the paradigm of commodified social relations. At the same time, they developed alternative notions about what work, in both its abstract social and its concrete individual sense, could mean. In the early twenty-first century, people are still opposing the idea of commodified labor and the power of unfettered markets. They are well advised to listen to the hopes and aspirations, as well as the criticisms and reservations, voiced a century and a half ago.

1. Introduction: Theory and Methods

1.1. The Polanyian Revival

This study investigates how working people, social-democratic intellectuals, labor reformers, and trade unionists in Berlin and New York City framed their demand to shorten the workday in reaction to the commodifying pressures of urban labor markets in the late 1860s and early 1870s. Before approaching their movements and analyzing the ideas they expressed, the following pages introduce the methodology and research context of this study. First and foremost, they explore the theoretical framework this study draws upon, a framework that is currently undergoing a major revival. Some 70 years ago, in the midst of economic chaos and global war, the political economist and social theorist Karl Polanyi published his magnum opus, *The Great Transformation.* Analyzing the rise of the self-regulating market in the late eighteenth and nineteenth centuries, Polanyi argued that it required the unrestricted and free supply not only of conventional commodities, but of all factors of production. Therefore, these factors had to be transformed into commodities; they had to become "commodified." To Polanyi, the commodification of labor, land, and money resulted from the fundamental transformation of the modern economy, which was caused by the massive introduction of machines. Large-scale mechanization became possible only through large-scale investments. For such investments to be profitable, it was vital that there were no supply shortages or any other interference that could disturb a steady production process. The machine had to be kept running. As a result, employers and investors cared little about religious observances, cultural practices, or physical constraints that would "de-commodify" the workforce on certain days of the week, during particular hours of the day, or even during entire periods of human existence, such as childhood or old age. Thus, an increasingly unrestricted market emerged that supplied not only goods, but also labor, land, and money. Since none of the latter were explicitly produced for market circulation, Polanyi called these commodities "fictitious." Its transformation from "natural entity" into "factor of production" thereby deprived the fictitious commodity of its earlier meaning.[14] For the first time in human history, an economy arose that was split from society itself, epitomized by a supposedly self-regulating market that was "'disembedded', freed from extra-economic controls and governed immanently by supply and demand."[15] Commodities such as land and labor were no longer produced and consumed according to a mixture of economic, social, religious, cultural, and political needs, but simply bought and sold. The market system gave rise to a new form of society, a market society, which regarded the demands and necessities of the economy more highly than the needs of society itself. Polanyi thus revealed how the notion of commodification was expanded to areas that other epochs or cultures regarded as essentially non-economic, such as the human capacity to work. This expansion stands at the center of *The Great Transformation.*

But Polanyi not only provided an analysis of the underlying processes of this transformation; he also offered a framework for the study of the social forces that promoted and opposed this truly revolutionary idea. According to Polanyi, the market societies of the late eighteenth to the early twentieth centuries were torn apart by a "double movement" that increasingly destabilized their social foundations. On the one side, adherents of the free-market movement struggled for the elimination of any institution or legislation that obstructed the supposedly universal benefit of self-regulating markets. Labor markets, liberal employers argued, needed to be rid of relief regulations that hindered the full commodification of human work and thus jeopardized the supply of labor and thwarted the development of wages.[16]

---

14 Burawoy, "From Polanyi to Pollyanna," 310.

15 Fraser, "Marketization, Social Protection, Emancipation," 141.

16 For a discussion of the English Poor Law in general and the abolition of the Speenhamland system in particular, see Polanyi, *The Great Transformation*, 81–107. Implemented by English authorities, the Speenhamland system was an early welfare measure that supplemented the low wages of the needy poor. Speenhamland has become an epitome for regulatory efforts to address the pauperism triggered by the massive dispossession of the English peasantry. To the dismay of liberal thinkers like Jeremy Bentham, Speenhamland forestalled the emergence of a self-regulating labor market. Instead of being forced to sell their labor power on the free market, dispossessed peasants and day laborers could rely on sources derived from an extra-market institution. The abolition of Speenhamland, finally realized in 1834, had therefore long been a central demand of proponents of the self-regulating market. For a more recent discussion of Speenhamland and the commodification of labor, see Block and Somers, "In the Shadow of Speenhamland."

Property markets, liberal thinkers maintained, were most effective when freed from tariffs, taxes, and any other regulation that interfered with the law of supply and demand. Currency markets, liberal financiers asserted, could only generate high rates of return if they were allowed to operate freely. In short, the liberal side of Polanyi's double movement insisted that only a self-regulating market would foster the "Wealth of Nations." Yet on the other side of Polanyi's twofold movement, a heterogeneous force emerged that struggled to protect society against the intrusive demands of the market. The movement for social protection encompassed not only the nascent labor movement and its social and political organizations, but also the various conservative movements of the landed gentry who wished to see their property protected and political parties and prominent politicians like Disraeli or Bismarck who tried to mediate between market forces and the social fabric.[17]

Given the aforementioned centrality of the free-market paradigm in present-day politics and social opposition, the current Polanyian renaissance is hardly surprising. In his foreword to the 2001 edition of *The Great Transformation*, Nobel laureate in economics Joseph E. Stiglitz stresses that "it often seems as if Polanyi is speaking directly to present-day issues."[18] In the eyes of eminent sociologist Fred L. Block, it is therefore no wonder that *The Great Transformation* is, "after years of relative obscurity, [...] increasingly recognized as one of the major works of twentieth-century social science."[19] Together with his colleague Margaret R. Somers, Block highlights Polanyi's enduring legacy for social, political, and economic thought.[20] Focusing on resistance movements to neoliberal hegemony, political sociologist Peter Evans argues that a thorough re-evaluation of Polanyi constitutes "a natural starting point for anyone interested in counter-hegemonic globalization."[21] James Caporaso and Sidney Tarrow show that Polanyi is even useful for

---

17 Analyzing the social composition of the forces that welcomed or opposed the introduction of the English Ten-Hour-Bill, Friedrich Engels came to a similar conclusion; see Engels, "Die Englische Zehnstundenbill;" Engels, "Die Zehnstundenfrage."

18 Polanyi, *The Great Transformation*, vii.

19 Block, "Karl Polanyi," 275.

20 Block and Somers, *The Power of Market Fundamentalism.*

21 Evans, "Alternative Globalization," 273. This contribution draws on his earlier critique of Polanyi's exclusive focus on local and national counter-movements. Contemporary social movements, Evans concludes, will have to organize and engage globally if they want to confront the hegemony of neoliberalism; see Evans, "Fighting Marginalization with Transnational Networks;" Evans, "Counter-Hegemonic Globalization."

analyses of present-day political processes such as European policy making and integration.[22] Interestingly, these prominent voices all testify to the astonishingly contemporary perspective that *The Great Transformation* provides for the study of the contradictions of free markets and the formation of social opposition to their commodifying logic. Although Polanyi had actually developed a theory for the nineteenth and early twentieth centuries, the vast majority of studies that have appeared over the past decade explore what his ideas mean for present-day societies.[23] This study, however, re-historicizes the Polanyian framework by applying it to the experiences of organized workers in mid-nineteenth-century Berlin and New York.

1.2. The Conceptual Toolbox

Rather than exploring general attitudes towards work, this study is interested in the historically specific ideas that mid-nineteenth-century urban *wage workers* expressed towards the *(de)commodification of labor (power)* and the emergence of a *free labor market*. In particular, the following chapters analyze the extent to which resistance to the commodification of labor influenced the discursive rationale for the demand for a shorter workday. Such an approach should obviously begin with a definition of the concept of *commodification*. As outlined above, commodification generally describes a transformative process that subjects a formerly non-economic entity to the ultimate power of the market.[24] Applied to labor, commodification thus refers to the reconfiguration of human work according to the logics of supply and demand. Labor commodification does not mean, however, that work had never been regarded an economically quantifiable and exchangeable unit before the introduction of capitalist production. Ancient, medieval, and early modern forms of labor often constituted extreme forms of commodified work. Enslaved or indentured workers, for instance, experienced the forced com-

22 Caporaso and Tarrow, "Polanyi in Brussels."

23 Among many others, see Dale, *Karl Polanyi*; Bugra and Agartan, *Reading Karl Polanyi*; Hann and Hart, *Market and Society*, Harvey, Ramlogan and Randles (eds.), *Karl Polanyi*; Kelsey, "Polanyi Revisited," McRobbie and Polanyi-Levitt (eds.), *Karl Polanyi in Vienna*; Mendell, "A Karl Polanyi Revival;" Stuhlberger Wjuniski and Fernandez, "Karl Polanyi; Thomasberger, "Karl Polanyi."

24 Cf. Prodnik, "A Note on the Ongoing Processes of Commodification," 274.

modification of their entire person, including their labor power. Yet as Polanyi stresses in his historical and ethnological studies, the free or forceful exchange or appropriation of labor power was just one element in the complex meaning of work in earlier or non-European societies.[25] The labor of peasants, clergymen, artisans, or officials was determined by a whole system of ideas and practices largely independent of market logics: They labored to guarantee subsistence, to satisfy the unwaged demands of lords, to perform religious services, to achieve spiritual fulfillment, to illustrate morale guidance, or to stabilize political rule. Though their labor might have contained a commodified element, it also included various elements of cultural and political significance.[26] Commodification now describes the stripping of such non-economic meanings from the notion of work. It defines a transformation or state in which the voluntary or enforced selling of labor on a market established precisely for this reason is either in the process of becoming or has become the dominant experience for the majority of the unpropertied classes. Freed from the power of social institutions, political regulations, or cultural practices that had once shaped the everyday reality of work and workers, commodified labor is characterized by the fact that the free play of supply and demand alone determines the conditions (price, length, continuity, etc.) under which it is bought, sold, and used. This, I propose, is the ideal-type definition of commodification which, as Polanyi reminds us, is best understood as a political program rather than a social reality. After all, the program's destructive power creates the very social opposition that thwarts the unregulated commodification of labor.

Having defined the general idea, we can turn to the question of what exactly it was that underwent commodification in the transformation of human work. Nineteenth-century workers often did not differentiate between *labor* and *labor power* when criticizing the commodification of labor. Therewith they attracted fierce criticism from Marx, who stressed that it was the ability to work rather than the work itself that became commodified under capitalism. This was, in Marx's eyes, what distinguished his own theory from classical political economy. Marx argued that economists before him had

---

25 Polanyi, *Primitive, Archaic, and Modern Economies*; Polanyi, "The Economy as Instituted Process."

26 For changing conceptions of work in history, see Kocka and Offe (eds.), *Geschichte und Zukunft der Arbeit*; Conze, "Arbeit." For the classic interpretation of the French Annales School, see Le Goff, *Für ein anderes Mittelalter*. Critical of Le Goff is Postel, *Arbeit und Willensfreiheit im Mittelalter*.

failed to offer a consistent explanation as to what constituted the value of labor. They were unable to show whether labor value was determined by labor's reproductive costs or its productive potential. According to Marx, in a system of capitalist production workers do not sell their labor, understood as a particular productive outcome. Rather, they sell their ability to perform certain productive tasks. The emphasis on the selling of labor power (rather than labor) helped Marx illustrate the complex reality of value that he saw hidden behind the formal rhetoric of *bourgeois* economics. If it was the workers' power that was purchased by the employer, then the value of labor was the respective quantity necessary to reproduce the power spent in production.[27] Therewith, the cornerstone was laid for Marx's theory of surplus value. In a system of capitalist production, the value of labor—just like the value of any other commodity—was determined by the time that was socially necessary for its production or, in the case or labor power, reproduction. Since wage workers put in longer hours than necessary to meet their reproductive costs, they created a surplus that went directly to their employers. Yet whether in Europe or the US, nineteenth-century workers had a much broader understanding of labor value.[28] To many of the workers, trade unionists, and labor reformers we are about to meet, the value of their labor was represented by *both* the power spent in production and a particular productive outcome.[29]

This study thus defines labor by both drawing on and going beyond the juxtaposition offered by Richard Biernacki. In his acclaimed study *The Fabrication of Labor*, Biernacki argues that workers in nineteenth-century Britain and Germany entertained very different ideas about how abstract labor emerged as the central category of commodity exchange. According to Biernacki, nineteenth-century British employers agreed with their workers that the value of labor was embodied in the product as a quantifiable unit that was realized at the point of sale. As a social category, labor thus allowed the exchange of equivalents by comparing the labor that had crystalized in the market product. In Britain, Biernacki argues, the concept of a "free producer" prevailed because the worker offered not his labor power, but a

27 Marx, *Das Kapital* I, 181–191; Marx, "Kritik des Gothaer Programms." See also Scharf, *Geschichte der Arbeitszeitverkürzung*, 40–47.

28 For a classic study of the supposedly exceptional tradition of working-class producerism in the US, see Perlman, *A Theory of the Labor Movement*, 154–176. For an anti-exceptionalist critique, see Reick, "We are the 99%."

29 Renzsch, "Einleitung," vii–viii; Welskopp, "Markt und Klasse," 19.

certain value he had produced himself. The labor of British wage workers was thus regarded as "a commodity delivered by contractors to manufacturers."[30] In Germany, in contrast, the worker offered his labor power for sale. Here, Biernacki argues, the value of labor was measured by the expenditure of labor power, by the physical or mental force that was spent and that required reproduction. Biernacki now suggests that the different ways in which labor was conceived of and conveyed as a commodity influenced not only the respective everyday practices of employment and production, but also how workers framed their demands and expressed protest. In his words, these cultural differences "create[d] and sustain[ed] decisive, systematic divergences in the formation of manufacturing practices and industrial relations."[31]

As original and—in the best sense of the term—thought-provoking as Biernacki's study is, the dichotomy of British notions of labor as the commodified output of free producers versus the German understanding of labor as commodified expenditure of labor power is not fully persuasive. Biernacki argues that since German workers had internalized the idea that they were selling or renting out their labor power to an employer who compensated them for the quantity of labor power spent at work, they grounded their opposition on particular flaws in this exchange. Yet as this book will demonstrate, mid-nineteenth-century German workers did not simply try to enforce favorable selling conditions for the commodity they had to offer. Rather, they struggled to end the system of wage work that commodified their labor in the first place. The producerist notion that Biernacki attributes to British workers mattered equally in German and, for that matter, American working-class discourse in the mid-nineteenth century. No less than their comrades in Britain, organized workers in Germany and the US cherished the ideal of independent and autonomous production that was increasingly jeopardized by the proliferation of wage labor. Depending on the trade in question, workers in Berlin and New York saw the value of their labor represented by *both* the value that materialized in the exchange product and the power spent in production. The one did not necessarily preclude the other. In fact, it seems that Biernacki's dichotomy separates not national cultures, but particular conditions of employment. What Biernacki interprets as nationally distinct, "cultural" constructions of labor value in many cases

30 Biernacki, "Labor as an Imagined Commodity," 185.

31 Biernacki, *The Fabrication of Labor*, 1.

reflected competing legal concepts of labor as a commodity that existed side by side in early industrial societies.[32]

The distinction between Marxist and artisanal understandings of labor value points to a peculiar conceptualization of freedom in nineteenth-century labor discourse. While the notion of *free labor* was in fact one of the prime goals of organized workers' struggles on both sides of the Atlantic, the *free labor market* was despised as an instrument used by employers and merchants to dominate labor. When trade unionists or skilled workers discussed the notion of a free labor market, they regularly opposed this market—or the underlying phenomenon of commodification—as an attack on their ability to control production and distribution. Yet when demanding free labor, they envisioned a state of independent working-class production that allowed workers to freely offer their labor—here understood as the crystallization of skill and diligence in a particular product. This critique of commodification reflected what they perceived as unjust competition from capitalized but "unproductive" merchants, bankers, and other "monopolists." Whereas the political rationale discussed in Chapter 3 draws primarily on workers' opposition to the loss of control over the products in which their *labor* had crystallized, Chapter 4 analyzes the social rationale that labor reformers and socialist intellectuals developed in order to reject the commodification of *labor power.*

Having defined the concepts of labor (power) and commodification, we can finally turn to the latter's antonym, *de-commodification.* The triumph of wage labor entailed a set of questions that organized workers did not want to leave to the market. From the eighteenth century onwards, workers pushed for some form of regulation regarding prices, wages, and working conditions. In his classic study on "The Moral Economy of the English Crowd in the Eighteenth Century," Edward P. Thompson explores how peasants and workers opposed the price-building mechanism of markets for daily needs. Thompson argues that the proto-working class was unwilling to accept what was explained to them as the natural development of prices according to the laws of supply and demand. Rather than erupting into uncontrolled violence when scarcity jeopardized their livelihood, the English lower classes tended to protest what they perceived as immoral practices or inexplicably high prices. According to Thompson, the English crowd struggled not so much for a free supply of goods as for a regulatory price setting by the local au-

32 Cf. Steinmetz, *Begegnungen vor Gericht*, 603.

thorities.[33] Christine Stansell observes a similar transformation of customary practices in early nineteenth-century New York City. In the 1820s, New York's Common Council ended the assize on bread, "an old municipal tradition that limited the price of bread in order to ensure the poor an adequate supply of food."[34] The local legislature's discontinuation of price settings for food staples reflected the liberal notion that bread prices, like prices for any other commodity, were best left to the market. To poor consumers, however, the idea that prices were simply the quantifiable result of the changing ratio of supply and demand perverted, as Thompson puts it, their perception of a *moral economy*. Yet there was one price that was exceptionally dear to the working class in the making—the price of labor. Organized workers thus struggled for the regulation of not only the prices for consumption goods, but also the price or level of wages. In fact, the demand to determine wages outside of the market, or, put differently, the demand for some form of wage protection, has accompanied trade and labor movements from the very beginning.[35] In addition to prices and wages, the suppliers of labor struggled for public or extra-economic regulation of their respective work conditions. Issues such as occupational safety, the availability of housing, the granting of breaks, and the use of machines caused workers to protest and demand public intervention.[36] However, one of the most contested aspect of nineteenth-century labor emerged over the length of the workday.

In the following, I concentrate on this particular aspect of free-market opposition, that is, the unwillingness to leave the length of the working day to the market. The struggles of workers and their movements, unions, and parties to reduce the length of the workday through legislation or collective force entailed the fervent hope for the de-commodification of labor. Clearly, a reduction of daily hours did not promise to suspend the experience of commodification entirely, nor did it end the logic of wage labor. After all,

33 Thompson, "The Moral Economy."

34 Stansell, *City of Women*, 35. See also Brody, *In Labor's Cause*, 6.

35 Eduard Bernstein pointed out that demands for minimum wages were already being made by proto-trade unions in the late 1840s and 1850s; see Bernstein, *Die Geschichte der Berliner Arbeiterbewegung*, 1–108.

36 While the English Luddite movement (including its notorious attitude towards machines and standardized work discipline) has received plenty of attention from social historians, other centers of the early industrializing world economy still await closer examination. For England, see Bailey, *The Luddite Rebellion*; Hobsbawm, "The Machine Breakers;" Thompson, *The Making of the English Working Class*, 604–659. For a rare discussion of German working-class attitudes towards machines, see Spehr, *Maschinensturm*.

labor would still be supplied in exchange for wages even if shorter hours were won, and wages or other working conditions would continue to depend on the market. And yet, to many working-class activists, the normal workday was a first step towards the de-commodification of work. As the following chapters will show, the notion of de-commodification carries both a social and a political quality. To Polanyi, who remained rather vague in this respect, de-commodification was a process of social *re-embedding*. Polanyi assumed that no society would be able to tolerate the unchecked powers of a free market for long. Faced with the menace of social disruption and chaos, society would eventually bring the market back under control and, in so doing, de-commodify labor, land, and money. To welfare-state sociologists, in contrast, de-commodification is a strictly political process in which legislative reforms restrain the power of the market. According to Gøsta Esping-Andersen and Claus Offe, for instance, the implementation and institutionalization of the Western welfare state in the second half of the twentieth century constitutes a rare case of massive de-commodification. With regard to human labor, the term implies that certain social groups are temporarily or permanently excluded from the pressure to sell their labor power on the market because they are assigned to institutions outside the market such as schools or universities, because they are entitled to financial provisions such as pensions, or because legislation or wage regulation frees them from the unrestrained forces of commodification.[37]

In this study, de-commodification appears in both its social and its political forms. Collective bargaining or strikes for shorter hours exemplify a social measure towards the de-commodification of labor, but so do discriminatory debates that shape the moral standards that facilitate or impede the commodification or de-commodification of distinct groups of workers. Petitions, electoral campaigns, and legislative initiatives for shorter hours, in contrast, are usually found in the repertoire of political struggles towards de-commodification. Whether workers understood de-commodification socially or politically depended very much on their occupation and gender. Thus de-commodification is defined here as both a political aim and a social practice. Applied to the experience of shorter-hour movements in the second half of the nineteenth century, the hope for de-commodification displays both an immediate quality and a long-term objective. On the immediate level, every hour not engaged in wage labor increased the amount of daily de-

37 Esping-Andersen, *The Three Worlds of Welfare Capitalism*; Offe, "Staatstheorie und Sozialpolitik," 160.

commodified time. From the perspective of organized labor, a reduction of hours thus blessed workers with a retrieval of time free from the pressure of the market. In its own words, the early workers' movement hoped that although shorter hours would not end exploitation, it would at least introduce a legal barrier. Thus, as a social-democratic paper from Berlin argued, the "capitalist who has bought a particular labor power can no longer use it for as long as he wishes."[38] On a more strategic level, however, the demand for shorter hours was seen as a crucial element in the broader struggle against market-determined social relations. It was a wedge that could be driven deeply into the hegemony of liberal economics. Workers in the mid- to late nineteenth century were confident that the enforcement of shorter workdays was only the beginning of the moral erosion, political delegitimation, and economic transformation of a social system that made men, women, and children into commodities—of a system, therefore, that made them into what, in their eyes, they could not, must not, be.

1.3. The Comparative Approach

Whereas the foregoing suggested why an analysis of working-class discussions on commodification may yield fresh insights into the emerging world of nineteenth-century organized labor, the comparative design still awaits explanation. After all, comparative or entangled research designs are not an end in themselves. This comparison of German and American labor-movement history offers two clear advantages over any single case account. The first reason draws upon the findings of the father of comparative historiography in the early twentieth century. Throughout his work, Marc Bloch highlighted the heuristic value of comparisons. Assuming that enclosures were an integral part of early capitalist developments in general, Bloch was able to demonstrate that they did not occur only in England, but also in France, where they had been largely neglected by historians.[39] The fact that

38 See "Der gesetzlich festgestellte Normalarbeitstag," *Social-Politische Blätter*, 7 February 1874, 3. ("Zwar bleibt der Arbeiter auch bei einem Normalarbeitstage noch immer der Ausgebeutete, aber die Ausbeutung ist doch einigermaßen eingeschränkt. Der Kapitalist, der dessen Arbeitskraft kauft, kann sie nicht mehr so maßlos lange ausnutzen wie bisher [...].")

39 For the heuristic category of historical comparison, see Haupt and Kocka, "Comparison and Beyond," 3.

the history of England's enclosures had been fairly well researched by the beginning of the twentieth century, in other words, allowed Bloch to trace back a largely overlooked French enclosure movement. This study applies a similar heuristic logic. In the American context, the movement to shorten the workday in the second half of the nineteenth century has attracted plenty of attention by historians, one of whom even speaks of the shorter-hour demand as the "Holy Grail" of postbellum American labor.[40] Given that the urban societies of mid-nineteenth-century Germany and the US shared important industrial characteristics, I assumed that if the demand for shorter working hours featured so prominently among American workers, it most likely mattered for German labor as well, although there exists no comparable body of research. While a considerable number of works has been published on national and local shorter-hour movements in the US—with the striking exception of New York City—there are very few studies of German hour struggles. The first objective of the comparative design, therefore, is to shed light on one of the most neglected movements in nineteenth-century German Social History.

Yet the comparative logic also works vice versa. Instead of further advancing the narrative of an American labor movement that has somehow failed to live up to the alleged standard of class consciousness and organization, the comparative design of this study reveals, second, the tremendous diversity and strength of organized labor in postbellum America.[41] By the late 1860s, American workers had championed an international struggle for shorter hours, a key demand of working people across the globe. They did so in a broad field of action, from community-based leagues to trade unions, from city-wide labor associations to early political parties. What the comparative approach therefore provides is a challenge to established notions of American exceptionalism. Social historians have regularly interpreted the US as a peculiar deviation from the supposedly ideal cases of Germany or France. For decades, transatlantic historiography implicitly accepted Werner Sombart's explanation of *why there was no socialism in the United States.* Approaching American Labor History with a rather monolithic understanding of socialism, it is not surprising that Sombart and his disciples detected a

40 Molloy, "Eight-Hour Movement," 153.

41 See Welskopp, "Birds of a Feather," 149.

lack of socialism in the US.[42] Yet this study suggests that not only was there a lot of socialism in the US during the 1860s and 1870s, there also was a great deal of republicanism in German working-class thought. The comparative perspective, in short, helps disturb notions of singularity.

Although this study compares, it also devotes careful attention to processes of transfer. For more than a decade, historians have debated the advantages and pitfalls of comparative versus transfer or entanglement studies. It was a group of cultural historians that first criticized comparative approaches for their neglect of the discursive reality of national identity and political institutions.[43] With their proposal of a *Histoire croisée*, Bénédicte Zimmermann and Michael Werner added a much discussed twist to this debate. In particular, Zimmermann and Werner argue that comparative historians implicitly create the very comparability they seek to analyze by pretending that a particular category—such as unemployment—carried the same meaning in two or more cultural backgrounds.[44] Yet, while comparisons were accused of reproducing national exceptionalisms or *Sonderwege*, transfer and entanglements were regularly denied the ability to develop the very conceptualization that allowed analytical insight in the first place. Hartmut Kaelble, for instance, argues that the much criticized comparison still offers crucial insights for historical research. After all, even transfer or entanglement approaches require comparison because only comparisons are able to reveal how cultures emanating or receiving transfers differed in their original composition and, therefore, how transfer and exchange affected these cultures.[45] Jürgen Kocka adds that History always needs to generalize and compare if it wants to remain a meaningful intellectual endeavor, especially in a globalized world. As enriching as the entangled perspective is, it

> must not lead away from but should incorporate rigorous comparison, which remains particularly indispensable for historical studies with global reach if they do not want to become merely speculative or feuilletonistic.[46]

---

42 Sombart, "Warum gibt es in den Vereinigten Staaten keinen Sozialismus?" For a critical discussion of Sombart's thesis, see Foner, "Why Is There No Socialism in the United States?"

43 For the critique by an early advocate of transfer studies, see Espagne, "Sur les limites du comparatisme."

44 Werner and Zimmermann, "Vergleich, Transfer, Verflechtung;" Werner and Zimmermann, "Beyond Comparison."

45 Kaelble, "Die Debatte über Vergleich und Transfer."

46 Kocka, "Comparison and Beyond," 44.

With a certain temporal distance, methodological battles often appear inexplicably rigid.[47] In my understanding, comparison and transfer or entanglement are approaches rather than fields of study. These approaches are different rather than better. They are, then, distinct but equally legitimate methods that entail particular logics of explanation: Historians apply designs of entanglement or transfer in order to enrich our understanding of influence and interrelation. Historians compare in order to reveal the particularity or universality of processes and transformations. Without losing sight of trans-Atlantic transfers, this study compares in order to highlight similarities in working-class thought. Rather than reproducing national peculiarities, it demonstrates that working-class ideas in fact tended to differ much more according to the divisionary lines of skill, trade, and prescribed gender than according to national background. A carpenter in New York City was much more likely to express ideas about labor power or the free market that were shared by a carpenter in Berlin than by a contracted seamstress in his very own neighborhood.

Having discussed why this study compares, the following clarifies the more concrete case selection. During the period under review, the early workers' movements in Germany and North America were primarily locally focused.[48] In the US, the North had just won a very costly war and the nation—including its vastly divergent working classes—continued to be heavily disunited. David Montgomery's conclusion still holds true that the historian searching for "effective manifestations of working-class reform aspirations in the 1860's must focus his attention on the local community."[49] In Germany, working-class activity was likewise scattered across the empire-to-be. Despite first attempts to unify the movement, German organized labor remained heavily localized for the time being, not least due to a considerable degree of repression, such as the Prussian Law of Association, which criminalized centralization.[50] At this local level, it was especially in cities that early labor opposition thrived in the 1860s and 1870s. And where better to study this opposition than in the two rapidly growing metropolises of Berlin and New York?

---

47 Cf. Budde, Conrad, and Janz, "Preface," 11–14; Cohen and O'Connor, "Introduction;" Green, "Forms of Comparison."

48 Klaus Tenfelde thus concluded that labor movements are hardly conceivable without the city; see Tenfelde, "Die Entstehung der deutschen Gewerkschaftsbewegung," 71.

49 Montgomery, *Beyond Equality*, 196.

50 For a short discussion of Prussia's Law of Association, see Chapter 2.

For a long time, the royal capital of Prussia had been stagnating rather than shining. Yet towards mid-century, Berlin was finally catching up politically, economically, and culturally with the great metropolises of Paris, London, and New York.[51] In 1855, Berlin was home to about 426,000 people.[52] A decade later, the newly established *Statistisches Bureau* already counted slightly more than 700,000 residents, an increase of more than a quarter of a million people. Another decade later, in 1877, Berlin finally surpassed one million inhabitants.[53] While the birth rate did exceed the mortality rate, it was the high degree of migration to the city, especially from nearby Brandenburg, West- and East-Prussia, Silesia, and Pomerania, that accounted for the enormous population increase.[54] For more than a century, the city had looked enviously at London for both inspiration and thrills. Yet as Berlin's *Magistrat*, the highest governing body of the city, declared in the late 1870s, Berlin increasingly turned its gaze away from London and towards the "fabulous development of the great cities in North America."[55] In particular, Berlin's officials were eager to stress that the city's spectacular pace of growth was paralleled only by that of New York.[56] The latter had already surpassed one million inhabitants in the late 1860s or early 1870s. In 1860, the State Census of New York counted slightly more than 800,000 residents.[57] The following census of 1875 recorded that the city now was home to more than a million people, with an additional 600,000 inhabitants residing in the neighboring counties of Kings (Brooklyn) and Queens. In the fifteen years since 1860, New York and its surrounding counties experienced an increase of about 400,000 new inhabitants.[58] Few other cities witnessed a

51 Dietrich, "Berlins Weg zur Industrie- und Handelsstadt," 191; Schoeps, "Berlin wird Weltstadt."

52 Dieterici, *Über die Zunahme der Bevölkerung*, 127, Table C.

53 Pafflhausen, "Fortschreibung des Bevölkerungsbestandes."

54 Magistrat der Stadt Berlin (ed.), *Bericht über die Gemeinde-Verwaltung der Stadt Berlin in den Jahren 1861 bis 1876,* vol. 1, 50, 52–53; Erbe, "Berlin im Kaiserreich," 696.

55 Cited in Dietrich, "Berlins Weg zur Industrie- und Handelsstadt," 191.

56 Magistrat der Stadt Berlin (ed.), *Bericht über die Gemeinde-Verwaltung der Stadt Berlin in den Jahren 1861 bis 1876,* vol. 1, 49. ("Es hat also in sechzehn Jahren eine Verdoppelung der Bevölkerung stattgefunden, ein Verhältnis, das, wenn auch bei der jetzigen Entwicklung des industriellen Lebens der Städte nicht unerhört, doch unter Städten dieser Größe sich nur bei New-York in ähnlicher Weise gezeigt hat.")

57 *Census of the State of New York for 1865*, 101.

58 *Census of the State of New York for 1875*, 2, Table no. 1 "Aggregate Population of New York by County." While this study focuses primarily on Berlin and New York within the historical boundaries of the 1860s and 1870s, it also covers incidents from areas not yet incorporated, such as Kings County (today's Brooklyn). Although these districts remained

population increase as intense as Berlin and New York in the 1860s and 1870s.[59]

During these one and a half decades, the two metropolises also underwent a tremendous transformation in urban industry, transportation, and services. But unlike the emergent steel and coal giants in Pennsylvania and Ohio or the Ruhr area, Berlin and New York also featured a strong legacy of artisanal occupations.[60] Workers in food processing, drink, and tobacco, like butchers, brewers, and cigar makers, flocked to the cities, where they joined the growing pool of clothing and textile workers. The expansion of Berlin and New York triggered a boom in the building sector, which swelled the ranks of carpenters, bricklayers, painters, paper hangers, and furniture makers. While New York's riversides gave employment to an army of shipbuilders, Berlin's north provided employment for a great number of locomotive and other skilled metal workers. In addition, an emerging urban *bourgeoisie* provided a wide array of employment possibilities from domestic services to typesetting, printing, musical-instrument making, and horse-carriage transportation.

What makes Berlin and New York especially interesting for a comparative history of labor struggles vis-à-vis the paradigm of commodification is the peculiar transformation of employment and production patterns that both cities witnessed, particularly in skilled and semi-skilled labor sectors. The vast group of urban construction workers, for instance, was changing dramatically around the early to middle part of the century. Traditional construction on order was increasingly replaced by speculative construction for a real-estate market—a change that also influenced artisanal hierarchies and

administratively independent until the incorporations of the five boroughs of Greater New York in 1898 and the establishment of Groß-Berlin in 1920, respectively, they were heavily entangled spaces of social, economic, and cultural exchange. For the administrative history of Berlin, see Erbe, "Berlin im Kaiserreich," 745–754; Escher, *Berlin und sein Umland.* For New York, see Burrows and Wallace, *Gotham*, 1219–1236.

59 Herzfeld, "Berlin auf dem Wege zur Weltstadt," 245.

60 Baar, "Berlin in der Industriellen Revolution;" Rock, "Independent Hours;" Stott, *Workers in the Metropolis;* Wilentz, *Chants Democratic.* This does not mean that, for instance, iron and steel workers did not experience a tremendous transformation of production and employment, including aspects of work control and autonomy, as Thomas Welskopp and David Montgomery stress; see Montgomery, *The Fall of the House of Labor*, 9–57; Welskopp, *Arbeit und Macht im Hüttenwerk.* But due to the scale and particular mode of production, changes in work organization as well as resistance by workers had very different trajectories in iron and steel works than in urban construction sites, sweatshops, and artisanal workshops.

employment conditions. The dominant clothing trades also experienced profound changes. Fewer and fewer independent tailors faced a rapidly growing number of outworkers and dependent masters who continued to work in their own shops, yet whose workday realities, from the purchase of material to the quantity and quality of finished goods, was entirely beyond their control.[61] Rather than large-scale factory production, formerly independent tailors came under pressure from putting-out systems, while journeymen found it increasingly difficult to leave the stage of dependent wage work behind. In addition, a quickly expanding army of sewing women was pushed into outwork that not only freed employers from responsibility for employees, but also intensified wage competition.[62] Clothing and construction trades thus faced an enormous transformation of their everyday work realities. This study therefore pays particular attention to the construction sectors (Chapter 5) and clothing (Chapter 6). Economic development and the transformation of employment patterns at the same time meant that Berlin and New York were becoming epicenters of organized labor.[63] Local trade-union groups or workers' associations mushroomed in the two cities from the mid-1860s onwards. Workers' mass meetings regularly filled New York's famous Germania Hall, run by a German socialist in the Bowery, or Cooper Institute, now as then a venue for public debate and progressive reform in what today is the East Village.[64] In Berlin, a growing number of pub landlords, especially in the city's northern and southern neighborhoods, opened their doors to workers' meetings. Among many others, the pubs called *Alcazar* and *Alhambra* brought a glimpse of Mauritanian grandeur to the working-class *tristesse* of neighborhoods in today's Kreuzberg, Friedrichshain, and Wedding. Organizational growth was both fueled and represented by the dramatic increase in local labor publications. As *The National Workman*, one of the new papers established in New York City at the time, declared in 1866, the city had long been an idea giver for the whole nation. From this, the paper concluded that "labor reform [could] only triumph in proportion to the exertions that are put forth in our city."[65] Berlin and New York are, in short, especially fruitful places for the study of

61 Baar, "Berlin in der Industriellen Revolution," 74.

62 Stansell, *City of Women*, 105–129.

63 Burrows and Wallace, *Gotham*, 986–988; Dietrich, "Berlins Weg zur Industrie- und Handelsstadt," 186–188.

64 Today known as Cooper Union. Burrows and Wallace, *Gotham*, 989.

65 "To Our Friends," *The National Workman*, 1 December 1866, 2.

working-class attitudes towards commodification because the two cities witnessed a tremendous transformation of work realities as well as a sharp increase in labor confrontation that was documented by a lively and diverse press.

Finally, there is a good reason to focus on the years between the end of the Civil War and the early phase of the Long Depression. In fact, there are two good reasons. First, the early to mid-1860s mark a crucial period in the organizational history of labor. In the midst of the Civil War, the severely thinned labor movement of the North began to regain strength. New York City's Draft Riot of 1863, popularized by Martin Scorsese' motion picture *Gangs of New York*, provides a telling example of this development. The predominantly Irish laborers of New York who participated in the riot rebelled against the unfair conscription that allowed wealthier New Yorkers to bail out from duty. At the same time, the rioters directed their anger against the freedmen in the city who competed with the Irish for unskilled wage labor. Numerous black New Yorkers were murdered in the course of the riot. Many American, English, and German workers who comprised New York's skilled labor force, however, opposed such uncontrolled violence. Struggling to disassociate themselves from the rioters, skilled workers felt the need to both appear as respectable members of the community and enforce their right to political and economic participation.[66] The Draft Riot therefore epitomizes both the increasing social tensions—including outbursts of racial hatred—and the reinvigoration of organized labor that the North experienced in 1863. For workers in Berlin, 1863 likewise ushered in a fresh start, following a phase of relative labor quiescence. The city's workers and reformers were deeply disappointed by the conservative counterstroke of the 1850s, which had revoked or shattered the freedoms won or hoped for in the revolution of 1848. Early labor organizations such as Stephan Born's *Allgemeine Deutsche Arbeiterverbrüderung* and its local representations had been prosecuted and banned by the mid-1850s. Similarly, young trade unions such as the Berlin-based Association of German Cigar Workers had been pushed out of the city. Towards the end of the decade, workers in the Prussian capital were deprived of an independent representation of their interests. The situation changed dramatically, however, with the dawn of the new decade, when liberal as well as social-democratic *Arbeitervereine* (workers' associations) mushroomed, especially in Saxony, the Rhineland, and cities like

66 Bernstein, *The New York City Draft Riots*; Burrows and Wallace, *Gotham*, 887–899.

Hamburg and Berlin, often in direct response to the repercussions of the economic crisis of the late 1850s. Yet for more than any other reason in the organizational history of German labor, 1863 stands out because it gave birth to the two nuclei of German social democracy, Ferdinand Lassalle's *Allgemeiner Deutscher Arbeiterverein* (General German Workers' Association, ADAV) and the *Vereinstag Deutscher Arbeitervereine* (Congress of German Workers' Associations, VDAV). The Long Depression finally marks the chronological end point of this study. Yet, rather than ending abruptly in 1873, this study slowly fades away in the early 1870s—just as the question of shorter hours gradually made room for demands for unemployment benefits and public works in the first years of crisis.

The second reason I have chosen to end this study in the early 1870s stems from the fact that the subsequent years witnessed a profound transformation of dominant political-economic thought. Promoting legislative intervention into the labor market, Prussia's *Kathedersozialisten* increasingly besieged the once uncontested paradigm of *laissez-faire*.[67] Under their influence, Reichstag commissions and public intellectuals began debating the need for protective labor legislation and, more broadly, the dangers of unfettered markets.[68] As Thomas Nipperdey stated, the free market was about to lose its hegemonic position in the mid- to late 1870s.[69] This eventually cleared the way for the birth of the German welfare state in the following decade. Across the Atlantic, the hegemony of *laissez-faire* was crumbling also. As David Montgomery has argued, the notion that government needed to play an active role in protecting the people's labor, land, and money from unrestricted markets won acceptance across the political spectrum.[70] Amy Dru Stanley likewise stresses that a new generation of economists increasingly opposed the long-cherished dogma of unfettered markets. Not unlike the *Kathedersozialisten* in Germany, these "ethical political economists" believed that class struggle and social disintegration could be avoided if only the state would acknowledge the inequalities that markets produced. And their cri-

67 This group of conservative academics opposed both the *laissez-faire* doctrines of liberalism and the transformative vision of social democracy. Instead, they argued for a more active role for the state in enforcing social protection from the market. The term *Kathedersozialist* refers to both their supposedly state-socialist convictions and their academic background.

68 See, for instance, the interpretation by Berlin's statistician Engel, *Die Industrielle Enquete*.

69 Nipperdey, *Deutsche Geschichte*, vol. 2, 325. Similarly, Kocka concludes that the end of the 1870s also marked the end of *laissez-faire* in Prussia; see Kocka, *Arbeitsverhältnisse und Arbeiterexistenzen*, 61. See also Wehler, *Deutsche Gesellschaftsgeschichte*, vol. 3, 638–640.

70 Montgomery, *House of Labor*, 5–7.

tique "began with the denial that human labor was a commodity."[71] Both in Germany and the US, this paradigm shift heralded a new era of state-sponsored protection and market intervention. Thus, the focus on the mid-1860s to early 1870s sheds light on the early organizational phase of working-class movements, which acted in a peculiar historical context marked by the beginning disintegration of an intellectual and political paradigm and the emergence of a new climate less hostile to the regulatory demands of organized labor.

As a consequence of the theoretical focus of this study, this is a history of ideas rather than of organizational structures. Toni Offermann has argued recently that a lack of attention to the organizational history of early labor has resulted in widespread misunderstandings.[72] Yet as much as Offermann is right to stress the importance of terminological clarity, the focus on organization might be one of the reasons for the dramatic marginalization of working-class historiography. The meticulousness of contributions that have studied the organizational background of early organized labor has undoubtedly enriched our understanding of the socio-cultural substrate that *made* the movement. It blessed a younger generation of historians with a wealth of handbooks, source collections, and monographs on local, regional, and national working-class associations, unions, and parties.[73] More than anything, it turned our attention away from the ideas of a vanguard leadership and towards the experiences of the working masses. And yet, this approach has reached a dead end. Paraphrasing Thomas Kuhn, the organizational-structural branch of labor historiography fails to raise the questions that could spark the discipline—let alone offer insights of interest to the wider public. Just as three decades ago the history of ideas made room for the socio-structural analysis of organized labor, the time now seems ripe for the return of ideas.[74] The comparative analysis of working-class ideas about commodification may help build bridges beyond the discipline of History proper. After all, focusing on discourse rather than organization makes Labor History both relevant for and compatible with contemporary debates in

71 Stanley, *From Bondage to Contract*, 169.

72 Offermann, *Die erste deutsche Arbeiterpartei*, 34–48.

73 See, for instance, the very helpful accounts and source collections by Dowe, *Aktion und Organisation*; Dowe (ed.), *Berichte über die Verhandlungen*; Na'aman, *Demokratische und soziale Impulse in der Frühgeschichte der deutschen Arbeiterbewegung*; Na'aman, *Von der Arbeiterbewegung zur Arbeiterpartei*; Na'aman, "Arbeitervereine, Arbeitertage und Arbeiterverband," IX–LI.

74 Cf. Schröder, *Arbeitergeschichte und Arbeiterbewegung*, 11–16.

social theory. Each of the main chapters therefore ends with a short conclusion that highlights how the chapter contributes to current discussions in social theory.

1.4. The Text Corpus

This study draws upon statistical surveys, legislative texts, personal accounts of activists, and, first and foremost, a great variety of social-democratic and working-class periodicals. Periodicals constitute, as Klaus Tenfelde emphasizes, one of the most important sources for our understanding of early organized labor.[75] Towards the late 1860s, Berlin was on its way to becoming one of the centers of independent social-democratic media.[76] The city was home to the ADAV's organ in Prussia, the *Social-Demokrat*, and its successor, the *Neuer Social-Demokrat.* The two papers extensively covered the discussions and events of organized labor in the Prussian and, eventually, German capital. By the end of 1873, the "*Neuer*" had more than three thousand subscriptions in Berlin alone.[77] Its editors were at the same time prominent members of Berlin's workers' movement, and they regularly addressed local meetings and assemblies. The ADAV paper was the organ of several organized trades, and as such it also published the debates and proceedings of very active trades, such as the city's bricklayers. In addition, Johann Baptist von Schweitzer's *Agitator*, a Lassallean weekly from Berlin, offers insights into theoretical debates. Unlike the *(Neuer) Social-Demokrat*, the short-lived *Agitator* aimed at working-class readers who might have felt close to but were not yet members of the ADAV.[78] Towards the end of the period under review, readers in Berlin could also resort to the *Social-politische Blätter*, which appeared in Berlin from 1873 to early 1875. Edited by Wilhelm Hasenclever and Wilhelm Hasselmann, the *Social-politische Blätter* combined political analysis, essays on working-class history, and Lassallean statements of principle with entertaining contributions like poems, songs, and serials. While these periodicals represented the majority fraction of Lassalleans in Berlin, the *Demokratische Zeitung* was the local mouthpiece of the rival socialist cur-

75 Tenfelde, "Die Entstehung der deutschen Gewerkschaftsbewegung," 106.

76 Renzsch, *Handwerker und Lohnarbeiter*, 17.

77 Bezirksleitung (ed.), *Geschichte der revolutionären Berliner Arbeiterbewegung*, 193–194.

78 Renzsch, "Einleitung," vii.

rent around August Bebel and Wilhelm Liebknecht. Where applicable, this study also makes use of the latter's *Volksstaat* (which appeared in Leipzig but regularly covered events in Berlin as well). Although—for reasons of availability—the ideas of local labor leaders feature prominently in this study, the small-scale approach also gives voice to rank-and-file members and common workers who sent letters to editors or spoke at local meetings.

The labor press of New York City was less neatly divided in the 1860s. German-American workers could turn to *Die Arbeiter-Union* as the organ of German trade unionism in the city, and, later, to the *Arbeiter-Zeitung* as the voice of Marxist Internationalism in New York. The only local English-language labor paper of the mid- to late 1860s was *The National Workman*, which appeared from 1866 to 1867. William J. Jessup thus recommended in 1870 that workers in New York refer either to *The Workingman's Advocate* of Chicago or the *American Workman of Boston*, or, if fluent in German, the German-language *Arbeiter-Union.*[79] Jessup could hardly hide his disappointment that "we, the English-speaking workmen, largely in the majority, have not even a weekly journal of our own in the State to advocate the cause of labor."[80] Only towards the end of the period under review did New York City experience an increase in English-language working-class publications. *The Toiler* of New York City launched in early 1874 with a bilingual edition in English and German. As the editors around Lucien Sanial declared, the new paper's purpose was "much less to speak ourselves than to let the people speak."[81] *The Toiler* regularly published letters sent in by local workers, which makes the paper a particularly valuable source for the study of ideas expressed by the working-class rank and file. Around the time *The Toiler* launched, several sections of the International Workingmen's Association (IWA), together with fractions of organized labor from the North-East, founded the Social Democratic Party of North America (SDPNA), a largely Lassallean forerunner of the Workingmen's Party of 1876, out of which, two years later, emerged the Socialist Labor Party of America (SLP).[82] From New York City, the SDPNA published two organs, the English-language *The Socialist* (later *The*

79 *Proceedings of the Sixth Annual Session of the Workingmen's Assembly*, 8.

80 Ibid., 12.

81 "The Labor Problem," *The Toiler*, 8 August 1874, 2. Unfortunately, the only available microfilm edition shows a paper in very poor condition with bits and entire pages missing. The paper seems to have existed for only about half a year.

82 Hillquit, *History of Socialism*, 188–192.

Labor Standard) and its German counterpart, *Der Social-Demokrat* (later *Arbeiter-Stimme*).

Though English-language working-class periodicals were somewhat underrepresented in New York between the mid-1860s and early 1870s, there were two important feminist papers that regularly discussed labor politics and covered working-class events. Susan B. Anthony and Elizabeth Cady Stanton's *The Revolution* and Victoria Woodhull and Tennessee Celeste Claflin's *Woodhull and Claflin's Weekly* were important sources for this study. On the other side of the Atlantic, the German *Neue Bahnen* provided rare first-wave feminist insights into questions of female labor.

In order to better embed working-class discourse in its historical context, this study has also drawn on non-working-class media. In Berlin, the liberal *Vossische Zeitung* followed the rise of the local labor movement with great suspicion.[83] In New York, *The New York Times* played a more ambivalent role in documenting organized labor. On the one hand, the paper published proceedings and declarations of local labor meetings and covered the eight-hour movement extensively. On the other, it usually dismissed the workers' struggle as an illegitimate interference with the free market. Quotations taken from *The New York Times* and other English-language sources appear unchanged in the following. German quotations are translated in the text and provided in German in the footnotes. Unless otherwise indicated, all translations are mine.

1.5. The State of Research

As mentioned briefly above, the struggle for shorter hours occupies an important place in nineteenth-century US Social History. From encyclopedic entries to historical monographs, it has produced a wide array of local studies and nation-wide approaches.[84] In his acclaimed micro-study of the eight-hour demand in Worcester, Massachusetts, Roy Rosenzweig argues that at the beginning of the twentieth century, historians of the shorter-hour movement succumbed to the dominant influence of John R. Commons and his

83 Though commonly known as "Vossische Zeitung," the paper actually appeared under the title "Königlich privilegirte Berlinische Zeitung von Staats- und gelehrten Sachen."

84 Molloy, "Eight-Hour Movement," 153; Newton-Matza, "Eight-Hour Day Movement," 521.

institutionalist school. For decades, Rosenzweig states, the movement was studied from a strictly political-economic perspective, exploring the organizations that promoted the demands and the economic developments that triggered them.[85] In one of the earliest studies of the shorter-hour movement in the US, Marion Cotter Cahill offered a characteristic example of this approach. Echoing the Progressive Era and anticipating the New Deal, Cahill was interested primarily in the role of what she termed the "direct measures" of legislation, trade-union action, and voluntary implementation by employers. Changing attitudes in society towards time and work, however, played but a minor role in her work.[86] It was not before the appearance of historians like David Montgomery and David Brody in the 1960s and 1970s that the spell of the Commons' school finally began to break.[87] Against the backdrop of New Labor History, scholars started exploring the shorter-hour demand in a broader context of leisure, religion, and culture. David R. Roediger's dissertation in particular, which was eventually published as a monograph together with Philip S. Foner, was a milestone in the historiography of the US shorter-hour movement.[88] Today, the struggle for shorter hours has become a regular feature of not only historical overviews, but also comparative volumes or studies that are primarily concerned with contemporary questions of time and work.[89] And yet, of all places, it is New York City that has somehow fallen through the cracks. Despite the city's significance for the history of organized labor in the US, the local shorter-hour struggle remains strikingly understudied. Not only are the few workday studies of historical New York rather dated, they also lack a synthesizing quality.[90] This is all the more surprising given the attention that, for instance, the shorter-hour movements of Chicago or New England have received.[91] The following pages thus contribute to the closure of this research gap. At the same time, this book fills a sort of chronological black hole. Though

85 Rosenzweig, *Eight Hours for What We Will*, 3.

86 Cahill, *Shorter Hours*, 5–7; see also Andrews, "Nationalisation," 102–110, 124–125; Feis, "The Attempt to Establish the Eight-Hour Day;" Fine, "The Eight-Hour Day Movement."

87 See, in particular, Brody, "Time and Work;" Montgomery, *Beyond Equality*, 230–260.

88 Roediger, *The Movement for a Shorter Working Day*; Roediger and Foner, *Our Own Time.*

89 See, for instance, Negrey, *Work Time*; Cross (ed.), *Worktime and Industrialization.*

90 See Hornbeck, "The Eight Hour Day," 214–217; Yellowitz, "Eight Hours and the Bricklayers' Strike," 78–100.

91 See Brexel, *The Knights of Labor*; Mirola, *Fighting in the Pews*; Mirola, "Asking for Bread;" Murphy, *Ten Hours' Labor*; Rosenzweig, *Eight Hours for What We Will.*

there exist many studies of urban labor both prior to the Civil War and following the end of Reconstruction, the immediate postwar years have received far less attention in this respect.[92]

Whereas the study of shorter-hour struggles in New York City can build upon a well-tilled field of historical scholarship on other places in the US or the nation in general, the same struggle has been virtually ignored by German historiography. The Friedrich Ebert Foundation's authoritative "Bibliography for the History of the German Workers' Movement" ("Bibliographie zur Geschichte der deutschen Arbeiterbewegung") lists about 400 publications between 1976 and 2014 that address the subject of working time.[93] Yet the vast majority of them cover the twentieth century only—although demands for shorter workdays were second only to wage demands in the strike wave of the late 1860s and early 1870s.[94] As Jürgen Kocka stresses, it was during this period that worktime became "a central element of struggle between employer and employee," and, he concludes, "it continues to determine labor struggles through to the present."[95] Acknowledging this fact, Helga Grebing, the *grande dame* of German social-democratic historiography, states that mass strikes for the introduction of shorter workdays were a crucial element of labor struggles in the 1860s.[96] Yet her acclaimed overview fails to provide insights into the German movement for shorter hours. Toni Offermann's abovementioned study offers an important socio-statistical contribution for nineteenth-century labor research, yet workday struggles are largely missing from his account as well.[97] In their comprehensive history of organized labor in the German Empire, Gerhard A. Ritter and Klaus Tenfelde analyze the emerging wage-labor market as an economic institution rather than a bone of contestation. Even where the authors discuss changes in daily hours of work, they remain largely focused on quantitative transformations.[98] This focus also applies to discussions from within the German

92 For antebellum New York, see Adams, *The Bowery Boys*; Blackmar, *Manhattan for Rent*; Rock, "Independent Hours;" Stansell, *City of Women*; Stott, *Workers in the Metropolis*; Wilentz, *Chants Democratic*. For Gilded Age New York, see Enstad, *Ladies of Labor*; Groyens, *Beer and Revolution*; Kosak, *Cultures of Opposition*; Michels, *A Fire in Their Hearts*; Peiss, *Cheap Amusements*.

93 See http://library.fes.de/cgi-bin/populo/bizga.pl.

94 Cf. Hermann, "Kampf um die Arbeitszeit;" Schneider, "Der Kampf um die Arbeitszeitverkürzung."

95 Kocka, *Arbeitsverhältnisse und Arbeiterexistenzen*, 486.

96 See Grebing, *Geschichte der deutschen Arbeiterbewegung*, 25.

97 Cf. Offermann, *Die erste deutsche Arbeiterpartei*; Welskopp, "Review."

98 Ritter and Tenfelde, *Arbeiter im Deutschen Kaiserreich*, 155–262, 354–371.

trade-union movement, which rediscovered the shorter-hour question in the 1980s.[99] Though also interested mostly in quantitative change, important contributions to an otherwise understudied field came from Christoph Deutschmann, Irmgard Steinisch, and Günter Scharf.[100]

While the history of shorter-hour struggles in Germany as a whole can thus be characterized as understudied, research on the history of the local movement in Berlin has not even begun. Despite the capital's significance for early social-democratic and working-class culture, virtually none of the city's historical overviews devotes much attention to the local labor movement. Instead of analyzing working-class agency and contestation, historical accounts of nineteenth-century Berlin often content themselves with references to general phenomena such as "industrialization" or "social misery."[101] To this day, Eduard Bernstein's three-volume *Geschichte der Berliner Arbeiterbewegung* constitutes the most detailed account of organized labor in Berlin, yet Bernstein was at least as much a protagonist of the movement he described as he was its chronicler.[102] A less personally involved but no less biased interpretation was presented by Annemarie Lange about two generations later. Loyal to state-socialist historiography, Lange interpreted the small Marxist faction of Berlin as the precursor of the later vanguard movement in the capital of the GDR. Despite the fact that Lassalleans dominated the early phase of working-class politics in Berlin, Lange downplays the local ADAV branch to little more than a temporary nuisance lacking the proper consciousness and strategic foresight.[103] Focusing on political repression and the struggle with capitalist production, Lange's account largely ignores workers' attitudes towards wage labor, the labor market, and ideas underlying the struggle for shorter workdays. Unsurprisingly, the volume edited by the *Sozialistische Einheitspartei Deutschlands* (Socialist Unity Party of Germany, SED) on the history of Berlin's revolutionary labor movement underscored Lange's bias, although it provides a more balanced view of the pro-

99 Jacobi, Schmidt, and Müller-Jentsch (eds.), *Arbeitskampf um Arbeitszeit*; Otto, *Die Arbeitszeit.*

100 Deutschmann, *Der Weg zum Normalarbeitstag*; Scharf, *Geschichte der Arbeitszeitverkürzung*, 47–64; Steinisch, *Arbeitszeitverkürzung und sozialer Wandel.*

101 See, for instance Demps, "Die Kaiserstadt;" Schoeps, "Berlin wird Weltstadt;" Stöver, *Geschichte Berlins.*

102 Between 1907 and 1910, Eduard Bernstein published a comprehensive three-volume account of Berlin's workers movement which covers the years from 1848 to the end of the century.

103 Lange, *Berlin zur Zeit Bebels*, 146–148.

portion of Marxists to Lassalleans in the city.[104] While the volume touches briefly upon the shorter-hour movement of the early 1870s, we learn little about what motivated organized workers in Berlin to demand the normal workday. This historiographical neglect has hardly changed since then.[105] In what is probably the most recent monograph on the history of organized labor in the German capital, Axel Weipert's very helpful *Das rote Berlin* offers a refreshing account of the diversity of the movement, spanning from protests against evictions to campaigns in defense of smoking in public places.[106] Local struggles for the reduction of daily hours, however, are missing from Weipert's otherwise rich and informative account as well. Wolfgang Renzsch's study on artisans and wage workers in Berlin's early labor movement constitutes a rare exception to this trend. Although Renzsch states that he is not primarily interested in a history of working-class ideas, his detailed study of early organized labor allows crucial insights into not only the socio-economic background of workers in Berlin, but also the motives for their struggle to shorten the workday.[107]

104 Bezirksleitung (ed.), *Geschichte der revolutionären Berliner Arbeiterbewegung*, 110–232.

105 For an overview of the few studies that appeared between 1945 and 1976 on early organized labor in Berlin, see Tenfelde and Ritter (eds.), *Bibliographie zur Geschichte der deutschen Arbeiterschaft und Arbeiterbewegung*, 258–260. For later studies, see http://library.fes.de/cgi-bin/populo/bizga.pl.

106 Weipert, *Das Rote Berlin.*

107 Renzsch, *Handwerker und Lohnarbeiter*, 11.

2. Market: The Commodification of Work and the Birth of Organized Labor

"The first step out of primitive barbarism
is the step into the market."[108]
John Prince-Smith, 1863

2.1. The Rise of a Free Labor Market

With the above words, the English-born economist John Prince-Smith introduced his German audience to the idea that only if all commodities, including labor, were offered for sale on free markets could liberty and civilization flourish unhindered. As mentioned in the Introduction, the phenomenon of work for wages is much older than the nineteenth century. Yet it was during the massive industrialization of this period that wage labor became the dominant social, economic, and cultural experience of a relentlesssly growing part of the population in urban Germany and America. In his comprehensive study on nineteenth-century work relations in Germany, Jürgen Kocka suggests that the period from 1800 to 1875 witnessed the transition to wage labor for the vast majority of dependent, non-agricultural workers, with the exception of female labor in domestic services and home production.[109] In the US, wage labor had already become the prevalent form of non-agricultural work by mid-century.[110] Encouraged by the powerful notion of individual freedom and made possible by the end of peonage and guild systems (or their partial lack in the US), the newly won liberty of the formerly bonded to sell their labor without restriction became one of the most fundamental preconditions for the rise of the modern market economy. The latter's intellectual pioneer dedicated the first book of his classic study on the *Wealth of Nations* to the division of labor. In Chapter 10, Adam Smith famously pronounced that the

> property which every man has in his own labour, as it is the original foundation of all other property, so it is the most sacred and inviolable. The patrimony of a poor

---

108 Prince-Smith, "Der Markt," 2. ("Der erste Schritt also aus der ursprünglichen Unkultur heraus ist der Schritt in den Markt herein.")

109 Kocka, *Arbeitsverhältnisse und Arbeiterexistenzen*, 508–509.

110 Gutman and Berlin, "Class Composition," 380–382; Montgomery, *Beyond Equality*, 25–44.

man lies in the strength and dexterity of his hands; and to hinder him from employing this strength and dexterity in what manner he thinks proper, without injury to his neighbour, is a plain violation of this most sacred property. It is a manifest encroachment upon the just liberty, both of the workman, and of those who might be disposed to employ him.[111]

According to Smith, a free and unrestricted market constitutes the most reliable means for the distribution of the "sacred" property of labor.[112] Since labor power is usually sacred to those who possess it because it is the only property they hold, labor tends to follow market shifts closely. In times of strong demand, providers of labor power can afford to offer their commodity at a higher price and under conditions of consumption more favorable to them. In times of decreasing demand, they are compelled to accept less beneficial prices and conditions.[113]

This notion was carved in stone by the nineteenth-century economic law commonly ascribed to Jean-Baptiste Say. According to "Say's Theorem," every supply created its own demand. If the suppliers of labor were flexible in terms of prices and working conditions, they would always find purchasers for their product.[114] The market would thus increase the responsiveness of labor and prevent workers from failing to find buyers during contractions of demand. Put differently, the laws of supply and demand would guarantee that laborers benefited from economic growth while being spared the experience of mass joblessness during economic downturns thanks to flexible wages and working times. According to this interpretation, there would be no structural unemployment as long as governments as well as trade associations and unions respected the liberty of all market players—an idea that was famously challenged by John Maynard Keynes in the following century.[115] Thanks to the integration of such ideas into a broader framework of political liberty, the commodification of labor in the nineteenth century was considered both an expression of individual freedom and

111 Smith, *Wealth of Nations*, 51.

112 For Smith's impact on the notion of contractual freedom in wage-labor relations, see also Stanley, *From Bondage to Contract*, 12–14.

113 Smith, *Wealth of Nations*, 27–36.

114 Although his name has fallen into oblivion outside the field of economics, Jean-Baptiste Say was considered one of the most influential political economists of the early to mid-nineteenth century. In the eyes of nineteenth-century economist August Oncken, there could be little doubt that Say provided the source for most traditional assumptions on economic thought; see Oncken, *Die Maxime laissez faire*, 9.

115 See Keynes, *The General Theory*, 18–21; Willke, *Keynes*, 30–51.

a guarantee against a lack of demand and the much-discussed pauperism resulting from it. Backed by the intellectual pioneers of late eighteenth and nineteenth-century liberalism, the free market became deeply rooted in modern society.

In Germany, the notion of a free market was taken up by various liberal employers and intellectuals from the 1840s onwards. From his adopted home town of Berlin, Prince-Smith argued that European societies were determined entirely by market relations. Although Prince-Smith was mainly interested in free-trade issues, he also attended to what he described as the "so-called labor question." In his same-titled article, he polemicized against the "degenerate and unpropertied classes" who had to learn that free labor constituted the only way out of poverty and deprivation. Prince-Smith concluded that

> he who is reserveless receives a price for his labor that is determined on the market, just like any other commodity price: He seeks the one who rates his labor the highest and is willing to pay the most.[116]

Striving to reduce the influence of early social democracy among German journeymen and workers, Prince-Smith dedicated a wide range of essays to the market as the central institution for the promotion of freedom and growth. In an article titled "The Market," he argued that the latter followed a natural, self-perpetuating logic. Market subjects, including those who offered the commodity of labor for sale, needed to understand the meaning of economic freedom in order to appreciate the promises of unfettered commercial relations. In Prince-Smith's eyes, the market was an almost organic phenomenon. As the embodiment of what he regarded as a natural movement that mediated between what men want and what men provide—or, put differently, between supply and demand—Prince-Smith idealized the market as the logical consequence of progress. Only through the laws of the market, he concluded, could efficiency and rationality for the sake of all triumph over selfish shortsightedness. Later in the essay, Prince-Smith debated what this meant for the market of this peculiar commodity that is human labor. The labor market provided the opportunity for the great mass of the unpropertied and uneducated to seek capitalized buyers and thereby meet

116 Prince-Smith, "Die sogenannte Arbeiterfrage," 38. ("Der Vorrathslose erhält für seine Arbeit einen Preis, welcher sich im Markte ebenso bestimmt, wie der Preis jeder Marktware: er sucht Denjenigen, der seine Arbeit am höchsten abschätzt und ihm dafür das meiste Geld geben will.")

the daily costs of reproduction. Workers would simply rent out their labor power to the qualified holder of capital. "The wage or rental charge for labor is, as with any commodity, dependent on the actual rate of supply and demand."[117] Prince-Smith expressed deep regret that some forces in society failed to recognize the beneficial impact of unrestricted markets. Instead of respecting the free play of supply and demand, both employers and workers tended to organize in order to set particular prices and working conditions that only the market could determine without violating the prospects of freedom and growth.

Yet Prince-Smith did not confine himself to the propagation of economic theory. Inspired by Richard Cobden's Anti-Corn Law League, which had successfully fought for the abolition of the protectionist Corn Laws in England, Prince-Smith contributed substantially to the formation of Germany's first free-trade association, the *Volkwirtschaftlicher Kongress* (Congress of German Economists). Founded in 1858, the congress featured prominently among the advocates of economic freedom in mid-nineteenth-century Germany. It was composed of a variety of economists and businessmen who wished to advance the liberalization of commerce and trade in their respective states. Though the congress was predominantly concerned with aspects of free trade and monetary policies, it also promoted the freedom of labor. At its first convention, Viktor Böhmert, an acclaimed statistician and professor of economics, declared that the congress opposed any legislative labor regulation. Instead, he stoutly defended the economic system that required the worker to depend upon his own labor and self-help, but also granted him the natural right to earn his bread in whatever way he wished, as long as he did not interfere with his neighbor.[118]

At the time the Englishman Prince-Smith found a new home in Berlin, Karl Heinzen was forced to flee his native land. A radical democrat and prolific publicist, Heinzen had already spent a brief time in American exile due to a publication critical of the Prussian government. Following his return to Germany and his active role in the failed revolution of 1848, Heinzen, like so many of his liberal fellows, faced political persecution once more from a reinvigorated Prussian state. Equipped with the fresh experience of conservative repression, Heinzen now crossed the Atlantic for good. From New

117 Prince-Smith, "Der Markt," 19. ("Sie vermiethet ihre Arbeitskraft an befähigte Kapitalisten. Der Lohn oder Mietpreis der Arbeit hängt, wie jeder Preis überhaupt, unmittelbar von dem Verhältniss [sic] zwischen Nachfrage und Angebot ab.")

118 Hentschel, *Die deutschen Freihändler*, 42–43.

York City, he made his way to Kentucky until, in the late 1850s, he settled permanently in Boston. There, in the politically much more permissive climate of New England, Heinzen merged his democratic vision with an American radicalism that was about to find new political shape in the form of the Republican Party. For Heinzen, the struggle for equality and liberty was the struggle of all freedom-loving citizens irrespective of their occupational status. With regard to the workingmen of America, Heinzen thus insisted that their hopes "could be realized only through the Radical party—the party of freedom."[119] He enthusiastically endorsed the democratic egalitarianism of the abolitionists, suffragists, and social reformers who energized the radical scene of New England during the 1850s and into the first years of the Civil War. At the same time, he welcomed the widely held notion that, in a republic of equals, there was no need for government intervention in domestic market processes. Already in the 1840s, Heinzen had criticized the young communist movement for its half-hearted internalization of republican ideals. The communists, he argued, cared little about freedom in the polity. Marx and his followers had retreated into a fantastic world of utopia because they were eager for attention rather than political transformation. At the earliest opportunity, they had betrayed the cause of the revolution of 1848 and, therewith, the cause of workers as well. Heinzen thus appealed to the workers to "leave the lecture halls of the communists and join the honest and honorable republicans."[120] Instead of fighting private property and the stimulating powers of competition, what both capital and labor required to prosper was a state that refrained from regulating their affairs.

While Karl Heinzen primarily addressed a German immigrant readership, the author and Unitarian minister Edward Everett Hale appealed especially to the native-born liberal mind. Though Hale generally welcomed the reduction of working hours, he fiercely opposed any intervention into what he believed was the natural movement of things. As David Montgomery emphasizes, Hale particularly rejected "any legislation other than that which 'tends to complete freedom in the sale by every man of his prime commodity, his labor.'"[121] However, American radicals of the 1850s and

---

119 Montgomery, *Beyond Equality*, 232. For competing political currents at the dawn of the Civil War, see ibid., 45–89. For "free labor" positions within the nascent Republican Party, see Foner, *Free Soil*, especially 11–39.

120 Heinzen, *Die Helden des teutschen Kommunismus*, 104. ("Auf, ihr Arbeiter, verlaßt die Hörsäle der Kommunisten und schließt euch ehrlichen und ehrenwerten Republikanern an!")

121 Montgomery, *Beyond Equality*, 246. See also Stanley, *From Bondage to Contract*, 75–78.

1860s did not promote *laissez-faire* ideals equally in all fields of commodity exchange. Rather, many in the radical camp openly favored protective tariffs over open international trade. But the demand for the protection of domestic consumer markets did not stop them from advocating free and unregulated markets for labor. The prominent political economist Henry C. Carey—in Marx's eyes "the only original economist of North America"—fiercely criticized *laissez-faire* doctrines in currency exchange and international trade.[122] The domestic labor market, however, was best left to itself, even though Carey was convinced that it had become glutted due to monopolization and low wages in Europe. Echoing Say's Theorem, he stated "that the true interests of labor and capital were identical and that supply and demand 'naturally' balanced each other out."[123] The eminent Republican thought leader Horace Greely promoted similar ideas in his *New York Tribune.* In Greely's eyes, if a worker found his hours too long or wages too low, "he should not 'stand idle' by striking, but should take another job or move to the West."[124]

Whether in Germany or the US, notions of individual liberty and contractual freedom contributed to the rapid demise of traditional work relations. At the same time, the increasing division of labor, the growing concentration of production, and the introduction of new machinery fueled the demand for mobile and flexible labor. The liberalization in economic thought and the revolution in production found their expression in the fundamental transformation of nineteenth-century labor legislation. Following the triumphant advance of the Napoleonic armies, the German states had abolished whatever was left of former serfdom regulations, while urban guilds were increasingly forced to remove entrance barriers and abandon protectionist price settlements. In 1810, the reform edicts commonly ascribed to vom Stein and von Hardenberg famously introduced the freedom of trade and occupation as a central pillar of a rejuvenated Prussian state. Though labor was thus technically freed by 1810, many restrictions continued to exist in various parts of Prussia, such that, in 1845, Frederick William IV passed a revised Trade Regulation Act. In Section 1 of said act, the king outlawed any local practice or provision that hindered his subjects from freely choosing a profession or offer their labor power for purchase.[125] The

122 Cited in Sylvers, "Marx, Engels und die USA," 31.

123 Montgomery, *Beyond Equality*, 86.

124 Cited in Foner, *Free Soil*, 26.

125 *Allgemeine Preußische Gewerbe-Ordnung vom 17. Januar 1845*, 1–2.

new Trade Regulation Act underscored the voluntariness of membership in guilds and other professional associations that had been introduced by reforms at the beginning of the century.[126] The act also contained regulations for dangerous crafts and professions that required special training, such as pharmacy. In addition, it provided that workers enjoyed particular rights such as fair and decent treatment and a very rudimentary form of employment protection. However, in Section 134 the act determined that the actual work relation between tradesperson or employer and apprentice, journeyman, or worker was entirely subject to free agreement.[127] This meant that, for instance, wages or daily working hours would not be fixed by legislation. In 1869, the Prussian trade act was woven into the Trade Regulation Act of the newly established North German Confederation. With the passage of this act in the member states of the confederation and, eventually, its adoption by the German Empire, the principle of economic freedom achieved general validity. With clearly defined exceptions, every adult citizen in the empire was given the right to offer his or her labor power on a free and unrestricted market. Such legislative restraint underscores the finding by Jürgen Kocka, who stresses that Prussia was virtually the only German state in the mid-nineteenth century that placed the market above even the state itself. While states like Bavaria strived to win control over urban labor markets, Prussia's officialdom enforced the reign of the free market especially in its cities. After all, unhindered competition and the spread of a free market for labor were hoped to boost productivity and foster economic growth.[128] As a consequence, aspects like daily hours of work were considered to be a matter of supply and demand rather than public intervention. This view clearly resonated with the liberal movement. Moritz Müller, a *bijouterie* manufacturer who regularly addressed the liberal *Arbeitertage* (workers' days) of the 1860s, expressed the view that workers surely enjoyed a right to recreation, but the actual length of the workday should be determined by free negotiation rather than law.[129]

At first sight, the US seems to offer a very different picture. In the course of the 1830s and 1840s, the labor forces of its eastern cities had mounted

126 See Section 94, ibid, 25–26.

127 See Section 134, ibid, 36. ("Die Festsetzung der Verhältnisse zwischen den selbstständigen Gewerbetreibenden und ihren Gesellen, Gehülfen und Lehrlingen ist Gegenstand freier Übereinkunft.")

128 Kocka, *Arbeitsverhältnisse und Arbeiterexistenzen*, 31.

129 Müller, *Eine Ansprache über die Arbeitszeit*, 6.

powerful campaigns for local, state, and federal intervention into the market.[130] If one concentrates exclusively on the workday legislation that followed in the coming two decades, the *laissez-faire* spirit of Jacksonian democracy appears to have been replaced by an interventionist ideal of public control and market regulation. In 1847, New Hampshire broke ground by passing the first ten-hour law and, therewith, the first state-wide regulation of the length of the workday. Year after year, municipal and state legislatures followed suit.[131] In the aftermath of the Civil War, legislatures at different levels introduced the first eight-hour bills, several of which applied to workers in New York. In 1866, New York City passed an eight-hour law for all city employees.[132] The following year, on May 9, 1867, the state of New York adopted an eight-hour law for all employees in the state (except domestic and farm laborers).[133] Another year later, on June 24, 1868, Congress passed an eight-hour law for all federal workers that President Johnson signed into law the following day.[134] Yet what all these bills had in common was their virtual ineffectiveness. From the earliest state regulation of working hours that New Hampshire passed in 1847 to the new initiatives of the 1860s, laws were designed or interpreted so broadly that they undermined any meaningful protection for workers. New Hampshire's initiative of 1847, for instance, provided that ten hours constituted a day's work "unless otherwise agreed by the parties."[135] Where laws lacked such explicit limitations, courts rendered existing hour restrictions meaningless. Judges regularly argued that no government, not even the democratically legitimized state or federal government of the US, could suspend the liberty of the individual to freely pursue their economic interests. As David Montgomery concludes, to nineteenth-century courts "the basic principles of the republic required defense of individual initiative in economic life against both governmental and social interference."[136] By granting the concept of free labor constitutional protection, courts thus withdrew aspects of wage work from democratic control.[137] In so doing, they contributed to the notion that the free exchange

130 Roediger and Foner, *Our Own Time*, 40.

131 Negrey, *Work Time*, 36–39.

132 Commons et al. (eds.), *History of American Industrial Society*, vol. 9, 278.

133 Ibid., 330.

134 Kuritz, "Ira Steward and the Eight Hour Day," 123; Roediger and Foner, *Our Own Time*, 93, 109–112; "Das Achtstunden-gesetz," *Die Arbeiter Union*, 2 January 1869, 6.

135 Roediger and Foner, *Our Own Time*, 58.

136 Montgomery, *Citizen Worker*, 49.

137 Montgomery, *Beyond Equality*, 321–323.

of the commodity of labor power was inscribed into the foundation of the Republic as a quasi natural law that no government, let alone collectively organized workers, could touch. According to the courts' peculiar interpretation, the eight-hour laws of the 1860s only determined that no worker could be forced to work longer than eight hours a day. But by no means did the law prohibit employees and employers from agreeing freely upon longer workdays if they wished to do so. Although workers in New York City were thus formally protected by municipal, state, and federal laws in the late 1860s, the spirit of non-intervention and free labor exchange in fact was unbroken.[138] Yet more and more suppliers of labor were unwilling to accept this situation quietly. Against the backdrop of unregulated markets, a transnational movement emerged in the first half of the nineteenth century that struggled against the paradigm of non-intervention.

As early as the 1820s, Robert Owen had popularized the demand for eight-hour workdays in the industrial laboratory of England. Based on his co-operative model of production, Owen promoted the idea that laborers needed to be protected from the cruel grasp of the factory system. Owen himself brought his ideas as far as the US, which he visited in the mid-1820s.[139] In the industrializing cities of the East, the battle call for shorter hours fell on fertile soil among the organized trades of Boston, New York, and Philadelphia.[140] From England and the US, the demand for a shorter workday spread to continental Europe, and indeed far beyond.[141] By mid-century, the shorter-hour movement literally spanned the globe, though probably not the world.[142] In the eyes of the prominent US labor leader and journalist George E. McNeill, the shorter-hour movement knew no nationality. According to him, even Bismarck trembled "before the power of this

138 Kuritz, "Ira Steward and the Eight Hour Day," 124.

139 Armytage, "Owen in America," 214–238; Hillquit, *History of Socialism in the United States*, 48–69.

140 Roediger and Foner, *Our Own Time*, 19–21.

141 Tsuzuki, "Robert Owen and Revolutionary Politics," 14–16.

142 Whether the demand for shorter hours resonated with non-Western or colonized societies is beyond the scope of this study. Given the rapacity of labor and land commodification in nineteenth-century colonies, struggles for de-commodification most likely played an important role for social opposition in colonial contexts as well. A rare discussion of the eight-hour system under colonial rule appeared in a report on South Africa on June 18, 1869. The *Arbeiter-Union* of New York City declared that, since 1862, all workers in South Africa worked on eight-hour shifts. It is very unlikely, however, that this actually applied to the entire working class irrespective of racialized differentiations; see "Das Achtstunden-System in Afrika," *Die Arbeiter-Union*, 18 June 1869, 1.

mighty movement."[143] And while German, Australian, French, Dutch, American, and English workers promoted the cause for shorter hours both locally and nationally, the International Workingmen's Association (IWA) gave the movement its transnational twist.[144] Convening in Geneva in September 1866, the First International promised to make the struggle for eight hours "the common platform of the working classes all over the world."[145]

Few labor activists epitomize the transnational character of the movement for shorter hours as impressively as Richard F. Trevellick, the "Harbinger of the Eight-Hour System."[146] Born in England in 1830, Trevellick became a shipyard worker in Southampton, where he witnessed firsthand the local struggles for eight hours. Since then, Trevellick took this demand with him wherever he travelled.[147] And travel he did. While he was still in his early twenties, Trevellick began an epic journey that took him to India, Australia, and New Zealand, where he participated in the great movement for eight hours that overran the British dominions at that time. Reporting from Australia on August 29, 1856, *The New York Daily Times* declared that "[w]hat is called the eight-hour movement had been pretty generally successful."[148] Similar reports came from neighboring New Zealand, where skilled workers in the building sector had won the eight-hour day. Equipped with fresh experiences of collective success, Trevellick embarked on a ship to South America, made his way from Peru to Panama and, around 1857, finally arrived in New Orleans. Over the coming years, Trevellick moved back and forth between New York City, Detroit, New Orleans, and many other US cities. Unlike few others, the future president of the National Labor Union (NLU) personified the new dawn of shorter-hours struggles that energized organized labor on both sides of the Atlantic.[149]

On its European shore, the industrial cities of England were not the only ones to witness powerful campaigns for normal workday legislation. A little

---

143 McNeill, *Argument on the Hours of Labor*, 20.

144 For France and England, see Cross, *The Quest for Time*; Weaver, "The Political Ideology of Short Time." For Australia, see Niland, "The Birth of the Movement for an Eight Hour Working Day;" Kimber and Love, *The Time of Their Lives*. For New Zealand, see Corliss and Parnell, *A Legacy*. For the Dutch perspective, see Karsten, *De Achturendag*, 191–304.

145 International Workingmen's Association (ed.), *Resolutions of the Congress of Geneva, 1866, and the Congress of Brussels, 1868*, 5.

146 Hicks, *Life of Richard F. Trevellick*.

147 Ibid., 12–13.

148 "News from Australia," *New York Daily Times*, 29 August 1856, 4. The New York Daily Times dropped the "Daily" in 1857.

149 See also Montgomery, *Beyond Equality*, 222–223.

further to the east, the capital of Prussia was on its way to becoming a hot-spot for shorter-hour agitation on the continent. Given the explosion of working-class residents, this was not surprising.[150]

2.2. Organized Labor in Berlin in the 1860s and early 1870s

Based on the general census returns of 1875, the *Magistrat* of Berlin published a report that showed that about half of Berlin's population was actively working, while the other half either depended upon incomes provided by the former or were engaged in some form of undocumented home production.[151] Of those documented as working, the single largest group was employed in the personal-service sector. The 76,440 coachmen, servants, chefs, and maids of the city represented about 15 percent of the entire work-force, with an additional 17,700 dependent relatives. This group was probably even larger, given the fact that washerwomen were either not included at all or subsumed under the category of clothing workers.[152] The 67,604 workers in clothing who supported 48,201 dependents constituted the largest group in the manual-labor sector. Taken together, clothing and cleaning were responsible for more than 13 percent of all productive labor. The roughly 56,000 unspecified laborers made up the second-largest group in manual labor, followed by the combined group of metal trades and machine, instrument and tool building. The construction sector employed about

150 Cf. Büsch, *Industrialisierung und Gewerbe.*

151 Magistrat der Stadt Berlin (ed.), *Bericht über die Gemeinde-Verwaltung der Stadt Berlin*, 55. The original census survey distinguished between independent producers ("Selbstthätige") and their dependents ("deren Angehörige"), but, as Lange and Rößler rightly point out, this distinction is to be treated with caution. Since such diverse occupational groups as manufacturers, artisanal masters, rentiers, pensioners, and peddlers all belonged to the same category of "Selbstthätige," it says very little about the ratio of self-employed to employed labor; see Lange, *Berlin zur Zeit Bebels*, 87; Rößler, *Zur Lage der Berliner Arbeiter*, 28. We also do not know how many of the dependent relatives were simultaneously involved in some form of productive work at home. Women were not recorded as "dependents" if they worked in some regular trade outside of their home. If, however, they worked irregularly or as members of a family workshop, they were usually listed as unproductive dependents. Obviously this resulted in the gross underrepresentation of working women; see. ibid., 31–32. For the statistical procedure, see Schwabe (ed.), *Die Resultate der Berliner Volkszählung vom 3. December 1867*, LXXVI–LXXVII.

152 Rößler, "Zur Lage der Berliner Arbeiter," 35.

25,000 workers, although their number was hard to determine due to seasonal unemployment as well as the fact that many carpenters and bricklayers often lived in surrounding municipalities.[153] Printing and the production of food, paper, and leather also featured prominently in the manual-labor sector. In addition to personal services and manual labor, about 73,500 people found employment in trade, transportation, and bar or restaurant keeping. Finally, about 12,000 Berliners were employed by the municipality, state, or empire, with an additional 20,000 employed as military personnel.[154]

Despite the enormous increase in productivity that accompanied the early phase of industrialization in Germany between 1830 and 1860, the workday had become longer rather than shorter for most trades.[155] Longer workdays did not necessarily mean that workers went to work earlier or returned home later, however. Often, the workday was stretched through the elimination of traditions like local holidays and Blue Mondays, the prohibition of family visits and alcoholic beverages, the ban of play and mischief at work, and, in general, the disciplining of the workforce.[156] According to Jürgen Kocka, the length of the workday climaxed in Prussia around the year 1860.[157] There are no reliable statistics for this period, yet local factory rules and the *Arbeitszeitordnung* (Working Time Act) passed by the *Berliner Gewerberat* (Trade Council) in 1854 indicate that the length of the workday officially oscillated between eleven and 13 hours in the Prussian capital.[158] Yet in fact, working days were often considerably longer. The bulk of Berlin's tailors, for instance, worked twelve to 14 hours a day, but even 16- to 18-hour days were not uncommon.[159] The city's bakers also knew workdays of 16 to 18 hours.[160] Domestic workers and home producers likewise faced extremely long workdays, but due to the irregularity and undocumented character of their labor, estimates are difficult. The bricklayers, carpenters, cabinetmakers, painters, paper hangers, plasterers, and other trades that comprised Ber-

153 Renzsch, *Handwerker und Lohnarbeiter*, 36, 42.

154 Magistrat der Stadt Berlin (ed.), *Bericht über die Gemeinde-Verwaltung der Stadt Berlin*, 55–56.

155 Otto, *Die Arbeitszeit*, 51–55, 59; Scharf, *Geschichte der Arbeitszeitverkürzung*, 76–88.

156 Cf. Pollard, "Factory Discipline;" Thompson, "Time, Work-Discipline, and Industrial Capitalism."

157 Kocka, *Arbeitsverhältnisse und Arbeiterexistenzen*, 481–486. For Germany in general, see Schröder, *Arbeitergeschichte und Arbeiterbewegung*, 194.

158 Scharf, *Geschichte der Arbeitszeitverkürzung*, 83. For the "Arbeitszeitordnung," see Bezirksleitung (ed.), *Geschichte der revolutionären Berliner Arbeiterbewegung*, 106.

159 Renzsch, *Handwerker und Lohnarbeiter*, 79; Scharf, *Geschichte der Arbeitszeitverkürzung*, 138.

160 "Vermischtes (Die Berliner Bäckereigesellen)," *Der Social-Demokrat*, 2 August 1868, 4.

lin's large building sector seem to have worked somewhere between eleven and 13 hours a day, yet, as with the tailors, the length of their workdays was heavily dependent on order and season.[161] Workers in Berlin's metal and machine-building trades usually worked for ten to twelve hours.[162] Although first businesses started introducing workday reductions in the 1860s, workers in Berlin (and, for that matter, urban workers all over industrializing Germany) still stood at the beginning of a long and stony march. It was not before the close of the century that the ten-hour workday became standard in most occupations.[163]

Berlin featured not only a very diverse work schedule, but also a highly uneven employment structure in the 1860s and early 1870s. In the north of the city, the districts of Moabit, Oranienburger Vorstadt, and Rosenthaler Vorstadt emerged as eminent centers for the metal industries that produced the railroad switches and locomotives that made Berlin the most important traffic hub in Central Europe.[164] Large-scale enterprises like Borsig and Schwartzkopff required workers to adopt to the specific challenges of factory work. For the skilled metal workers employed there, the experience of wage work had become an everyday reality. Yet despite the development of water- and railways, the import of natural resources remained relatively costly, a fact that thwarted the expansion of resource-intensive production. Labor-intensive production, in contrast, had been on the rise since the 1830s.[165] In the suburbs of the Wilhelmine Ring, a circle of new constructions clustered around the old inner-city neighborhoods, industries like tailoring and shoemaking gave work to the masses of newcomers who swamped the city.[166] The southern districts of Luisenstadt and Stralauer Viertel alone, which constitute large parts of today's Kreuzberg and Fried-

---

161 Bezirksleitung (ed.), *Geschichte der revolutionären Berliner Arbeiterbewegung*, 106; Lange, *Berlin zur Zeit Bebels*, 158; Scharf, *Geschichte der Arbeitszeitverkürzung*, 139–140. Renzsch suggests that between 1848 and 1869, Berlin's construction workers usually worked eleven hours a day; see Renzsch, *Handwerker und Lohnarbeiter*, 49.

162 Ibid., 160–168. See, for instance, the local blacksmith journeyman who declared in 1869 that he worked 14-hour shifts, including a two-hour break, "Lokal-Nachrichten," *Die Zukunft*, 7 July 1869, 3. Metal workers at Siemens in Berlin worked about ten hours a day in the early 1870s; see Kocka, "Von der Manufaktur zur Fabrik," 272.

163 See Deutschmann and Dybowski-Johannson, "Wirtschaftliche und soziale Determinanten der Arbeitszeitpolitik," 314–315.

164 Dietrich, "Berlins Weg zur Industrie- und Handelsstadt," 180; Richter, "Zwischen Revolution und Reichsgründung," 657.

165 Baar, "Berlin in der Industriellen Revolution," 72.

166 For the emergence of the Wilhelmine Ring, see Weipert, *Das Rote Berlin*, 37.

richshain, were home to almost a third of the entire urban population.[167] These young suburbs featured labor- and life-worlds characterized by the very lack of separation between the two worlds. Many of the notoriously overcrowded tenements served not only as dwellings, but also as production units that hosted a myriad of different work arrangements. If they did not work directly in their homes, many artisans found work in neighborhood workshops, small-scale manufactories, or remises in rear-end courtyards. Here the city's tailors and shoemakers worked as independent artisans or, increasingly, as petty contractors, a peculiar occupational position that blurred the concept of wage work.[168] The intensification of home production also undermined the boundaries of self-employment. Often entire families either produced independently for local markets or assisted the contracted labor of the family head.[169] In the late 1860s and 1870s, many of Berlin's contracted artisans already produced ready-made clothing that was exported to as far away as New York.[170]

The coexistence of factory wage work, fictitious and real self-employment, and unwaged female and child labor in home production resulted in very diverse employment and work experiences. In 1861, the municipality conducted a survey that showed that the group of craftsmen who worked primarily for local markets was still considerably larger than the group of producers working mainly for national and international markets. Among the former group, the average ratio of employees to masters was about two to one (with the exception of construction, which had a ratio of about six to one). In the second group, however, the average ratio was almost eleven to one. In the metal trades, the ratio was even between 21 and 23 to one. This comparison shows that, while Berlin already featured a small sector of centralized industrial wage labor in the early 1860s, far more citizens either worked as self-employed craftsmen or found employment in small workshops with a single employer and very few fellow employees.[171] Although labor concentration had grown in a few industries, the urban economy of Berlin was still dominated by small workshops.[172] In 1874, Berlin's newly established factory inspector conducted a survey that showed that almost

167 Rößler, "Zur Lage der Berliner Arbeiter," 27.
168 Dietrich, "Berlins Weg zur Industrie- und Handelsstadt," 181–188.
169 Richter, "Zwischen Revolution und Reichsgründung," 660–661.
170 Dietrich, "Berlins Weg zur Industrie- und Handelsstadt," 189–190.
171 See Engel, "Die Industrie der großen Städte," 143.
172 Rößler, "Zur Lage der Berliner Arbeiter," 105.

half of all "factories" in the city employed ten workers or fewer, with an additional quarter that employed 25 workers or fewer. There were only three factories in 1874 that employed more than 1,000 workers. By no means can the early urban labor force thus be described as heavily concentrated in large factories that fostered proletarian class consciousness, as state-socialist historiography would later have it.[173]

Despite its eventual prominence as the "capital of German labor," Berlin was in fact somewhat of a latecomer in the second wave of working-class organizing that followed the careful withdrawal of state repression in the early 1860s.[174] To the regret of Eduard Bernstein, the city's working class was notoriously reluctant to embrace social-democratic ideas or build independent associations.[175] During the turbulent months of the 1848 revolution, the first independent workers' associations had mushroomed across the city, yet Berlin's organized workers also advanced their democratic demands side by side with their employers.[176] The ideological and organizational foundations laid here proved rather solid, so much so that—at a time when Ferdinand Lassalle was winning ground in Saxony, Hamburg, and elsewhere—the majority of Berlin's labor force remained firmly rooted in the liberal-democratic tradition.[177] And Berlin's liberal movement actively strived to prevent the local working class from falling under the Lassallean spell. In 1859, the aforementioned Congress of German Economists used its influence and helped establish the *Deutscher Nationalverein* (German National Association), a rather broad coalition movement spanning from radical democrats to right-liberal nationalists who aimed to advance industrialization and political unity. Two years later, the affiliated *Deutsche Fortschrittspartei* (German Progress Party) was launched as a political arm of the movement that dominated municipal politics for years. In Berlin, Hermann Schulze-Delitzsch, a political veteran of 1848 and a prominent figure in both the National Association and the Progress Party, became one of the most outspoken voices advocating consumer and saving co-operatives, workers' education, and a general program of economic liberalism. On January 18, 1863, the city witnessed the birth of a new organization of workers that

173 Cf. Bezirksleitung (ed.), *Geschichte der revolutionären Berliner Arbeiterbewegung*, 104–105.

174 Dietrich, "Berlins Weg zur Industrie- und Handelsstadt," 183–184; Erbe, "Berlin im Kaiserreich," 764; Welskopp, *Das Banner der Brüderlichkeit*, 141.

175 Bernstein, *Die Geschichte der Berliner Arbeiterbewegung*, 108.

176 Cf. Hachtmann, *Berlin 1848*, 94–103.

177 Bezirksleitung (ed.), *Geschichte der revolutionären Berliner Arbeiterbewegung*, 126–128. See also Lassalle, *An die Arbeiter Berlins.*

largely embodied Schulze-Delitzsch's stance. Distancing itself from principles laid down by Lassalle and Marx, the *Berliner Arbeiterverein* (Workers' Association of Berlin, BAV) represented the fraction of the urban working class that saw its interests as being in harmony with those of its employers.[178] Instead of fighting for protective legislation, the BAV openly advanced the further commodification of labor.[179]

Due to the strong position of the BAV in Berlin, Lassalle's rival ADAV initially struggled to gain a foothold in the Prussian capital.[180] Founded in Leipzig in 1863, the ADAV challenged the paternalism of liberal organizers and promoted the centralization of an independent workers' movement that, in its own eyes, remained loyal to the democratic heritage of 1848. Yet due to the untimely death of its charismatic leader in 1864, the early years of the ADAV were characterized by fractional conflict between the entourage of the prominent Countess Sophie von Hatzfeld, who claimed to keep to the true teachings of her deceased mentor and friend Lassalle, and the group around Johann Baptist von Schweitzer, who had recently moved to Berlin, from where he strived to extend the ADAV's influence under his authoritarian leadership.[181] Faced with internal trench warfare and the preeminence of Schulze-Delitzsch, it was no wonder that the Berlin branch[182] of the ADAV was initially, as Bernstein put it, its "problem child." In February

178 Na'aman, *Von der Arbeiterbewegung zur Arbeiterpartei*, 9–23; Weipert, *Das Rote Berlin*, 29.

179 The BAV thus hoped that the Trade Act would "enable the full liberalization of labor and employment" ("[…] die Gewerbe-Ordnung im Sinne vollster Gewerbefreiheit zu amendiren"); see Geheimes Staatsarchiv Preußischer Kulturbesitz (henceforth GStA PK), I. HA Rep. 120 A, I, 1, Nr. 56: "Die beim Reichstage des Norddeutschen Bundes eingegangenen Petitionen," 1867–1873; here: "Reichstag des Norddeutschen Bundes, 1. Legislatur-Periode, Sitzungs-Periode 1868, Sechstes Verzeichnis der beim Reichstage des Norddeutschen Bundes eingegangenen, an die Petitions-Kommission abgegebenen Petitionen," 1868, Record Number 22.

180 Bergmann, *Das Berliner Handwerk*; Dietrich, "Berlins Weg zur Industrie- und Handelsstadt," 184; Renzsch, *Handwerker und Lohnarbeiter*, 26–27.

181 Mayer, *Johann Baptist von Schweitzer*, 71; Welskopp, *Das Banner der Brüderlichkeit*, 38–40.

182 Toni Offermann stresses that local ADAV memberships were best understood as *Gemeinden*—that is, as congregations or communities—since *Gemeinde* conveys their organizationally dependent background as well as their quasi-religious character most accurately. Given both the ADAV's take on centralization and the existing legal restrictions in Prussia, the ADAV insisted that local memberships were part of the central association in Leipzig rather than autonomous associations; see Offermann, *Die erste deutsche Arbeiterpartei*, 36–38. The term "branch" is thus not unproblematic, but it helps avoid misunderstandings in the English language.

1864, it had no more than 35 members, compared to the roughly 2,000 workers who actively supported the liberal BAV.[183]

Yet the young Lassallean movement in Berlin faced not only internal conflict and a strong liberal competitor, but also the iron fist of the state. There can hardly be a more reliable source to testify to the degree of political repression than the following legal overview provided by the Prussian authorities themselves. In 1871, the Prussian State Ministry complied eagerly with a request by the new Reich Chancellor, who wished to receive a detailed overview of the Laws of Assembly and Association that had been passed in Prussia up to that point.[184] Until 1848, the ministry declared, there had been no separate code of law for assemblies and associations. Instead, individuals and associations were subject to the common law of the land, which provided for a wide array of legal restrictions for political and economic associations. Facing massive pressure by a revolting citizenry in 1848, the Prussian Crown saw itself forced to consider the granting of greater associational freedoms.[185] Passed on December 6, 1848, and revised on January 31, 1850, Article 29, No. 1 of the new constitution determined that all Prussians enjoyed the right to convene unarmed and peacefully in closed rooms without prior permission. The following article provided that all Prussians enjoyed the right to form associations, as long as they did not run contrary to the penal code. Though the constitution thereby granted basic associational rights, these newly won freedoms were far from comprehensive.[186] The right to convene freely, for instance, did not apply to gatherings in the open, as the second sentence of Article 29 made clear. In addition, both the right of assembly and the right of free association were modified by Article 30, No. 2, which declared that legal intervention was permissible in the event of any threat to public order and safety. Finally, Article 30, No. 3 introduced a curtailment that would become particularly obstructive for the labor movement in Prussia. The article determined that

183 Bernstein, *Die Geschichte der Berliner Arbeiterbewegung*, 112; Offermann, *Die erste deutsche Arbeiterpartei*, 150.

184 GStA PK, I. HA Rep. 90 A, Nr. 2257: "Regelung des Vereins- und Versammlungsrechts," Bd. 1, 1794–1893, Record Number 121.

185 GStA PK, I. HA Rep. 90 A, Nr. 2257: "Regelung des Vereins- und Versammlungsrechts," Bd. 1, 1794–1893, Record Number 126. See also Paschen, *Demokratische Vereine und Preussischer Staat.*

186 See also Richter, "Zwischen Revolution und Reichsgründung," 642–643.

any *political* association could be subject to legislative restriction and temporary prohibition.[187]

The thus "freed" Prussians did not have to wait long to see what legislative restrictions would look like. On March 11, 1850, the *Vereins- und Versammlungsgesetz* (Law of Assembly and Association; henceforth Association Law) went into effect. The law determined the rights and obligations of associations, the conditions under which they could be disbanded, and the qualifications for active membership. In addition, Section 8 determined the provisions that applied in particular to associations that the law considered political (rather than religious or economic). For instance, political associations were prohibited from accepting female or juvenile members or forming coalitions with other political association striving for the same goal. Women and apprentices were not only barred from membership, but also forbidden to attend public meetings of a political character.[188] Any gathering of a political character could be observed by up to two police officers, who were given authority to disband the meeting if a speaker made an unlawful statement, if the meeting jeopardized public order and safety, or if the organizer failed to remove female or underaged attendants from the audience. Meetings in closed rooms that debated public affairs had to be registered with the local police, while conventions in the open required written authorization at least 48 hours prior to the meeting.[189] Since the law also prohibited the combination of local associations or committees striving for the same political goal, social-democratic branches in Berlin regularly experienced the shutdown of their sections. As a consequence, election committees, which were permitted by the state as preparatory electoral commissions in the respective constituencies, played an important organizational role in Berlin and other Prussian cities.[190]

As mentioned in the Introduction, 1863 witnessed the birth of not only the ADAV, but also a second workers' association, the *Vereinstag Deutscher Arbeitervereine* (VDAV). From the very beginning, this rather loose coalition of local and regional workers' associations struggled to quell the conflict between its liberal leadership and the rank and file who yearned for self-repre-

187 Kletke (ed.), *Die Verfassungs-Urkunde für den Preußischen Staat*, 9.

188 GStA PK, I. HA Rep. 90 A, Nr. 2257: "Regelung des Vereins- und Versammlungsrechts," Bd. 1, 1794–1893, Record Numbers 126–127.

189 GStA PK, I. HA Rep. 90 A, Nr. 2257: "Regelung des Vereins- und Versammlungsrechts," Bd. 1, 1794–1893, Record Number 127.

190 Fricke, *Handbuch*, 47; Weipert, *Das Rote Berlin*, 44.

sentation and democratic participation. The industrialists and liberal reformers who dominated the VDAV's leadership took great pains to keep organized labor under control, yet they were less and less able to stop the growth of a social-democratic fraction that insisted on direct democratic reform. August Bebel's assumption to the presidency of the VDAV in 1867 was thus the culmination rather than the beginning of this development.[191] Within a year, the social-democratic fraction enforced the VDAV's acceptance of the principles laid down by the First International. The liberal leadership and sympathizing members consequently left the association. Thus the way was clear for the fusion of the now social-democratic VDAV and several defectors who had left von Schweitzer's ADAV.

At a congress in the summer of 1869 in the city of Eisenach—which gave them the name of *Eisenachers*—the *Sozialdemokratische Arbeiterpartei* (Social Democratic Workers' Party, SDAP) was launched. The following years were characterized by the social-democratic rivalry between the ADAV—which promoted Lassalle's demand for state-sponsored co-operatives and advocated the *Kleindeutsche* or "Lesser German solution" that had been looming since the Austro-Prussian war of 1866—and the Eisenacher SDAP, which had moved closer to the IWA approach of Marx and Engels, stressed the importance of internationalist trade unionism, and struggled against a Germany dominated by Prussia.[192] This national antagonism was mirrored in the microcosm of organized labor in Berlin. Already in 1866, an oppositional group within the Berlin branch of the ADAV had established one of the first local sections of the IWA in Germany. Once the VDAV majority had embraced the Internationalists' approach in 1868, the liberal BAV was pushed to react. Since many in the BAV rejected the acceptance of the IWA's inaugural address as the leading organizational principle, a social-democratic fraction left the BAV and, in the autumn of 1868, established the *Demokratischer Arbeiterverein*.[193] Comprised of a diverse group of workers, intellectuals, and industrialists—among them Paul Singer, who later became one of Berlin's most prominent social democrats—the *Demokratischer Ar-*

191 Dowe, "Die deutsche Sozialdemokratie," 41–42.

192 Wehler, *Deutsche Gesellschaftsgeschichte*, 348–352; Weipert, *Das Rote Berlin*, 30–32.

193 For some time, Berlin's radical-democratic *Demokratischer Verein* existed side by side with the social-democratic *Demokratischer Arbeiterverein*; see, for instance, "Lokales (Demokratischer Verein)," *Demokratische Zeitung*, 28 April 1872, 6; "Lokales (Demokratischer Arbeiterverein)," *Demokratische Zeitung*, 28 April 1872, 6. See also Na'aman, *Von der Arbeiterbewegung zur Arbeiterpartei*, 171–173; Gemkow, "Berliner Sektion der I. Internationale," 527–530.

beiterverein henceforth represented the Eisenacher fraction in Berlin.[194] Though the Eisenacher fraction in Berlin remained fairly small compared to the local ADAV branch, it became an important reservoir for deviant social-democratic positions in the capital, where the rivalry proved especially bitter.

Despite regular clashes in the streets as well as the pages of its press, the workers' movement in Berlin continued to grow—not least thanks to an increase in trade-union activity. In fact, trade unions were pivotal for the revitalization of organized labor in the late 1860s.[195] Union growth resulted from both the decade's economic boom and Prussia's careful relaxation of the legal regulations that had hampered labor organizations earlier. From 1867 onwards, workers' coalitions were increasingly tolerated until, two years later, the Trade Regulation Act of the North German Confederation officially granted the right to organize.[196] Against this backdrop, Berlin's trade-union scene began to prosper. Some local associations, most prominently the *Verein der Buchdruckegehilfen* (Association of Book Printer Assistants) and the *Berliner Zigarrenarbeiter-Verein* (Cigar Workers' Association of Berlin), had already re-emerged in the early 1860s. Others took shape as the decade matured. Trades like bricklaying and carpentry proved especially active. Renzsch estimates that between a fourth and a third of all members of Berlin's social-democratic movement belonged to one of the construction trades that organized in the late 1860s and early 1870s under the roof of the ADAV.[197] The building trades therewith put the generally trade-union-hostile ADAV under considerable pressure. Due to the notorious "iron law of wages," which it had inherited from its founding father, the Lassalleans traditionally opposed wage strikes and unionization as futile. According to Lassalle's iron law of wages, the free reign of supply and demand inevitably reduced wages to whatever minimum enabled the plain survival of the working class. From this law, it followed that wages would eventually fall back to near-destitution levels even if strikes were won. Workers were thus better advised to focus their energies on political organization and suffrage demands. In the late 1860s, this strict rejection of trade unionism began to soften. The ADAV leadership still distrusted unionization as an inappro-

194 See Eduard Bernstein, "Zum Gedächtnis Paul Singers," *Der Wahre Jacob*, 14 February 1911, 6961; Renzsch, *Handwerker und Lohnarbeiter*, 25; Weipert, *Das Rote Berlin*, 31.

195 Grebing, *Geschichte der deutschen Arbeiterbewegung*, 25; Tenfelde, "Die Entstehung der deutschen Gewerkschaftsbewegung," 114–122.

196 Scharf, *Geschichte der Arbeitszeitverkürzung*, 120; Tenfelde, "Die Entstehung der deutschen Gewerkschaftsbewegung," 107–110.

197 Renzsch, *Handwerker und Lohnarbeiter*, 49.

priate means to improve the lives of workers, yet it conceded that strikes might be useful for, as President von Schweitzer put it at a meeting at Berlin's prominent working-class venue *Universum*, the building of class consciousness and the abolition of the most scandalous working conditions.[198] Against considerable resistance, von Schweitzer enforced the foundation of the *Allgemeiner Deutscher Arbeiterschaftsverband* (General Federation of German Workers' Association, henceforth *Arbeiterschaftsverband*), a heavily centralized trade-union federation that represented workers in broad sectors rather than occupational fields.[199]

In Berlin, the *Arbeiterschaftsverband* competed with two rival organizations.[200] On the one hand, the liberal unions that were usually referred to as *Hirsch-Dunckersche Gewerkvereine* promoted social-security benefit funds in line with their harmonious understanding of labor relations. On the other hand, von Schweitzer's *Arbeiterschaftsverband* was also challenged by the less centralized movement of the *Internationale Gewerksgenossenschaften* (International Trade Associations). Close to the IWA and the direct-democratic approach of the Eisenachers, the internationally oriented unions allowed for much more autonomy at the local level, a fact that also made them popular among several unions in Berlin. Despite his remarkable turn-around, von Schweitzer appeared less and less able to integrate the thriving trade-union movement into his union-hostile approach. In addition, his dictatorial leadership posed a serious burden for the ADAV. Facing a steep decline in support and fresh allegations of collaboration with Prussian authorities, von Schweitzer stepped down in 1871. With the removal of von Schweitzer and the foundation of the German Empire, the preconditions for a gradual convergence were laid.[201] Despite continuous clashes in both local meeting halls and the press, the rank and file in Berlin pushed towards unification. While the great strike waves of the late 1860s and early 1870s taught workers and union members that solidarity required co-operation across party divides, the social-democratic leadership was increasingly bound together by the shared experience of legal repression and hostilities in parliament.[202] In 1875, after a decade of bitter conflict, the ADAV and SDAP convened in Gotha

198 "Vereins-Theil (Für den Allg. Deutsch. Arb-Verein)," *Der Social-Demokrat*, 10 July 1867, 2–3; Bernstein, *Die Geschichte der Berliner Arbeiterbewegung*, 173–174.

199 Dowe, "Die deutsche Sozialdemokratie," 47; Wehler, *Deutsche Gesellschaftsgeschichte*, 352.

200 Needless to say, the Catholic trade-union movement was less influential in Protestant Berlin; see Tenfelde, "Die Entstehung der deutschen Gewerkschaftsbewegung," 119.

201 Renzsch, *Handwerker und Lohnarbeiter*, 22.

202 Dowe, "Die deutsche Sozialdemokratie," 47.

and launched the *Sozialistische Arbeiterpartei Deutschlands* (Socialist Workers' Party of Germany, SAP). From now on, the workers' movement thus marched under a unified banner, until, in 1878, the Anti-Socialist Law ended the constitutional phase of organized social democracy for years to come.

About twelve years earlier, on October 4, 1866, a young man named Sigfrid Meyer was bidding farewell to his home town of Berlin.[203] For years, the mining-engineer student had been active in the young workers' movement of the city. As a member of Berlin's ADAV branch, co-founder of the local IWA section, and ardent admirer of Marx, he embodied the richness and diversity of early social-democratic life in the Prussian capital.[204] It was, as Meyer expressed in a letter to Liebknecht, the sheer lack of employment opportunities that pushed him to return to New York where he had been active already in the previous decade.[205] Little is certain about the specifics of Meyer's departure, yet we have reason to believe that, like so many others who came from or passed through Berlin, he took the famous *Amerikalinie* that linked the Prussian capital with Bremen and Bremerhaven. Here, Meyer embarked the emigrant ship "Hermann," which, on October 22, 1866, turned into the Upper Bay of Manhattan.[206] Following a long and perilous

203 In a letter that Meyer sent to Ernestine Liebknecht on October 3, 1866, he informed her about Liebknecht's arrest and the fact that Meyer intended to depart the following day; see "Sigfrid Meyer an Ernestine Liebknecht," 190–191.

204 Meyer was referred to as either Siegfried or Sigfrid. For his occupational background, see also Henderson, *The Life of Friedrich Engels*, vol. 2, 411; Welskopp, *Das Banner der Brüderlichkeit*, 411. Henderson wrongly dates Meyer's emigration to the following year. Meyer achieved some prominence when he published a new edition of the Communist Manifesto in Berlin and urged Marx (together with Theodor Metzner and August Vogt) to come to Berlin and lead the local movement. For Meyer's role in the early movement in Berlin, see "Ein Brief Berliner Arbeiter an Marx (Ein Beitrag zur Berliner Parteigeschichte)," *Vorwärts*, 8 December 1913; Dlubek and Akimovna Stepanova, *Die I. Internationale in Deutschland*, 89–90; Gemkow, "Berliner Sektion der I. Internationale," 518–520; "Sigfrid Meyer an Wilhelm Liebknecht," 116–118, 118–120, 142–145. Once in New York, Meyer appears, if at all, as recipient of letters from Marx, who urged the young comrade to build a strong IWA chapter on American soil; see Messer-Kruse, *The Yankee International*, 66–73; Montgomery, *Beyond Equality*, 166. Meyer apparently died in 1872 at the age of 36, see "Sigfrid Meyer an Wilhelm Liebknecht," 116, Footnote 1.

205 Ibid., 117.

206 The passenger records digitized and made available by the Battery Conservancy list a certain Siegfried Meyer, a 30-year-old immigrant from Berlin, who arrived in New York on October 22, 1866. Unless there was another Si(e)gfri(e)d Meyer in the same age cohort who also emigrated in late 1866 from Berlin to New York, this is our Meyer. For a digital name search, see http://castlegarden.org/searcher.php.

journey, the young Berliner once more laid eye upon his new home, the city of New York.[207]

2.3. Organized Labor in New York in the 1860s and early 1870s

Surely Meyer's fellow expats from Berlin were overwhelmed by the many sights, smells, and sounds that descended upon them once they had made their way through the immigration facility at Castle Clinton.[208] Yet, as they were soon to discover, not everything in New York differed from what they knew. Thanks to the explosive growth of *Kleindeutschland* or Little Germany in Lower Manhattan, the new arrivals quickly found entrance into what had become the third-largest German-speaking community in the world, outranked only by Vienna and Berlin.[209] The latter played an important role in this stream of migration. As Berlin's *Demokratische Zeitung* reported in 1873, at times entire Prussian villages left the city for New York, taking with them long- and short-time Berliners in pursuit of a better life in the US.[210] Those who chose to settle in New York quickly realized that the city's occupational structure bore a striking resemblance to the Prussian capital. According to the ninth federal census of 1870—one of the earliest national censuses that paid "close and detailed attention to the occupations of the people"—manufacturing was the largest employment sector in New York.[211] It was followed by the personal and professional services sector and the trade and transportation sector, which provided work for roughly half as many people as the manufacturing sector. In the trade sector, the great majority were employed as traders and dealers or clerks and salesmen, whereas the largest group of workers in transportation was employed as carmen, draymen, or teamsters.

207 According to Foner and Messer-Kruse, Meyer had been one of the co-founders of New York's notorious Communist Club; see Foner, *History of the Labor Movement*, 413; Messer-Kruse, *The Yankee International*, 71–73.

208 Castle Garden had been turned into the Emigrant Landing Depot in 1855. It served as official emigration center until the opening of Ellis Island in 1892; see Burrows and Wallace, *Gotham*, 738, 1111. The passenger lists at Castle Garden alone show more than 1,000 Berliners who arrived in New York City between 1860 and 1870.

209 Burrows and Wallace, *Gotham*, 745.

210 BC., "Lokales (Die Auswanderung)," *Demokratische Zeitung*, 27 March 1873, 3.

211 Montgomery, *Beyond Equality*, 28.

Almost half of all people in the personal and professional service sector worked as domestic servants, with an additional quarter employed as common laborers. Except for the 855 people registered as gardeners, nurserymen, and winegrowers, the agriculture sector was virtually nonexistent.[212] By far the largest number of workers in the manufacturing sector were tailors and seamstresses, a number almost twice as large as the distant second, carpenters and joiners. In the 1860s and 1870s, New York's labor landscape was thus dominated by common laborers (including longshoremen), domestic servants, workers in the clothing industry (especially tailors, seamstresses, boot and shoe makers, milliners, and dress and mantua makers), the building trades (especially carpenters and joiners, bricklayers and stonemasons, painters and varnishers, plasterers, paper hangers, plumbers, and gasfitters), and the food, drink, and tobacco sector (especially bakers, butchers, brewers, and cigar makers). In addition, the number of printers and upholsterers was relatively large. Mining, in contrast, was obviously irrelevant, and although the metal trades did give employment to roughly 7,500 New Yorkers in 1870, there were more butchers and bakers in the city than the combined number of blacksmiths, tinners, and iron and steel workers.[213] In sum, the census of 1870 counted almost 240,000 workers in manufacturing and services. Like Berlin, New York had become a capital of labor.

Across the US, mechanization and the spread of non-agrarian labor had resulted in a sharp rise in productivity. Yet despite the fact that labor was becoming more productive, the length of the workday had generally been increasing over the first half of the nineteenth century. It seems to have peaked around mid-century.[214] When comparing the length of the workday in nineteenth-century Berlin and New York, absolute numbers can be misleading. In the US case, hours often referred to pure working time. In Germany, hours usually included lunch breaks, which, depending on trade and region, could be as long as two hours. Even among German workers themselves, there existed confusion as to whether their demand included breaks or not. At the first Weavers' Day in 1871, for instance, August Bebel urged

212 This excludes subsistence farming and gardening in the periphery of the city, which was especially common among African American New Yorkers.

213 "Selected Occupations, with Age and Sex, and Nativity."

214 Robert Whaples argues that–despite compositional flaws–the two surveys that were compiled towards the end of the century clearly show that the length of the workday began to decrease somewhere between 1830 and 1850; see Whaples, "Hours of Work in U.S. History."

the delegates not to make unrealistic demands by asking for a ten-hour day, including a two-hour lunch break. He argued that even in England and the US, the eight-hour workday had thus far materialized only in a few public enterprises. Those delegates who insisted on a ten-hour workday *including* two hours of rest replied, however, that German workers must not fall behind the achievements of other industrial societies. According to the minutes of the convention, Bebel later repeated his demand for a ten-hour workday "including a two-hour break." Since this was a direct contradiction of what he had said just a moment before, it probably reflected the general confusion of the minute taker rather than a change of mind by Bebel.[215]

Though absolute workdays in Berlin tended to be longer, the occupational pattern of variation corresponds neatly to that of New York. Together with car and coach drivers, New York's bakers faced the longest workdays, which often ranged from 16 to 18 hours. Even 20-hour shifts were apparently not uncommon during busy weeks.[216] The city's tailors also toiled for twelve to 15 hours a day, as did other workers in the textile and clothing sector. The more formal and centralized labor was, the more likely it was to be employed for shorter hours. New York's metal and construction trades, for instance, had largely adopted a ten-hour workday by mid-century, although overtime hours were common.[217] The city's employment structure was likewise very similar to that of Berlin. Wage work had become prevalent in large workplaces like the city's shipyards or gas companies. Similarly, the mass of workers in the building trades were used to waged work. Many of the bakers and butchers, tailors and weavers, and cigar and artificial-flower makers, however, worked in arrangements that often defied clear definition. Full employment, seasonal semi-employment, fictitious self-employment, actual self-employment, as well as various forms of un or under-waged home employment existed simultaneously.[218] In the ready-made-clothes sector, for instance, a few workshops employed an expanding number of wage workers, while an even larger number of tailors worked as formally independent, contracted producers. As in Berlin, such formally independent masters were in fact heavily dependent upon the merchants who determined everything

215 See Deutsches Weber-Central-Comitee (ed.), *Ausführlicher Bericht*, 53–55.

216 "Die Bäcker von New York," *Die Arbeiter-Union*, 13 February 1869, 3.

217 Bates, *Bricklayers' Century of Craftsmanship*, 12; *Proceedings of the Sixth Annual Session of the Workingmen's Assembly*, 25–26; Montgomery, *Beyond Equality*, 234; Roediger and Foner, *Our Own Time,* 34, 66–67.

218 Burrows and Wallace, *Gotham*, 739–744.

from the quantity ordered to the quality expected.[219] Berlin and New York City featured another important characteristic. Due to the lack of resources and natural energy as well as—at least initially—very high costs of transportation, both cities witnessed an enormous rise in labor-intensive production in the first half of the century. Although some of the large employers that later became symbols of industrial life in New York had already opened factories by mid-century, the 1860s were still characterized by small and mid-scale businesses and an army of contracted and quasi self-employed workers.[220] "Rather than superseding the artisan system with large, mechanized factories," Christine Stansell stresses rightly, "employers transformed it from within, avoiding high overhead costs through the proliferation of small-scale, labor-intensive enterprises."[221]

New York's world of labor differed from that of Berlin in terms of national segregation, however. In his widely acclaimed study of the city's working class in the first decades of the nineteenth century, Sean Wilentz argues that New York's early labor movement was comprised of predominantly native-born artisans and craftsmen who claimed to defend the ideals of 1776.[222] Yet two decades of mass migration had thoroughly transformed New York's laboring class by the early 1860s. Increasing national segregation thus distinguished postbellum New York from European cities like Berlin, but also its own past.[223] As Stanley Nadel shows, German-born artisans and workers accounted for almost a quarter of all employees in New York City in 1870. While their number was very low among domestic servants and common laborers, they provided 41 percent of all tailors in the city and about half of New York City' butchers, tobacco workers, bakers, and boot and shoemakers. Of the cabinetmakers and upholsterers, an impressive 61 percent were born in Germany, exceeded only by the 70 percent of brewers and distillers.[224] Irish immigrant surpassed American-born workers in the field of common laborers and domestic servants. Together with Americans, the Irish dominated the building trades, providing more than three times as many brick and stone masons and marble and stone cutters as the second

219 Ernst, *Immigrant Life in New York City*, 18.

220 Stott, *Workers in the Metropolis*, 23–28.

221 Stansell, *City of Women*, 107.

222 Wilentz, *Chants Democratic*, 61–103.

223 Stott, *Workers in the Metropolis*, 3. In fact, increasing national segregation was characteristic of the US working class in general; see Gutman and Berlin, "Class Composition," 380–382.

224 Nadel, *Little Germany*, 63, Table 11.

largest group, their American-born counterparts. The latter supplied the highest number of carpenters and joiners as well as skilled metal workers (with the exception of Irish blacksmiths), followed by the Germans. Similarly, the vast majority of New York's printers and bookbinders were American-born. American workers competed with the Germans over leadership in the tailoring trade.[225] Finally, the census of 1875 listed roughly 20,000 African Americans living in New York and the counties of Kings and Queens.[226] By mid-century, many African Americans had been driven out of the construction and waterfront jobs they had occupied earlier. In postbellum New York, male African Americans found employment as waiters and personal servants, while female African Americans were forced to the bottom of the urban labor market, where they worked as washerwomen, maids, or prostitutes.[227]

The growth of urban employment resulted in a parallel increase in local unions. In fact, Edwin G. Burrows and Mike Wallace suggest that more workers in New York City "enrolled in trade unions between 1865 and 1873 than during any other period of the nineteenth century."[228] The predominantly Irish dock workers flocked to the powerful Longshoremen Union, while the Laborers United Benevolent Society opened its ranks to the mostly unskilled workers of the city, among whom the Irish likewise featured strongly. The New York local branch of the Journeymen Tailor's National Trades Union, which was established in 1865 in Philadelphia, represented the interests of the vast group of tailors in the city.[229] In the same year, the first national Union of Bricklayers was founded and quickly emerged as one of the most prominent unions in the building trades. By the late 1860s, the Bricklayers International Union of the United States of America had granted charters to several locals both in Brooklyn and Manhattan. These local branches—of which many members had already been active in 1850, when the New York Bricklayers Union merged with the Bricklayers and Plasterers Beneficial Society of New York—displayed an intense strike activity and shaped labor discourse far beyond its occupational boundary.[230] Though the group of printers was relatively small in comparison to the vast group of

225 "Selected Occupations, with Age and Sex, and Nativity."

226 "Population by County 1790–1870," 51.

227 Burrows and Wallace, *Gotham*, 854.

228 Ibid., 986.

229 Stowell, *The Journeymen Tailors' Union*, 9–12.

230 Bates, *Bricklayers' Century of Craftsmanship*, 1–34; Yellowitz, "Eight Hours and the Bricklayers' Strike," 78–100. The union dropped its prefix "International" in the late 1860s.

clothing and construction workers, the local branch of the Typographical Union proved to be a powerful catalyst for labor demands. Looking back at a proud legacy of organizing efforts at the dawn of the century, Local 6 was in fact a key figure in the labor movement of New York City.[231] Similarly to the printers, the cigar workers of New York were able to resume earlier organizational ties in the aftermath of the Civil War, when the city became one of the focal points of cigar making in the nation. At a New York convention in 1864, the National Union of Cigar Makers of America was established, and it shortly thereafter transformed into the Cigar Makers' International Union (CMIU) in order to accommodate Canadian locals.[232] In New York City, Local 15 of the CMIU competed with the rival United Cigar Makers of New York, which eventually joined the former as Local 144. The city's organized cigar makers henceforth occupied a central position in the local labor movement.[233]

Like our expat Sigfrid Meyer, many of the members of organized labor and socialist opposition arrived in New York City in the mid- to late 1860s. Coming from Germany, England, Ireland, Austria-Hungary, France, Bohemia, and Belgium, these predominantly young workers were provided fertile ground in New York for the ideas and experiences they brought from their homelands. In 1863, the family of Samuel Gompers left London for Manhattan, where Gompers learned the trade of cigar making from his father. Around the time Gompers joined the local union of cigar makers, he first met Peter J. McGuire, a child of Irish immigrants who also had settled in the neighborhood. They were soon joined by the Austrian-Hungarian immigrant Adolph Strasser, one of the founders of the United Cigar Makers of New York.[234] Together, the three men helped fashion the city's labor discourse and union struggles in the late 1860s and 1870s, long before they became the prominent founders of the American Federation of Labor (AFL). While the lives and deeds of men like Gompers have attracted a great deal of attention, the vast majority of New York's trade unionists and working-class activists of the 1860s vanished as quietly from the stage as

231 Tracy, *History of the Typographical Union*; Rock, "Independent Hours," 21–39; New York Public Library, ZL-352, Reel 2: New York City Typographical Union No. 6, Regular Meetings Minutes, 1870–1917, Item "Sept. 5, 1871, Regular Monthly Meeting of NY Typographical Union No. 6."

232 Andrews, "Nationalisation," 70.

233 Cooper, *Once a Cigar Maker*, 19–20. For a discussion of German cigar-making unionism in New York City, see Schneider, *Trade Unions and Community*, 50–118.

234 Cooper, "What Ever Happened to Adolph Strasser;" Reed, "Strasser, Adolph," 532–533.

they had entered it. The German-born Conrad Kuhn, for instance, was a prominent supporter of New York City's eight-hour movement in the 1860s. He represented the German Cigar Makers and, later, the *Arbeiter-Union* of New York at various conventions of the NLU. Yet, like so many other wage workers who temporarily became active members of the movement, he quickly passed into oblivion.[235] We know little about men like Carl (Karl) Speyer, who was a member of the administrative board of the *Arbeiter-Zeitung* as well as corresponding secretary of the *Vereingte Tischler New Yorks*, the city's German-speaking joiner's union.[236] For some of these union men and socialist activists, even their national background remains uncertain. Robert Blissert, for instance, is alternately referred to as of German, Irish, and English descent.[237]

Though immigration was a crucial factor for working-class politics and labor organization in the city, some of the most prolific figures in the movement were in fact American-bred. Following employment as a printer, the Connecticut-born William J. Jessup joined the multitude of ship carpenters in New York, among whom he rose to prominence as an apt organizer and brilliant speaker. His active support of the local eight-hour movement brought him in contact with George Edwin McNeill. Born and raised in Massachusetts, McNeill frequently visited New York to promote the eight-hour cause among the city's workers.[238] Later, in an obituary for McNeill, *The New York Times* would vest him with the honorable title of "Father of the Eight-Hour Movement."[239] Activists like Jessup and McNeill proved

235 Montgomery, *Beyond Equality*, 198.

236 Ibid., 469. Speyer had been a member of the German IWA branch in London in the late 1860s; see his letter to the workers of Germany: Carl Speyer, "An die Arbeiter Deutschlands," *Der Botschafter*, 24 December 1868, 221–222. He continued to serve the IWA as a leading member of New York's Section 1.

237 Montgomery states that Robert Blissert was born in 1843 in England, where he participated in London's tailor strikes of the 1860s; see Montgomery, *Beyond Equality*, 463. According to Timothy Messer-Kruse, Blissert was Irish; see Messer-Kruse, *The Yankee International*, 144. Blissert himself indicated that he was German. In a speech to a workers' rally in Philadelphia in 1874, he made the interesting comment that, as a worker, he knew no nationalities. Though born in Germany, he was as good as any an American, "yes, better than the Americans themselves, for he had sworn to be a good American, which they never did." See "Philadelphia: Workingmen's Festival and Demonstration," *The Toiler*, 22 August 1874, 1.

238 Montgomery, *Beyond Equality*, 467.

239 "George E. McNeill Dead," *New York Times*, 20 May 1906, 9. See also Roediger and Foner, *Our Own Time*, 113–115.

crucial in organizing urban labor. Not unlike Berlin, New York City witnessed a concentration of local unions into powerful, city-wide umbrella groups in the aftermath of the war. Echoing pre-war initiatives like the Industrial Congress of 1850, so-called city trade assemblies soon emerged as decisive actors in the postbellum landscape of organized labor in New York City.[240] Already in 1864, delegates of local shipyard, construction, and printing unions had launched the Workingmen's Union, New York's most prominent English-speaking trade assembly at the time.[241]

While the Workingmen's Union adopted an antagonistic approach towards organized employers, its German-speaking equivalent initially took a less confrontational position. Representing various unions of German craftsmen in the city, the *Arbeiter-Bund*'s emphasis on consumer cooperatives and self-help resembled the program Schulze-Delitzsch propagated on the other side of the Atlantic.[242] Nowhere was this liberal tradition more evident than in the local paper of the *Bund*. In its first number of September 3, 1864, the *New Yorker Arbeiter-Zeitung* (not to be confused with the same-named local Marxist paper of the early 1870s) revealed its political program to the German-speaking readers of the city. Unlike any other country, the editorial stressed, the US was the country of free labor, where neither birth nor social rank, but only diligence and ambition, determined individual progress and wealth. Here, workers were not "proletarians," but equal partners in the quest for prosperity. The American worker therefore did not stand below the capitalist, but next to him.[243] Through the pages of the *New Yorker Arbeiter-Zeitung*, the *Arbeiter-Bund* urged local unions to focus on the establishment of savings banks and consumer cooperatives and leave the question of wages and hours to the free play of supply and demand.[244] Yet the association had clearly failed to read the signs of the times. Stubbornly

240 Burrows and Wallace, *Gotham*, 771; Montgomery, *Beyond Equality*, 161.

241 In the 1860s and 1870s, a confusing multitude of local associations referred to their organizations as "Workingmen's Union." In fact, G.P. Taylor, the president of the Workingmen's Union referred to here, found it necessary to call a special meeting in order to debate possible actions "in reference to the name of the Workingmen's Union being used by political parties throughout the city," see "Labor Movements, New York, Workingmen's Union," *The National Workman*, 20 October 1866. See also Montgomery, *Beyond Equality*, 163.

242 The Arbeiter-Bund had been established by Joseph Weydemeyer in the 1850s, but it had abandoned its Marxist outlook already by the end of the decade; see Ernst, *Immigrant Life in New York City*, 118–119.

243 "Arbeiter-Vereine," *New Yorker Arbeiter-Zeitung*, 3 September 1865, 4.

244 Montgomery, *Beyond Equality*, 164.

adhering to the paradigm of non-intervention, both the *Bund* and its organ vanished from the landscape of organized labor. As David Montgomery puts it, the notion of self-help "no longer excited the organized craftsmen of New York."[245]

The *Arbeiter-Bund* was soon replaced by an association of German-speaking workers that stood firmly on the ground of independent organizing. Established in 1866 with a largely Lassallean outlook, the *Allgemeiner Deutscher Arbeiter-Verein* (General German Workingmen's Association, GGWA) of New York became a local recruitment base for the countless working-class transplants who poured into New York City in the late 1860s.[246] Among many others, it became home to such prominent imports as Edward Grosse, former private secretary of von Schweitzer.[247] For members like Grosse, the new American context challenged some of their most cherished Lassallean beliefs. Given the ability of local unions to enforce sustainable wage increases in a polity that had already introduced universal manhood suffrage, neither Lassalle's iron law of wages nor his focus on suffrage demands over trade-union activity offered strategic help in a new political surrounding.[248]

But the inability of Lassallean theory to make sense of American realities initially facilitated a surprising degree of co-operation with German-Ameri-

245 Ibid., 165. Burrows and Wallace do not clearly distinguish between *Arbeiter-Bund* and *Arbeiter-Union*; see Burrows and Wallace, *Gotham*, 986–988.

246 Accounts of working-class organizing in New York City during the 1860s vary considerably. Hillquit states that the association was founded in 1868, and he interchangeably refers to it as the General German Labor Association or the General German Working-Men's Association; see Hillquit, *History of Socialism in the United States*, 163–180. Philip S. Foner stresses that the association first appeared in 1866 as the General German Workingmen's Association; see Foner and Chamberlin (eds.), *Friedrich A. Sorge's Labor Movement*, 9. According to Bernstein, the association was formed in 1865, see Bernstein, *The First International in America*, 37.

247 See also the self-description that the association published in the pages of its Berlin-based paper; "Vereins-Theil: New York [Allg. Deutsch. Arb.-Verein: Ausbreitung desselben in Amerika]," *Der Social-Demokrat*, 27 February 1865, 3–4. This study gives preference to the translation General German Workingmen's Association rather than General German Labor Union; cf., for instance, Messer-Kruse, *The Yankee International*, 73. The term *Verein* or "association" had a peculiar connotation of independence and autonomy that distinguished it from both political parties and trade unions (which, for that matter, Lassalleans opposed).

248 Montgomery, *Beyond Equality*, 166.

can Marxists.[249] Whereas many of the predominantly German Lassalleans were newcomers to New York's world of organized labor, a handful of Marxists had already made their way to New York in the preceding decade. In 1852, the Saxon Friedrich A. Sorge had settled in Hoboken, from where he popularized Marxist teachings in the greater New York region. Five years after his arrival in the US, Sorge joined New York's recently established Communist Club, a successor to the metropolitan Communist League and the only Marxist organization in New York that survived through the Civil War years.[250] Not least thanks to the help of Sorge, the disintegrating Communist Club, together with members of the local GGWA, launched the Social Party of New York and Vicinity in 1868.[251] Although the party failed to draw voter support, it did succeed in bringing together a broad spectrum of socialist activists. The failure and dissolution of the Social Party was followed by a reconstitution of the GGWA, which continued to foster socialist thought among immigrant workers in New York City.[252] In 1868, the local movement of German workers managed to install Adolph Douai as editor of the *Arbeiter-Union*, a local trade-union paper that therewith experienced a decisive turn towards the left. Owing to its rather diverse ideological background, the *Arbeiter-Union* reprinted articles from different German and US labor periodicals alike. In so doing, it quickly became one of the central working-class mediators between the proletarian communities of Berlin and New York. The paper not only covered labor topics from the Prussian capital, it also published personal correspondence that German migrants sent home to Berlin—as it did in 1869, when it printed the correspondence between a German worker in New York City and his friend in Berlin.[253]

In the summer of the same year, about two dozen German unions in New York formed a new city-wide trade assembly, the *Arbeiter-Union*, which adopted the same-named paper as its organ.[254] From now on, the new German-speaking city central struggled side by side with its English-speaking counterpart, the Workingmen's Union. Around that time, the remnants of

249 This split re-emerged in the early 1870s, however, when Marxist IWA sections and local Lassallean labor parties competed for working-class support; see Hillquit, *History of Socialism in the United States*, 188–192.

250 Foner and Chamberlin (eds.), *Friedrich A. Sorge's Labor Movement*, 4–6.

251 Hillquit, *History of Socialism in the United States*, 177.

252 Messer-Kruse, *The Yankee International*, 73.

253 "Auch ein politisches Glaubensbekenntnis: Einem Briefe eines New Yorker Deutschen an seinen Freund in Berlin entnommen," *Die Arbeiter-Union*, 19 October 1869, 2.

254 Montgomery, *Beyond Equality*, 169.

the unsuccessful Social Party officially joined the IWA by establishing the German-speaking New York Section 1, the first International section in the US.[255] Over the coming years, new German, Irish, French, Italian, Bohemian, and American sections enriched the landscape of socialist opposition in New York, but they also provided ample cause for internal conflict.[256]

While Lassallean and Marxist organizing efforts proved especially fruitful among immigrant communities in New York, many native-born workers pinned their hope on the national centralization of trade unionism. On August 20, 1866, representatives of various labor unions and trade assemblies convened in Baltimore, where they founded the National Labor Union. As the first national federation of organized trades, the NLU reflected the growing conviction among unionists that only concerted action could enforce substantial improvements for the nation's working classes.[257] New York's labor movement occupied a prominent place in the history of the short-lived NLU. The city was starkly overrepresented at the preliminary NLU congress in March 1866, and it continuously supplied a great number of delegates over the coming years.[258] Various local trade unions joined the NLU during these years, as did the aforementioned GGWA, which registered as Labor Union No. 5 of New York.[259] New York City regularly served as host for NLU committee meetings and conventions such as the general convention of 1868, out of which emerged one of the characteristically ephemeral labor parties of the time. Though utterly unsuccessful at the polls, the National Reform Party reflected the political determination and self-confidence of organized labor in postbellum America.[260] New York also supplied some of the NLU's most active personnel. Together with William H. Sylvis and Jon-

---

255 "German Workingmen's Union," *The New York Times*, 20 July 1869, 8; Montgomery, *Beyond Equality*, 168–169; Foner and Chamberlin (eds.), *Friedrich A. Sorge's Labor Movement in the United States*, 9.

256 Foner, *History of the Labor Movement*, vol. 1, 233; Foner and Chamberlin (eds.), *Friedrich A. Sorge's Labor Movement in the United States*; Burrows and Wallace, *Gotham*, 988–989. For a compelling study of the Internationalists' influence on organized labor in the US, see Messer-Kruse, *The Yankee International*.

257 Foner, *History of the Labor Movement in the United States*, 370–388; Zinn, *A People's History*, 240–242.

258 Commons et al. (eds.), *History of American Industrial Society*, vol. 9, 126.

259 Bernstein, *The First International in America*, 31; Foner and Chamberlin (eds.), *Friedrich A. Sorge's Labor Movement in the United States*, 8–11.

260 Hillquit, *History of Socialism in the United States*, 169–170.

athan Fincher, the Brooklynite William Harding was a driving force in the preparation of the founding congress of the NLU in Baltimore.[261]

At this congress, the aforementioned William J. Jessup served as delegate from New York, and he subsequently acted as vice president of the NLU in the state of New York. Therewith, Jessup embodies the peculiar organizational ties that linked the mostly English-speaking faction of local labor to the state and federal levels. As secretary of the Workingmen's Union, president to the state-wide New York Workingmen's Assembly, and as trade-union delegate to the NLU, he was, as Montgomery highlights, one of the first professional unionists who led "a national union, a city central, and a state assembly."[262] Jessup held close contact with immigrant activists in New York City like Sorge or Meyer; he kept up correspondence with Marx and the International in Europe; and he tirelessly attended meetings of trade unions, labor associations, and nascent independent parties in order to build a vibrant workers' movements.[263] Jessup, in short, personifies the extraordinary diversity of organized labor in postbellum New York. And whether Yankee or immigrant, trade unionist or labor reformer, self-employed or waged, skilled or unskilled, Lassallean, Marxist, or neither—there was one demand in the 1860s and early 1870s that filled every heart and mind of working-class New York City: "Eight Hours For What We Will!"[264]

261 Foner, *History of the Labor Movement in the United States*, 371.

262 Montgomery, *Beyond Equality*, 164.

263 Bernstein, *The First International in America*, 28–29; Hillquit, *History of Socialism in the United States*, 173; Messer-Kruse, *The Yankee International*, 61–63; Marx and Engels, *Collected Works*, vol. 43, 147.

264 The origin of this slogan is not entirely clear. Regularly used by English and American workers, it eventually found entrance into the labor hymn "Eight Hours;" see Rosenzweig, *Eight Hours for What We Will*, 1.

3. Polity: Shorter Hours and the Struggle for Equality

"Resolved, that we steadily and persistently maintain that the reduction of the hours of labor should be compulsory on all, and that human labor is not a commodity to be regulated by the law of supply and demand."[265]
Resolution of a Workers' Mass Meeting at Cooper Institute, New York City, 1874

3.1. The Movement for Shorter Hours in New York

Initially, the outbreak of the American Civil War had pushed the shorter-hour struggle to the background of social conflict.[266] On the one hand, the strength of the antebellum movement declined as high conscription rates thinned out the nation's working-class hot spots. On the other, the remaining workforce was cautious not to appear as exploiters of a political state of exception. After all, the war could easily be mobilized against working-class movements that supposedly jeopardized the unity of the Union. With the Republic at stake, workers initially tended to refrain from pushing large political campaigns and focused on local wage struggles instead.[267] Yet whereas the war had temporarily helped suppress the movement, it increasingly became a rhetorical weapon for organized labor as it dragged on. When the first working-class veterans returned to their former jobs and trades, the Northern industrial centers witnessed a powerful return of the struggle for shorter hours.[268] Unlike the ten-hour movement of the previous generation, the postbellum movement emerged with a standardized demand for eight

265 "Cooper Institute: Working-Men Mass Meeting," *The Toiler*, 23 May 1874, 1.

266 For a detailed overview of the antebellum movement, see Roediger, *The Movement for a Shorter Working Day*.

267 While there were few wartime shorter-hour campaigns, New York City witnessed a relatively high amount of wage strikes, especially towards the end of the war; see Burrows and Wallace, *Gotham*, 883–884; Wilentz, *Chants Democratic*, 395. For general strike activity during the Civil War, see Montgomery, *Beyond Equality*, 97–101. Roediger and Foner refer to 1864 as the year when the shorter-hour movement returned to New York; see Roediger and Foner, *Our Own Time*, 92–93.

268 Kuritz, "Ira Steward and the Eight Hour Day," 118.

hours. From his exile in London, Marx thus famously observed that the Civil War's first fruit "was the eight hours' agitation that ran with the seven-leagued boots of the locomotive from the Atlantic to the Pacific, from New England to California."[269] In New York City, the eight-hour demand was promoted by a diverse group of actors. Local trade unions launched individual campaigns at the workplace for the introduction of eight hours. Together, these unions built city and state assemblies that forged broad coalitions of working-class solidarity. Following the example of Boston, several New York City unions formed sector-wide eight-hour leagues and lobbied for eight-hour legislation.[270] At the same time, some local unionists contributed to the short-lived, cross-trade Central Eight Hour League in order to channel their efforts. In addition, the local eight-hour movement also enjoyed the support of the aforementioned coalitions of Marxist and Lassallean immigrants from Europe who popularized the demand in their organizations, from the GGWA to the Social Party to the local IWA sections. The latter brought together several trade unions in the city and formed The Eight Hour Enforcement League as a means to enforce the observance of the law.[271] In 1873, the Enforcement League eventually merged with the remnants of the English-speaking Workingmen's Union into the Workingmen's Central Council of New York.[272]

Compared to such a firm commitment, the political parties in the city took a more ambivalent position towards the question of shorter hours. On the one hand, neither of the two parties rejected the eight-hour demand *per se*. While the radical wing of the Republican Party in particular tended to sympathize with the prospect of shorter workdays as a precondition for moral refinement and individual betterment, New York's Democrats recognized the potential that the eight-hour demand had for securing the working-class vote. On the other hand, however, both parties feared the strength of an independent labor movement that pushed for class legislation, thereby

269 Cited in Roediger and Foner, *Our Own Time*, 82.

270 As in other centers of the urban North, the building trades were especially important for the spread of these leagues; see ibid., 87–90, 112.

271 "The Internationals and the Eight-Hour Law," *New York Times*, 23 April 1873, 12. The IWA soon withdrew from the League because of the "prejudices" of many trade unionists against them; see "The Eight-Hour Enforcement League," *New York Times*, 10 May 1873, 7; "Correspondenzen," *Arbeiter-Zeitung*, 24 May 1873, 4.

272 "Die Arbeiterbewegung," *Arbeiter-Zeitung*, 19 July 1873, 2; "Arbeiterbewegung," *Die Arbeiter-Zeitung*, 2 August 1873, 2.

challenging the reign of the market.[273] Yet whether the parties liked it or not, the demand for eight hours greatly excited working-class New York in the first peace-time spring in years.

New York's organized workers struggled on both a political level for shorter-hour legislation and an economic level for its enforcement in particular businesses or trades. For a short period in the aftermath of the Civil War, it seemed as if the economic approach would prevail when the ship joiners and caulkers waged the first eight-hour strike the city had seen.[274] Despite widespread signs of support that kept the entire region in suspense, the shipyard workers' resources proved too thin to sustain a prolonged strike. After seven weeks, the striking workers were forced to return to ten-hour shifts.[275] Faced with failure, organized labor in New York turned towards politics. According to *The National Workman*, the short-lived organ of the English-speaking Workingmen's Union, the central objective of the city's labor movement had to be the passage of an eight-hour law.[276] This required that workers base their voting decision strictly on the eight-hour question. Deeply disappointed by the municipality's neglect of their interests, the paper issued a warning to local authorities that if they continued to disregard working-class demands, they could no longer count on the support of organized labor. Directed at New York's city officials, it stressed that "[w]e made and we can unmake them."[277] In order to increase the pressure on all law-giving bodies, *The National Workman* published a circular that had been sent to candidates running for county, state, or national election.[278] The circular was pretty straightforward. It read simply:

> Will you, if elected to the position for which you are nominated, vote for and use your influence in making eight hours a legal day's work, and in case such bill is not introduced, will you, when called upon by the working classes, or their representatives, introduce such a bill?[279]

273 Burrows and Wallace, *Gotham*, 987.

274 "The Strike at the Ship-Yards: The Test of the Eight Hour Question," *The New York Times*, 1 May 1866, 4.

275 Yellowitz, "Eight Hours and the Bricklayers' Strike," 84.

276 "The Work before Us," *The National Workman*, 20 October 1866, 2.

277 "The Vagaries of American Social Science," *The National Workman*, 27 October 1866.

278 At that time, there already existed a number of Eight Hour Leagues at the ward level; see "Central Eight Hour League," *The National Workman*, 22 November 1866, 3.

279 "Central Eight Hour League," *The National Workman*, 3 November 1866.

To the delight of *The National Workman*, only one candidate sent a negative reply. With this pawn in hand, the workers of New York felt confident that, as a letter to the editors predicted, "we will [soon] have the eight hour system as a law."[280] By the end of 1866, virtually no union, workers' association, or labor-reform group had failed to endorse the demand. From the bricklayers to the ship joiners, from the cigar makers to the tailors, from the GGWA to the offices of the labor-friendly papers, the demand for eight hours united the local movement as seldom before. Whether at mass rallies, public picnics, labor conventions, beer-hall festivities, or in the pages of its press, the movement made sure that the call for eight hours was heard by New York's legislators and employers.[281] Representing about 50 unions, New York's city-wide umbrella association of English-speaking labor proved especially decisive in orchestrating the local shorter-hour movement. Unlike individual trade unions, which focused on the enforcement of eight-hour demands in particular businesses or sectors through negotiation or, if necessary, strikes, the Workingmen's Union addressed the urban working class at large and strived to influence public opinion and political discourse alike.[282] As a consequence, the city central's approach differed markedly from trade-union strategies (which will be discussed in Chapter 5).

On May 29, 1865, the Workingmen's Union organized one of the earliest post-war expressions of renewed working-class confidence. Thousands of workers were drawn that day to a mass picnic at Jones' Wood, a commercial picnic ground and prominent working-class locality near the East River.[283] As *The New York Times* reported, the well-attended picnic displayed a peculiar mix of proletarian orderliness and hearty enjoyment.[284] The paper did what it could to downplay the political character of the picnic, covering at length the outdoor activities of young men and pretty girls. Yet even the *Times*,

280 "Letter from 'Hemlock Knot,' Brooklyn," *The National Workman*, 17 November 1866, 2.

281 Burrows and Wallace, *Gotham*, 986–988.

282 I generally follow Yellowitz's distinction between political and economic campaigns for eight hours, yet I do not see the city-wide trade-union associations as purely economic organizations. As the examples discussed here indicate, city centrals struggled simultaneously for the enforcement of shorter-hour regulations in individual trades and for universal legislation; cf. Yellowitz, "Eight Hours and the Bricklayers' Strike," 84.

283 Burrows and Wallace, *Gotham*, 791–792, 994.

284 "The Workingmen's Union: Grand Demonstration Yesterday and To-Day at Jones' Wood, Sixteen Thousand Tickets Sold, Dancing and Frolicking," *The New York Times*, 30 May 1865, 2.

which was known for its critical stance towards interventions into the omnipresent "free play of supply and demand" could not hide the fact that the picnic was, first and foremost, an impressive demonstration of the Workingmen's Union's determination to win the normal workday.[285] To the proletarian attendees who were about to forge one of the most powerful movements in the nation, the fight for eight hours was much more than simply a get-together for jolly dance and lager beer. Rather, New York's workers were demanding what they saw as the fulfillment of a promise given to them by none other than the Republic itself. For years, they had given their lives defending it. Now it was time that the nation attended to the plight of the working man. Luckily for them, they soon found the support of a powerful ally.

As Timothy Messer-Kruse puts it, there existed much potential in the aftermath of the war for a new coalition of reformers to "recombine the fragments of radicalism that had been scattered by the victorious closing of the abolitionist umbrella."[286] It was in this climate of ideological re-evaluation that abolitionists turned their attention towards the fate of the working classes of the nation. In the South, they strongly promoted a land-reform movement that promised to support a class of independent black yeomen. In the North, and especially in its urban centers, abolitionists concentrated on the question of wage labor. According to long-time reform veterans like Wendell Phillips, the proliferation of the wage system threatened to erode the republican ideal of an educated, independent, and equal citizenry. Addressing Boston's Eight Hour League, Phillips invited his audience to picture nearby New York, that "metropolis of crime and monstrous inequality." No Christian civilization could tolerate the coexistence of such splendid wealth and leisure on the one hand and grinding poverty despite endless toil on the other. He wholeheartedly defended the eight-hour movement, therefore, on the basis of not only economic deliberation, but also political belief. Even if, as employers regularly warned, the shortening of the workday would hamper productivity and therefore economic growth, it was surely worth it if the overworked masses gained the time necessary for civic perfection. *This*, he argued, the struggle to gain leisure time for collective betterment, was the

285 "The Workingmen's Union: Continuation of the Grand Festival at Jones' Wood, Second Day of the Demonstration," *The New York Times*, 31 May 1865, 2.

286 Messer-Kruse, *The Yankee International*, 93. See also Stanley, *From Bondage to Contract*, 60–62.

deeper significance of the movement for eight hours.[287] Phillips and other prominent abolitionists thereby drew a close connection between the evolution of an unregulated market for wage labor and the evils of chattel slavery. Even if more subtle and less institutionalized, a free labor market featured elements of the despised slave system. In drawing this connection, abolitionists equipped the young workers' movement with powerful anti-slavery rhetoric that it successfully integrated into its own quest for equality and participation.[288] And as the aftermath of the war revealed, New York City's eight-hour movement made frequent use of this anti-slavery bridge.

In December 1865, local eight-hour activists organized a mass meeting to discuss and celebrate their cause at Cooper Institute. The great number of English and German-speaking men and women who attended the meeting were greeted by a large banner that decorated the hall. It read, pure and simple: "Freemen, no slaves!"[289] As the ensuing debates showed, working-class New York was horrified by the idea that an unregulated workday turned free citizens into slaves. Speakers warned the large audience that the system of wage labor threatened to revive the system of chattel slavery they had helped defeat through enormous sacrifices. According to postbellum working-class analysis, a worker who had no control over his labor—here understood as a particular amount of skill and diligence crystalized in a product—resembled the social figure of the slave since both were deprived of the most sacred precondition for active citizenship: Autonomy. Like that of chattel slaves, the labor of wage workers was highly productive, yet it did not give workers control over the manufacturing and distribution of the goods they produced. Discussing the everyday plight of workers in New York City, the German-language *Arbeiter-Zeitung* thus concluded several years later that "one of the main causes of our misery is that we work for someone else, for an employing master."[290] Put the other way around, the

---

287 "The Eight-Hour Movement: Wendell Phillips' Advice to the Working Men," *The New York Times*, 24 May 1870, 2.

288 See Messer-Kruse, "Eight Hours, Greenbacks and 'Chinamen,'" 135–136; Roediger, "Ira Steward." For the influence of abolitionist theory on postbellum labor in general, see Messer-Kruse, *The Yankee International*, 23–35; Montgomery, *Beyond Equality*, 25–44.

289 "Local Intelligence: The Eight Hour Movement, Mass Meeting of Working Men at the Cooper Institute: A Dignified and Enthusiastic Meeting," *The New York Times*, 8 December 1865, 8.

290 "Aus dem Alltagsleben," *Arbeiter-Zeitung*, 8 February 1873, 3. ("Eine der Hauptursachen unseres Unglücks ist, daß wir für andere, für Arbeitsherren, arbeiten, also die Lohnarbeit […].")

Arbeiter-Zeitung here scandalized the fact that wage laborers no longer *worked for themselves*, that is, that they no longer controlled the products of their labor. Based on this analysis, the same paper reminded its immigrant readership that there were shops in New York City that were as exploitative as the slave system. The only thing missing was the whip, "and these workshops would be no less of a disgrace than the plantations of the South."[291]

This perception was widely shared by native-born abolitionists and social reformers. In a fierce rant against Alexander Turney Stewart, the Irish merchant who was about to open the world's largest retail store in New York City, one of the editors of *The Revolution* argued that Stewart's business undermined the republican foundations of the US. Exposing strong anti-Irish and anti-Catholic sentiments, Parker Pillsbury's lead article denounced that there were about five thousand workers in New York City who were completely in Stewart's power,

> to be retained or discharged, in youth or old age, in health or sickness, in plenty or poverty, as ever could have been a plantation of chattel slaves! True, he cannot offer them for sale to the highest bidder in front of City Hall. But he and others have so adjusted the laws of capital that they all appear before his mighty temples of Mammon and offer themselves to him at such prices as he will pay.[292]

Like a vampire, Pillsbury continued, New York's "merchant prince" sucked the fruits of their labor from his victims without ever having produced any value himself. To reformers like Pillsbury, the wage system was thus a new form of slavery, or, as he put it, "the high art of slavery."[293] This analysis resonated with the city's diverse movement of workers. Richard F. Trevellick, the well-traveled trade unionist and president of the NLU introduced earlier, insisted that the eight-hour workday was not merely a right of the free worker. Rather, he stressed in an address to the Bricklayer's Union of Brooklyn, it was an obligation for any free citizen of the Republic.[294] For how should a worker whom the cruel logic of the market forced to labor for twelve, 14, or 16 hours a day fulfill his civic duties? How was he supposed to become a well-informed member of society who could base his voting decision on

291 "An die Mühevollen und Geplagten," *Arbeiter-Zeitung*, 15 February 1873, 1. ("[...] um diese Anstalten den südlichen Plantagen—schändlichen Angedenkens—ebenbürtig an die Seite stellen zu können.")

292 P.[arker] P.[illsbury], "Largest Store in the World," *The Revolution*, 3 September 1868, 136.

293 Ibid., 137.

294 "Labor Movements, New York: Bricklayers' B. and P. Union, No. 1," *The National Workman*, 5 January 1867, 3.

rational deliberation? How could he join a political association, run for office, or sharpen his wits in public debate? Looking back at one and half decades of struggle, the *Labor Standard* of New York brought these questions to a simple conclusion. The organ of the recently founded Workingmen's Party of the United States left no doubt that a person who was

> compelled to spend from ten to fifteen hours a day and even more in any kind of labor, [...] cannot be a true citizen of a free state, a responsible, intelligent, self-governing agent.[295]

For the local eight-hour movement, the shorter workday was thus a first step towards enforcing the republican ideal of autonomy and democratic participation by liberating the worker from the yoke of "wage slavery."[296] As Parker Pillsbury's aforementioned commentary in *The Revolution* indicates, opposition to the system of "wage slavery" was thereby but the negative expression of the producerist ethos that was still widely shared by American workers. In their study on the decline of the concept of "wage slavery" in working-class discourse towards the end of the nineteenth century, sociologists Helga Kristin Hallgrimsdottir and Cecilia Benoit provide a very useful definition of the concept of producerism. According to the authors, the producerist vision,

> referencing the mythical republican past, held that self-ownership, through control over conditions and relations of production, was the only guarantor of individual autonomy, personal freedom and liberty in society. Autonomy, freedom and liberty were idealized as the natural condition of the male producer who owned both his labor and the means by which his labor was translated into economic goods.[297]

This was indeed precisely what New York's eight-hour movement was struggling for. In the mid-1870s, *The Socialist* argued that wage labor had always been a stage in the development of a craftsman from childhood to adulthood. The young apprentice accepted the limitation of his freedom as citizen and producer because he understood that the limitation was temporarily only:

295 "The Normal Workday," *Labor Standard*, 3 February 1877, 2.
296 "Die 'New York Times' und die Arbeiterbewegung," *Die Arbeiter-Union*, 4 June 1869, 2.
297 Hallgrimsdottir and Benoit, "From Wage Slaves to Wage Workers," 1401.

When working for wages, the young man was looking forward to the time when he should work for himself, with as distinct a hope, as the schoolboy was looking forward to the time when he should vote.[298]

Yet the promise of self-employment and autonomy materialized for fewer and fewer young workers. According to the paper's analysis, the massive increase in permanent wage labor had left an entire class of free men unable to control their everyday lives. The eight-hour struggle now appeared as a weapon in the hands of workers who opposed this development. Echoing the ten-hour movement of the first half of the century, the postbellum movement referred to the shortening of hours as a precondition for the survival of the Republic.[299] In so doing, it drew heavily upon the notion that labor was not a common commodity.[300] The peculiar mélange of German socialists, American labor reformers, and English trade unionists that comprised New York's eight-hour movement insisted that it was the commodification of labor that degraded the worker to a status little better than that of a slave. Although liberal rhetoric pretended that wage workers were free, they were actually disturbingly unfree due to their inability to control the products of their labor. Just like any other commodity, their labor was offered on a market that exclusively benefitted the "unproductive" propertied classes. At first sight, a shorter workday would not abolish the commodification of labor, but merely decrease the amount of time during which the worker existed as a commodity. Yet to eight-hour activists, their struggle meant much more. On the one hand, the ability to enforce workday restrictions upon their bosses epitomized that they were not a soulless and powerless commodity that could be used by employers as they wished. It was thus a crucial element in the struggle against the dehumanization of workers (which will be discussed in the following chapter). On the other hand, the eight-hour workday was seen as a first step in a long battle to end the current system of wage work. Eight-hour activists envisioned a world of production and exchange in which every worker proudly offered a product that represented the value of his labor. To them, the eight-hour demand was, as Hallgrimsdottir and Benoit put it, a way to defend the concept of the worker as a producer *who owned both his labor and the means through which his labor was translated into economic goods.* In the words of New York's *Toiler*, the producerist

298 "Social Tracts: Wage Slavery," *The Socialist*, 27 May 1876, 4.

299 Roediger, *The Movement for a Shorter Working Day*, 18–42.

300 For an excellent study on the impact of discussions about slavery and the free-market on labor thought in the US, see Stanley, *From Bondage to Contract*, 60–97.

ideal was fueled by the belief in a near and better future when workers would enjoy the "sweet boon to be one's own master and to work for one's self."[301] This hope was based on the assumption that workers on shorter shifts would use their electoral power in order to transform the entire system of "wage slavery." Formulating widespread opposition to the commodification of their labor, a mass rally of New York City workers resolved to

> steadily and persistently maintain that the reduction of the hours of labor should be compulsory on all, and that human labor is not a commodity to be regulated by the law of supply and demand.[302]

The local eight-hour struggle of the 1860s and early 1870s took up the legacy of those "chants democratic" that had been sung across the city in the first half of the century.[303] To workers in New York, the normal workday was a means for greater political liberty, democratic participation, and full citizenship. It was both a symbol and the promise of the free republic they had fought for. Deeply entrenched in this logic was the conviction that the socio-economic system of "wage slavery" was akin to the system of chattel slavery because both deprived producers of their political autonomy.

Interestingly, workers in Berlin had no firsthand experience with chattel slavery or a free republic. And yet, the rhetoric of anti-slavery and a genuine republican spirit also swept through the ranks of the movement that emerged in the Prussian capital in the mid- to late 1860s.

3.2. The Movement for Shorter Hours in Berlin

Contrasting political freedoms in Prussia and the US, Louis Kröber, Secretary of Section 25 of the IWA in North America, argued passionately that in

> America there existed complete freedom of association, freedom of speech; there does not even exist a law that regulates the press or associations. People are free to

301 "Social Tracts: Wage Slavery," *The Socialist*, 27 May 1876, 4.
302 "Cooper Institute: Working-Men Mass Meeting," *The Toiler*, 23 May 1874, 1.
303 Wilentz, *Chants Democratic*.

gather as they wish, without prior registration and without the supervision of a brigade of constables and cops; if one of the latter dared to show up at a meeting, he has to expect to be kicked out rather ungently.[304]

Kröber's assessment indicates that even in the eyes of organized labor, the US had accomplished what Berlin's liberal movement had been preaching for years. Large cities like New York in particular were blessed with a free labor market, unrestricted freedom of association, and a flourishing landscape of institutions promoting thrift and self-help. And yet New York's working class seemed as miserable as that of Berlin.[305] The American city thus offered plenty of ammunition for social-democratic agitation at home. Yet at the same time, the vitality and strength of organized labor in postbellum New York also commanded a great deal of admiration among workers in Berlin. The struggle for shorter hours thereby constituted an important point of contact between the working-class communities of New York and Berlin.

The first ADAV chapter on American soil, founded in New York City in February 1866, was characteristic of this trans-Atlantic exchange of news and ideas. While historical research has recently turned attention towards the geography of early German social-democracy, it has largely failed to notice that the ADAV established local branches even in non-German speaking lands (beyond Switzerland and the Habsburg Empire, that is). ADAV's decisions to establish branches so widely not only illustrates the manifold working-class bonds that linked cities like Berlin and New York, it also epitomizes the internationalist self perception of Lassallean socialists in Germany—a fact that had long been overshadowed by the explicit internationalism of their Eisenacher and Marxist rivals. Early in 1866, the American ADAV *Bevollmächtigter* (representative) in New York, August Schlag, informed readers at home that although the local ADAV branch's main objective was to propagate Lassallean principles in New York, its members could not help but be attracted to the powerful movement for a shorter

---

304 "Aus Amerika," *Der Volksstaat*, 20 January 1872, 2. ("[...] Amerika besteht vollständige Versammlungs-, Rede- und Preßfreiheit, es giebt überhaupt gar kein Gesetz über die Presse und die Vereine. Man kann sich versammeln, wie es einem beliebt, ohne es anzumelden, und ohne unter einer Oberaufsicht von einer Brigade Gensdarmen und Polizisten zu stehen; würde sich einer der Letzteren in Versammlungen erblicken lassen, so müsste er es sich gefallen lassen, wenn er sanft oder auch unsanft an die Luft gesetzt würde.")

305 "Ausland: Amerika (Über das Elend der New Yorker Arbeiterbevölkerung)," *Der Social-Demokrat*, 28 November 1865, 3–4.

workday.[306] Discussing a large eight-hour demonstration on May 5, 1866, Schlag argued that the mobilization success was a clear expression of the ability of the local eight-hour movement to put pressure on all levels of government.[307] It seemed that the eight-hour movement offered workers in the US the opportunity to finally overcome ethnic and political divisions.[308] While New York City featured prominently in Berlin both as a place of hope and despair, Berliners were very conscious about how they were perceived abroad. Observers from Berlin seemed especially content that their revolutionary reputation preceded them. As the *Neuer Social-Demokrat* bragged rather proudly,

> working-class Berliners have already won notoriety to rank next to the Parisians when it comes to revolutionary sympathies. The *New Yorker Daily Bulletin* reported that there were apparently many elements from Paris and Berlin engaged in the numerous strikes that have recently swept across America, as the frequent calls to violence suggested.[309]

Stories from Berlin proved especially popular among inhabitants of *Kleindeutschland*, who were keenly interested in how their new home town fared in comparison to the Prussian capital. In the winter of 1868, their community hotly discussed a report that compared wages in Berlin and New York City. While some openly conceded that wages were considerably higher in New York and life therefore generally better, others replied that living costs were likewise much higher in New York and the difference between the two cities actually less dramatic. The latter emphasized that working-class life was in fact equally miserable on both sides of the Atlantic.[310] Such transatlantic discussions suggest that many of the working-class inhabitants of Little Germany had at least spent some time in the Prussian capital before making

306 "Ausland: Amerika [Die Arbeiterbewegung]," *Der Social-Demokrat*, 13 February 1866, 3–4. The usage of the term "Bevollmächtigter" in the party press indicates that the New York section was seen as an official offshoot abroad.

307 "Ausland: Sch. New York [Acht Stunden Arbeitszeit]," *Der Social-Demokrat*, 9 May 1866, Supplement.

308 "Ausland: Amerika [Die Arbeiterbewegung]," *Der Social-Demokrat*, 13 February 1866, 3.

309 "Politische Rundschau: Die Berliner Arbeiter," *Neuer Social-Demokrat*, 26 June 1872, 2. ("Die Berliner Arbeiter sind bereits in den Ruf gekommen, was social-revolutionäre Gesinnung betrifft, gleich neben den Parisern zu rangieren. So schreibt das 'New Yorker Daily Bulletin' wie folgt: Bei den zahlreichen Strikes, die in neuerer Zeit in Amerika vorkamen, scheinen vorherrschend viele Pariser und Berliner Elemente betheiligt zu sein, weil häufig gewaltsame Maßregeln anempfohlen werden.")

310 Geo. Gaide, "Eingesandt (Verspätet), New York, Okt. 27 1868," *Die Arbeiter Union*, 5 December 1868, 6.

their way to the new world. Some, like Gustav Lübkert, passed through New York only briefly before settling elsewhere.[311] Others, however, had come to stay. Late in 1872 the *Neuer Social-Demokrat* published a short letter it had received from New York. Addressing the German working class of New York City, it read:

> Party comrades! We Lassalleans in New York have also founded an association based on Lassalle's principles. Our meetings take place every Wednesday, 8 pm, 165 Bowery, chaired by a party comrade from Berlin.[312]

This "party comrade from Berlin," A. Mundt, replaced the aforementioned Schlag as the new ADAV delegate for New York in the early 1870s. From there, he regularly sent correspondence to the office of the *Neuer Social-Demokrat*, therewith adding to the stream of information that already flowed back and forth between relatives, friends, and co-workers in New York and Berlin. What workers in Berlin found particularly appealing was the connection that American eight-hour activists drew between unregulated labor markets and the "enslavement of work."

In the years prior to his emigration to New York City, where he would become one of the most visible German socialist of the decade, the shoemaker August Vogt followed closely the struggle of the American Republic against slavery.[313] Vogt, a veteran of the Communist League and founding

311 Lübkert eventually settled down in Pennsylvania where he became president of the local association of German workers; see August Weist, "Alleghany (Allgemeiner Bericht: Agitation gegen die Mäßigungsvereinler)," *Neuer Social-Demokrat*, 28 May 1873, 2. As former president of the *Allgemeiner Deutschen Zimmererverein*, Lübkert was actively involved in the shorter-hour struggles of the building trades that shook Berlin in the late 1860s. According to Renzsch, he immigrated to the US in 1870 or 1871; see Renzsch, *Handwerker und Lohnarbeiter*, 54.

312 "Die New-Yorker Lassalleaner," *Neuer Social-Demokrat*, 22 December 1872, Supplement, 5. ("Parteigenossen! Auch wir Lassalleaner in New-York haben uns jetzt zu einem Verein nach Lassalle'schen Prinzipien zusammengethan und versammeln uns jeden Mittwoch, Abends 8 Uhr, Bowery Nr. 165, unter Vorsitz eines Berliner Parteigenossen.") The Berliner *Parteigenosse* was Mundt, as the regular correspondence that followed show; see, for instance, "Vereins-Theil: Aus New York," *Neuer Social-Demokrat*, 16 March 1873, 2.

313 "August Vogt und Wilhelm Liebknecht an Julius Vahlteich," 3, Footnote 1. Following his relocation to New York, Vogt eventually became an adversary of the local Marxists, and Sorge in particular. The latter wrote to Liebknecht in 1872 that the group of "frondeurs" around Vogt and Grosse had turned a café in New York into the home base for German Lassalleans and other "deviators" in the city. According to Sorge, Vogt had supported the defecting Yankee sections of the IWA in New York; see "F. A. Sorge an Wilhelm Liebknecht," 342, 416–417.

member of the Berlin section of the IWA, was a characteristic supporter of the young workers' movement.[314] Drawn equally to the theories of Marx and Lassalle, he had joined the Berlin branch of the ADAV in the mid-1860s together with his close friend Sigfrid Meyer, whom we have met before. Vogt quickly rose to prominence as a regular speaker at local working-class meetings. At one of these gatherings in the *Alhambra*, he analyzed the recent end of the American Civil War and the abolition of chattel slavery in the US. Vogt was certain that the emancipation of the "black slave" would inevitably lead the way for the emancipation of the "white slave" as well. To him, the end of slavery in the US was but a prelude for the emancipation of working classes everywhere.[315] The transatlantic comparison allowed working-class Berliners like Vogt to entrench the metaphor of "wage slavery" deeply in social-democratic discourse. As long as wage labor existed, working people would remain as unfree as chattel slaves.

Consistently with this discourse, Berlin's *Social-Demokrat*, in a contribution titled "The Wage Slave," demanded: "Love to humanity, death to slavery, the last slavery of all."[316] Opposition to the dreaded enslavement of workers fueled demands for shorter hours in Berlin as well. When the delegates to the *Allgemeiner Deutscher Schuhmacher-Kongreß* (General German Shoemakers' Congress) convened in the German capital in November 1872, they resolved that the normal workday was of paramount importance, "lest big industry exploit the shoemaker as a slave."[317] Facing enormous pressure from a putting-out system fueled by merchant capital, textile and clothing workers were especially critical of the proliferation of wage labor, which they regarded as an attack on their position as independent producers and, as a result, on their ideal of political self-determination. These distressed workers saw the legislative introduction of shorter hours as a weapon in the struggle against the "slavery of wage work." As was true for organized labor in New York City, in Berlin the slave analogy clearly expressed widespread fears that

314 Bezirksleitung (ed.), *Geschichte der revolutionären Berliner Arbeiterbewegung*, 126.

315 "Allgemeine Arbeiter-Versammlung in der Berliner 'Alhambra,'" *Der Social-Demokrat*, 7 November 1865, 4. ("Und so wie dort [in the US] die schwarze Sclaverei gefallen ist, so wird auch die weiße Sclaverei fallen durch die Produktivassoziationen, das ist das eiserne Muß der Geschichte.")

316 "Die Lohnsclaven," *Neuer Social-Demokrat*, 25 September 1872, 1. ("Liebe dem Menschenthum, Tod der Sclaverei, der letzten Sclaverei.")

317 f., "Lokales (Der Allgemeine Deutsche Schuhmacher-Kongreß)," *Demokratische Zeitung*, 19 November 1872, 3. ("[…] damit die Groß-Industrie den Schuhmacher in Zukunft nicht als Sklaven ausbeuten kann.")

a free labor market undermined republican ideals of equality, autonomy, and participation. The *Neuer Social-Demokrat* often drew this connection by publishing correspondence from New York City that served to highlight their common struggle. A letter from the "Eight-Hour League in New York," for instance, revealed that German social democrats shared the hope of their US comrades that shorter hours were the first step on the path towards the eventual emancipation of labor. Today, the league noted, even those economists who only a couple of years earlier had preached strict non-intervention into the labor market now acknowledged the legitimacy of the eight-hour demand. Workers everywhere were united in their struggle for shorter hours, even though the Germans were yet more modest in their actual hour demands than their American brothers. The correspondent here referred to the fact that both the ADAV and the SDAP had long hesitated to make concrete hour demands for all trades. When they eventually did, they usually settled for ten hours rather than eight. The ADAV officially adopted the ten-hour demand for large industries at its Berlin convention in 1867. For the time being, the convention declared, more radical hour demands were simply not realistic, given the current balance of power. The SDAP refrained from making concrete hour demands altogether. At its Eisenacher Convention of 1869, it merely listed *the introduction of a normal workday* as part of its program.[318] Irrespective of the distinct strategies employed in Germany and the US, the New York correspondent urged readers at home to emphasize that their cause followed directly from industrial development. The more labor was mechanized, centralized, and divided, the more workers were deprived of their right to self-determination.

> We can no longer determine How? What? or Where? we want to work because we no longer work for ourselves. We are left with but one consideration. If we do not want to starve to death, we have to work for others so that they can batten on the sweat of our labor.[319]

Rallying against the omnipresent "unproductive" employer, workers bitterly protested their loss of control over the distribution of the surplus value they had produced in the first place. In their eyes, this was a highly unjust system

---

318 Cf. "Erste Beilage," *Der Social-Demokrat*, 29 November 1867, 1–4; "Das Eisenacher Programm," *Demokratische Zeitung*, 30 November 1871, 2.

319 "Aus Newyork," *Neuer Social-Demokrat*, 31 May 1872, 3. ("Wir können nicht mehr bestimmen, wie? was? oder wo? wir arbeiten wollen, weil wir nicht mehr für uns arbeiten. Uns ist nur noch eine Erwägung übrig geblieben. Wenn wir nicht verhungern wollen, müssen wir für Andere arbeiten, damit diese sich vom Schweiße unserer Arbeit mästen.")

that needed to be transformed in the name of republican equality. Followers of the *Neuer Social-Demokrat* could thus read:

> Fellow workers! We do not want to be enslaved! We want to be humans! We want to remain in control of the utilization of the products of our labor. Our next task is therefore to win back at least a part of the time we are now forced to spend in senseless toil so that we might find the energy, leisure, and intellect necessary to organize; so that we can come together, discuss our situation, and prepare ourselves for the self-representation of our interest in the body politic.[320]

As the foregoing has shown, workers in Berlin widely shared this critique of unregulated workdays as a threat to their civic rights. At a meeting of local paper hangers, a certain Mr. Rost argued that the shorter workday was in fact a crucial precondition for the very democratic participation workers were struggling for. After all,

> of what use are the rights of assembly and association to the worker who has to put in twelve, 13, or more hours a day? Under such conditions he is neither physically nor mentally in a position to defend his political rights.[321]

Following Rost's talk, the assembled paper hangers passed a resolution calling for the introduction of a nine-hour workday.[322]

Like the paper hangers, the local *Verein der Berliner Buchdrucker und Schriftgießer* (Association of Book Printers and Type Founders of Berlin) demanded legislative intervention into the free labor market. Without shorter-hour protection, the printers reasoned, the laborer becomes a "weak-willed and mechanic limb in both polity and community."[323] Rather than a violation of

---

320 Ibid. ("Mitarbeiter! Wir wollen nicht versklaven, wir wollen Menschen bleiben. Wir wollen in Zukunft über die Verwendung und Verwerthung unserer Arbeitsprodukte mitbestimmen. Unsere nächste Aufgabe muß deshalb darin bestehen, mindestens einen Theil der Zeit, die wir jetzt mit für uns zweckloser Arbeit auszufüllen gezwungen sind, wieder zu erobern, damit wir die nötige Kraft und Muße finden, und intellektuell ausbilden zu können; damit es uns ermöglicht wird, zusammen zu kommen, um über die Verbesserung unserer Lage zu berathen und uns darauf vorzubereiten, im staatlichen Organismus unsere Interessen selbst vertreten zu können.")

321 "Berliner Arbeiter-Bund (Tapezierer-Strikeverein)," *Neuer Social-Demokrat*, 23 August 1872, 3. ("[...] was nütze dem Arbeiterstande jetzt das Vereins- und Versammlungsrecht, wo er noch 12, 13 und mehr Stunden arbeiten müsse, er könne dann unmöglich seinen körperlich und geistig abgespannten Körper noch dazu benutzen, um seine Interessen als Staatsbürger zu wahren.")

322 Almost a year later, the paper hangers were still protesting for a nine-hour normal workday; see "Verbands-Theil: Berliner Arbeiter-Bund (Versammlung des Strikevereins der Tapezierer)," *Neuer Social-Demokrat*, 9 March 1873, 3.

323 "Zur Arbeiterbewegung," *Demokratische Zeitung*, 25 July 1872, 2.

economic freedom, shorter-hour legislation constituted a legitimate intervention by the state into the false liberty of the employer to take unfair advantage of the unpropertied worker. The *Neuer Social-Demokrat* concluded that "the normal workday is therefore not a barrier to freedom, but a breach in this barrier."[324] As in New York City, the urban craftsmen who constituted the backbone of Berlin's workers' movement in the 1860s and early 1870s despised the wage system that, in their eyes, jeopardized their right to political equality and democratic participation. Thus, when workers in Berlin struggled for the protection of their labor via the introduction of normal workday legislation, they defended the notion of the craftsman as the independent producer of value who was entitled to the "full fruits" of his labor.

In his detailed study of working-class Berlin in the early to mid-1870s, Wolfgang Renzsch shows that the increasing loss of producer autonomy was one of the prime motives for opposition among urban craftsmen.[325] The more these workers lost control over production and distribution, the more firmly they endorsed a struggle that promised to protect their autonomy as independent producers and free citizens. The producerist rhetoric thereby tied in closely with opposition to what organized workers in Berlin perceived as the commodification of labor. Similarly to working-class discourse in New York City, the notion of de-commodification became a crucial element in the political rationale of Berlin's nascent movement for shorter hours. Around the time the Workingmen's Union intensified its pressure on New York's legislature, a large group of workers in Berlin followed Schulze-Delitzsch's invitation to the *Alhambra*, one of the most spacious working-class venues in the city. Once again the liberal convener used the opportunity to advocate the free labor market as the precondition for economic prosperity, individual betterment, and political equality. Social differences, he argued, would always exist. What democratic polities needed to provide was equality before the law and access to education for all. Johann Baptist von Schweitzer fiercely rejected this notion of a free labor market in a workers' meeting that was organized at the same location one week later. Rather than the mockery of liberal freedom, von Schweitzer thundered, workers needed protection from a rapacious market. An unregulated labor market clearly undermined political rights. After all, the commodification of labor resulted

324 H.[asselmann], "Der Normalarbeitstag und das Prinzip der Freiheit," *Neuer Social-Demokrat*, 16 October 1872, 1. ("Der Normalarbeitstag ist somit nicht Schranke der Freiheit, sondern eine Bresche in dieser Schranke.")

325 Renzsch, *Handwerker und Lohnarbeiter*, 18.

in extremely long workdays that left little room for active participation. In von Schweitzer's eyes, Schulze-Delitzsch's naïve conception of free labor reflected the general shallowness of liberal thought.[326] Hoping to break the spell of the latter, local activists organized a debate tournament that was supposed to give liberals and social democrats the opportunity to present their respective views on labor. The preparatory committee tried to attract Prince-Smith, Julius Faucher, and Otto Michaelis as free-labor advocates, yet apparently none of them was willing to share a rostrum with von Schweitzer.[327] Thus, the mass meeting that took place on November 6, 1865 was firmly in the hands of local social democrats. Rejecting free-market teachings, the speakers fiercely embraced the notion that labor was not a commodity. Therefore, workers could not be exposed to the unchecked powers of unregulated labor markets.[328]

On both side of the Atlantic, the idea that shorter hours would help decommodify labor and enforce democratic participation tied in with widespread hopes for intellectual betterment. In 1866, the eight-hour normal workday became the subject of a lengthy discussion between New York's *National Workman* and its adversary, *The Economist and Dry Goods Reporter*. As the organ of the manufacturers and dry-goods traders in New York City, the latter declared that no one would rejoice as much as employers to see their employees strive for cultural and intellectual refinement. Yet the great mass of workers did not show signs of individual improvement as citizens or collective betterment as a class. It was highly doubtful, the paper concluded, that shorter hours would actually result in a more educated, refined, and responsible citizenry. Rather, eight-hour workdays were much more likely to give rise "to a wretched bunch of inebriated paupers."[329] This verdict provided more ammunition to *The National Workman* than it could ask for. The paper replied sharply that the moral and intellectual betterment of the working classes could not precede the shortening of hours, as the *Dry Goods Reporter* implied. Rather, workers first had to be freed from the intolerable burden of long hours before they could begin investing time in education, organizing, and political self-determination:

---

326 "Vortrag vor der Allgemeinen Arbeiter-Versammlung in der Berliner 'Alhambra,'" *Der Social-Demokrat*, 11 October 1865, 1.

327 See "Politischer Theil: Zur morgigen Arbeiterversammlung in der 'Alhambra,'" *Der Social-Demokrat*, 5 November 1865, 3.

328 "Allgemeine Arbeiter-Versammlung in der Berliner 'Alhambra,'" 7 November 1865, 3–4.

329 "The Eight Hour System," *The National Workman*, 8 December 1866, 1.

All the teachings of experience are calculated to confirm the workingmen of America in their demand for the adoption of the Eight Hour system as the most effective means that can be devised by human ingenuity for their elevation.[330]

At a mass meeting at Cooper Institute a couple of years earlier, delegate Purcell of the organized painters had illustrated this aspect very vividly. According to the local painter, employers in the city opposed the eight-hour day because they claimed that workers would spend their leisure time at the rum house rather than the evening school. Yet Purcell replied that the workers of New York were respectable men who had nothing in common with the urban underworld of drunkards and thieves. He insisted that what their employers really feared was that New York's class of skilled workers would use their free time to study and become educated and independent members of the polity.[331] Workers like Purcell were confident that the shorter workday would promote an emancipated citizenry that visited libraries and lectures, engaged in public debate, or studied—and understood—the programs of the existing political parties. Underscoring this point, New York's *Toiler* suggested that during the short phase when eight-hour shifts were actually enforced in the early 1870s, proletarian attendance at evening schools had grown by 44 percent.[332] The paper was in agreement with its readers that the shorter workday would enable workers to acquire the education and knowledge necessary to fulfill their civic duties.

Workers in Berlin made the same connection between a normal workday and the education of a democratic citizenry. At a general meeting of the local *Streik-Verein der Sattler* (strike association of Berlin's upholsterers), a certain Mr. Berg argued that the normal workday promised intellectual betterment through education. Once workers were protected from the long hours that the free market imposed on them, they could become the responsible and self-governing citizens of a future republic.[333] Yet education was seen as not only a republican prerequisite for active citizenship, but also a quasi-revolutionary demand. At a meeting of New York's bricklayers in the summer of 1868, a delegate reminded his audience of a master mason who had re-

330 "The Dry Goods Reporter and the National Workman," *The National Workman*, 29 December 1866, 2.

331 "Die Massenversammlung am 16. April im Cooper-Institute," *Die Arbeiter-Union*, 24 April 1869, 4.

332 "Labor Notes," *The Toiler*, 25 July 1874, 3.

333 "Lokales (Strike-Verein der Sattler)," *Demokratische Zeitung*, 10 January 1872, 5. ("Nur dadurch allein sei es möglich, eine erhöhte leibliche und geistige Ausbildung zu erlangen.")

cently stated that the journeymen lacked the intelligence to enforce their idea. The speaker replied that this was "precisely what the eight-hour movement was for—to get time to obtain intelligence."[334] Given the bitter eight-hour strike that the local bricklayers had been staging at that time (see Chapter 5), the hope of obtaining intelligence through more leisure time was clearly not limited to questions of civic participation. Rather, workers were certain that the shorter workday would allow them to educate themselves, develop a common understanding of their situation, and act upon this shared idea. The nexus of better education as a result of shorter hours, in other words, was also seen as a step towards the development of class consciousness. Here, too, the American shorter-hour movement provided a crucial point of reference for organized labor in Germany. In an article that appeared in the pages of the VDAV's *Demokratisches Wochenblatt*, August Bebel reasoned that an increase in leisure time would allow the worker to obtain the intelligence and education necessary for the emancipation of the working class. Herein, Bebel concluded, lay the political significance of the eight-hour movement in England and the US.[335] Bebel's Lassallean rivals came to the same conclusion. An article in the Berlin-based *Social-politische Blätter* argued that if workers were given more time off work, they would make good use of it. They would free themselves from the intellectual hegemony of liberal thought and advance socialist alternatives instead. Shorter hours would thus prove decisive for the political mobilization of workers. Rather solemnly, the paper declared that a normal workday would foster independent working-class thought and "rekindle the spark to a blazing fire in a thousand places."[336]

Closely linked to the producerist vision of political autonomy, shorter-hour debates in Berlin and New York were also influenced by dominant notions of manhood. As Thomas Welskopp shows, the concept of masculinity mattered greatly in the social-democratic discourse of the time. Local unions and political associations provided male workers with a platform and social space for mutual self-assurance. To belong to a union and/or party, especially in times of massive state repression, demonstrated both courage

334 "Bricklayers' Meeting," *The New York Times*, 28 July 1868, 8.

335 Scharf, *Geschichte der Arbeitszeitverkürzung*, 132.

336 "Der gesetzlich festgestellte Normalarbeitstag," *Social-Politische Blätter*, 7 February 1874, 4. ("[...] an tausend Orten den glimmenden Funken zur lodernden Flamme anfachen.") The same article by Hasselmann had already appeared several years before in the pages of Agitator; see Wilhelm Hasselmann, "Der gesetzlich festgesetzte Normal-Arbeitstag," *Agitator*, 15 April 1870, 1–2.

and defiance. The support of striking comrades was likewise a question of honor and solidarity that was often characterized as a sign of manliness.[337] The free labor market, in contrast, was regarded as a menace to working-class notions of masculinity. Discussing a report that had recently appeared in the business friendly *Concordia*, the *Volksstaat* argued that it was little wonder that workers who had known nothing else but slavery and submission for their entire lives lacked the manliness necessary to oppose the employment of child labor. The paper continued that both physical misery and ideological influence had demoralized and eventually emasculated (*entmannt*) workers. The latter no longer recognized the moral perversion of child labor, nor did they understand that the commodification of underage labor power put pressure on their wages and working hours.[338]

The fear of emasculation was especially prevalent in the political rationale of the shorter-hour movement. Looking back at the movement for normal workday legislation, New York's *Labor Standard* argued that as much as the advocates of the free market pretended that the latter promoted the freedom of workers, what it really did was undermine working-class participation in the polity. It was therefore, the paper concluded, "the paramount duty of the state to guard [...the] manhood of its citizens from economic dependence on private capitalists."[339] The paper's predecessor had found a similar correlation between working-class resistance against the free market and proletarian understandings of masculinity. In its first issue, *The Socialist* lectured its prospective readers that buying the paper was an unmistakable expression of their manliness and commitment to the common cause. "Rise in all the dignity of manhood," the paper thundered, "and remove the foul blot of wage slavery from the star-spangled banner as we removed the curse of chattel slavery."[340] This idea traveled the Atlantic freely. The New York City-based correspondent of the *Volksstaat* informed his followers at home that everywhere around the globe the same social maladies prevailed. In a char-

337 Welskopp, *Das Banner der Brüderlichkeit*, 335–337, 482–484. For a compelling discussion of proletarian concepts of masculinity, see Lucas, *Vom Scheitern der deutschen Arbeiterbewegung*, 45–69. See also Hoffrogge, *Sozialismus und Arbeiterbewegung*, 117–120; Roediger, *The Wages of Whiteness*, 55.

338 "Zur Frauen- und Kinderarbeit," *Der Volksstaat*, 13 November 1874, 1. ("Arbeiter, die ihr Leben lang in erdrückender, hoffnungsloser Sklaverei vegetieren, vermögen natürlich in der Regel nach nicht sich zu mannhafter Unabhängigkeit der Gesinnung emporzuheben [...].")

339 "The Normal Workday," *Labor Standard*, 3 February 1877, 2.

340 "An Appeal," *The Socialist*, 15 April 1876, 1.

acteristic effort to discourage migration, he therefore concluded that "there is no salvation through escape, but only through manly, iron will and brave, bold deeds."[341] In Berlin, the prominent bricklayer and socialist Paul Grottkau told the members of the *Allgemeiner Deutscher Maurerverein* (General German Bricklayers' Association) that the struggle for shorter hours provided class-conscious workers with an opportunity to demonstrate their manliness.[342] As free republican *men*, they could not allow the labor market to control their lives.

To shorter-hour activists, the right to physical and mental integrity was yet another essential precondition for active citizenship. Backed by statistical surveys and official reports, organized labor on both sides of the Atlantic stressed that the unregulated labor market undermined the health and well-being of the local working classes. At the first *Webertag* (Weavers' Day) in 1871, delegate Uhlmann from Berlin thus demanded the legislative reduction of the workday as a fundamental right of workers. Portraying a heavily overworked proletariat in the German capital, Uhlmann argued that the normal workday would ease the physical plight of the worker and end the further dulling of the mind.[343] Other trades agreed. At a meeting of the International Association of Manufacturing and Manual Laborers in Berlin that was dedicated to a discussion of the shorter-hour struggle, speaker Kayser stated that the introduction of a normal workday was of paramount importance for any working man. After all, "this alone could protect the worker from mental enfeeblement and physical harm."[344] The Association of Book Printers and Type Founders of Berlin likewise argued that their long workdays had ruined the health of the entire trade. Typesetters in particular, who worked at night in poorly lit offices where they prepared the morning editions of the local press, suffered from the lack of workday protection.[345] Local shoemakers were certain that it was they who suffered the most from unregulated workdays. Convening in Berlin in late 1872, they resolved that only the legislative introduction and rigorous enforcement of shorter hours could stop the trag-

---

341 "Aus Amerika (Schluß)," *Der Volksstaat*, 22 December 1869, 2. ("Es giebt keine Rettung vor ihnen [the social maladies] durch die Flucht, sondern nur durch den ernsten Manneswillen und die muthige unerschrockene Thatkraft.")

342 Paeplow, *Zur Geschichte der deutschen Bauarbeiterbewegung*, 245.

343 Deutsches Weber-Central-Comitee (ed.), *Ausführlicher Bericht*, 53.

344 "Lokales (Versammlung der Internationalen Manufaktur- und Handarbeiterschaft)," *Demokratische Zeitung*, 14 March 1872, 3. ("[…] weil dieser [the shorter workday] nur allein im Stande ist, die Arbeiter vor geistiger und körperlicher Versumpfung zu schützen […].")

345 "Zur Arbeiterbewegung," *Demokratische Zeitung*, 25 July 1872, 2.

edy that every year thousands of workers perished in the prime of their lives due to excessively long workdays.[346] Health concerns were also a central argument among eight-hour activists in New York City who struggled against the morally corrupting and socially destructive reign of the free market. The organ of the city's Workingmen's Union, for instance, defended the introduction of a normal workday as a much-needed protection against the further deterioration of workers' well-being. Disregarding actual work realities in farming and the impact of the market on American agriculture, *The National Workman* claimed that American farmers enjoyed a long life and good health because the only thing they had ever known was an eight-hour workday. The American wage worker, in contrast, saw his health worsen every year due to excessively long work hours. Echoing working-class analysis in Berlin, the paper concluded that the unrestricted commodification of labor power made workers sick. In so doing, the free labor market caused the untimely death of an entire class of citizens.[347]

3.3. Chapter Conclusion

To readers today, it is disturbing how readily American white male workers equated the fate of the formally and materially unfree chattel slaves with their lives as wage laborers—only to discard this comparison quickly as an insult to their dignity. As David R. Roediger argues in his pathbreaking study on working-class notions of whiteness, the metaphor of "white slavery" had been a crucial element in the formation of working-class identity across Jacksonian America. According to Roediger, whiteness thereby represented more than a bread-and-butter privilege. Surely, he argues, white workers profited materially from ideas of white supremacy, but the "wages of whiteness" entailed a psychological value, too. Drawing on W.E.B. DuBois' *Black Reconstruction*, Roediger suggests that this psychological wage actually helped white workers set themselves apart from even less fortunate groups in society. Unlike their non-white counterparts, they did not need to fear that they would be prevented from voting, performing jury service, or exercising any

346 f., "Lokales (Der Allgemeine Deutsche Schuhmacher-Kongreß)," *Demokratische Zeitung*, 20 November 1872, 2.

347 "The Dry Goods Reporter and The National Workman," *The National Workman*, 29 December 1866, 2.

other constitutional right. They thus learned that, no matter how depressing their lives as workers might be, at least they were politically privileged. In Roediger's words, "[c]hattel slavery provided white workers with a touchstone against which to weigh their fears and a yardstick to measure their reassurance."[348] Against this backdrop, Jacksonian workers used the concept "white slavery" as an explicit warning that they would not quietly consent to the further deprivation of autonomy and selfhood inherent in permanent wage work—a deprivation that in their eyes might have been suitable for dependent blacks, but not for free white producers. The latter term, Roediger states, encompassed a broad social spectrum. Agricultural workers, home producers, and petty masters could hardly be subsumed under the category of wage workers since, strictly speaking, they did not receive a wage. They could easily be subsumed, however, under the category of "enslaved whites" who suffered under merchant capital, urban landlords, and industrial bosses. The term "white slavery" also resonated with non-working-class Democrats since ending "white slavery" did not require the abolition of the wage system, but merely the amelioration of hardships for whites by improving their living standards and employment conditions.[349] As a matter of fact, the notion that working-class whites' peculiar "slavery" was somehow as cruel as or even crueler than chattel slavery—because it was imagined as more subtle or sophisticated or because it supposedly freed the employer from the paternalistic duties of the master—drew upon ideas that resonated even with proslavery whites.[350] Though postbellum labor continuously highlighted its abolitionist legacy, the equation of wage labor and chattel slavery had brought the antebellum movement into proximity with ideas like those infamously expressed in George Fitzhugh's deeply reactionary critique of free markets and free labor.[351] The fact that American white labor so easily relativized the experience of enslaved African American workers in order to delegitimize the despised system of wage labor irritated even a few contemporary observers. Though primarily interested in the neglect of abolitionists to consider coercion arising directly from free labor markets, Jonathan A. Glickstein's study of anti-slavery discourse shows that some abolitionists openly rejected

348 Roediger, *The Wages of Whiteness*, 66.

349 Ibid. 72–73.

350 See also Stanley, *From Bondage to Contract*, 19–20.

351 Fitzhugh published two major works in the 1850s; see Fitzhugh, *Sociology for the South*; Fitzhugh, *Cannibals All*. For opposing views on free wage labor and slavery in antebellum North and South, see also Foner, *Free Soil*, 40–72.

workers' equation of wage labor and chattel slavery.[352] This equation not only relativized the suffering of millions of African Americans; it also made sure that black wage workers were further estranged from the young workers' movement in places like New York City.

Roediger argues that references to "white slavery" increasingly gave way to references to "wage slavery" in the second half of the century.[353] During the 1830s and 1840s, white Northern workers had broadly associated servility and dependency with African Americans. When criticizing "white slavery," they articulated a complex fear of the impending loss of political liberty while simultaneously expressing the conviction that their very whiteness would protect them from disenfranchisement. Towards the 1850s and 1860s, however, it became more and more difficult for white workers to uphold the counter-image of "naturally dependent" blacks. After all, racist ideas about black dependency did not go well with the proliferation of wage labor and widespread military service by African Americans. At the same time, republican notions of labor also shifted. While wage labor had once symbolized an inferior state of dependency, many radicals now embraced free wage labor as the antithesis to slave labor. By the end of the Civil War, Roediger argues, Northern white workers had largely adopted this rhetoric when they defended the concept of free labor as an ideal of independent production. Rather than contrasting "free labor" with "white slavery," they now contrasted "free labor" with "wage labor."

Despite its many penetrating insights, Roediger's *Wages of Whiteness* remains strikingly vague in this respect.[354] The producerist notion the author describes was not an invention of the 1860s. Antebellum workers had already distinguished very carefully between "free labor" (symbolizing the freedom of manual workers to control the products of their labor) and the "free labor market" (which epitomized the loss of self-determination due to the destructive powers of capital). Nor did postbellum workers simply accept the republican interpretation of "free labor" as the antinomy of slavery. On the contrary, organized labor increasingly opposed what it understood as a shallow notion of contractual freedom on the labor market. Postbellum workers in New York City did not understand "free labor" as something already gained. Rather, they continued to interpret "free labor" as a future goal that—despite the abolition of slavery—continued to be threatened by

352 Glickstein, "'Poverty Is Not Slavery,'" 213–215.

353 Roediger, *The Wages of Whiteness*, 65–92.

354 See also Brody, "Review of The Wages of Whitenes."

enslavement.[355] The fact that references to "white slavery" faded in postbellum discourse does not mean that workers abruptly stopped contrasting the systems of wage labor and chattel slavery in deeply racialized terms.[356] Although white workers could no longer compare themselves to chattel slaves after emancipation, the historical concept of black slavery remained an important foil against which organized labor formulated its demands. When opposing "wage slavery," postbellum shorter-hour activists did not compare their fate to some abstract social institution far away or in the distant past, but to the very vivid memory of black chattel slavery. With respect to postbellum working-class discourse, it actually did not matter much whether workers explicitly described their slavery as "white" or not because the concept of "wage slavery" was already fraught with racial prejudice.[357] As this study has shown, postbellum sources demanding a shortening of the workday regularly display a deeply internalized sarcasm that decried the alleged absurdity or pervasion inherent in the fact that "even" the black slave of the past had been freer than the white worker of today. At least in New York City, the comparison of white wage labor and black chattel slavery still entailed the conviction that these groups in fact were incomparable. It thus did not lead organized workers towards color-blind multiculturalism. Instead, it helped sustain a collective identity that was stylized as particularly worthy of protection.

At first glance, organized labor in Berlin refrained from racialized comparisons of wage labor and slavery. When highlighting the unfreedom of the wage system, working-class sources regularly scandalized it by reviving the bygone world of ancient and medieval slavery or peonage. Although social democrats in Berlin understood slavery as an unfree institution, they also highlighted the paternalistic duty of the master towards the slave. Not unlike apologists of slavery in the US, early social democrats in Germany found the fate of the slave less appalling than that of the wage worker. Like the slave, the wage worker was deprived of liberty, but, unlike the slave, he also was deprived of protection. Berlin's *Social-politische Blätter* therefore declared that

355 Cf. Stanley, *From Bondage to Contract*, 84–97.

356 Cf. Smith, *Debating Slavery*, 1.

357 It would take another decade or so until "white slavery" became the term predominantly used for white women's labor and, especially, female prostitution.

materially, the situation of slaves and bondsmen was golden compared to the situation of nineteenth-century wage slaves, who are not the bodily property of other men, but a commodity for others to purchase.[358]

Examples such as these suggest that German workers compared wage labor to slavery historically rather than racially. But the conviction that commodification made the system of wage labor equivalent to the system of *black* chattel slavery in fact appealed to workers in Berlin as well, many of whom had probably never met a black person or a chattel slave.[359] And yet they readily compared their experience as white workers to the *black slaves of the Americas*. Shortly before moving to New York City in 1866, the social democrat August Vogt used a public appearance in Berlin to express his view that the end of "black slavery" in the US was just a prelude to the end of "white slavery" everywhere.[360] Several years later, the short-term secretary of Berlin's IWA section and the SDAP branch of Spandau, Ferdinand Jozewicz, published his novel *Weiße Sklaven* (White Slaves), which criticized the spread of wage labor as a threat to working-class notions of autonomy and independence.[361] The VDAV's *Demokratisches Wochenblatt* of Berlin even featured a special section titled "Weiße Sklaven" that regularly compared "white wage slavery" to "black chattel slavery."[362] Similarly to working-class rhetoric in the US, German sources criticizing "white slavery" reveal the same degree of sarcasm and outrage when comparing wage work and chattel

358 "Der Unterschied," *Social-Politische Blätter*, 15 June 1873, 125–126. ("Materiell war die Lage der Sclaven und Leibeigenen golden gegenüber der Lage der Lohnsclaven des neunzehnten Jahrhunderts, die allerdings nicht das leibliche Eigenthum andere Menschen sind, die aber als Waare anderen Menschen zur Verfügung stehen.")

359 Very little is known about an Afro-German presence in Berlin prior to the 1880s. Unlike US surveys of that time, German statistics lacked the category of "skin color." Surveys about migration and religious beliefs, however, testify to a striking homogeneity. The census of 1875 shows that only about one percent of Berlin's inhabitants were not of Prussian or other German origin. Most of these non-German immigrants had Austrian-Hungarian or Russian backgrounds. While the number of Catholics and Jews was increasing, Berlin remained a Protestant city. Of the slightly less than one million inhabitants in 1875, about 850,000 were Protestants, about 67,000 Roman Catholics, and about 45,000 Jews. According to this survey, there were only 48 "Mohammedans and [members of] other religions" in the entire city; see Magistrat der Stadt Berlin (ed.), *Bericht über die Gemeinde-Verwaltung der Stadt Berlin*, 53.

360 "Allgemeine Arbeiter-Versammlung in der Berliner 'Alhambra,'" *Der Social-Demokrat*, 7 November 1865, 4.

361 Bezirksleitung (ed.), *Geschichte der revolutionären Berliner Arbeiterbewegung*, 173; Welskopp, *Das Banner der Brüderlichkeit*, 174. The novel seems to be lost.

362 Cf. Scharf, *Geschichte der Arbeitszeitverkürzung*, 138.

slavery. Here, too, workers compared their situation as wage laborers to that of unfree black slaves because they trusted that readers or listeners read the same moral compass, a compass that pointed directly towards doom. Comparisons to black slavery were therefore often made in the form of warnings. If the spread of free labor markets continued unhindered, workers would have no choice but to rise in rebellion against a system that degraded them to the status of the unfree, dependent, and allegedly servile blacks across the sea.

Roediger thus errs when he suggests that, at least prior to unification, the German states did not witness references to terms like "white" or "wage slavery" as a dystopic characterization of wage relations.[363] The fact that societies were "virtually slaveless," in other words, does not necessarily mean that they lacked a racialized concept of "wage slavery."[364] Rather, German working-class discussions of slavery in the US and the Caribbean reveal that here, too, early organized labor did not merely understand slavery as the metaphorical antonym to liberty, but as a social practice that had just recently ended. As this chapter has shown, it was especially immigrant workers' associations and labor papers that helped distribute a racist critique of wage labor in a society that had no direct experience of chattel slavery. The transnational comparison of concepts criticizing the "enslavement of labor" at the same time reveals a scholarly lack of attention to the impact of *race* on working-class thought, especially in those young European nation states that had not yet established colonial empires of their own—such as mid-nineteenth-century Italy, Belgium, and Germany.[365] It seems likely that here, too, terms such as "white slavery" helped legitimize racialized disparities in transnational contexts, especially in the decades preceding the emergence of anti-imperialist and anti-colonial theory.

The comparison of the political rationale for shorter hours has demonstrated that, although, formally speaking, New Yorkers enjoyed everything Berliners hoped for, their analysis and rhetoric differed surprisingly little. Though workers in Berlin had no firsthand experience with republican polities—they suffered from the restrictive regulations of the Law of Association, their papers were regularly censured and banned, and they did not

363 Cf. Welskopp, *Das Banner der Brüderlichkeit*, 73.

364 See Roediger, *The Wages of Whiteness*, 28, 66.

365 Cf. the forthcoming volume by Bruns and Hampf (eds.), *Wissen, Tranfer, Differenz*.

enjoy equal suffrage rights[366]—they expressed a genuine republican commitment. Organized labor in Berlin and New York agreed that the free exchange of the products of labor was the right of every producer, yet labor itself could not be severed from the worker and sold to someone else without violating the worker's right to self-determination. The commodification of labor thus threatened to transform the allegedly free wage worker—whom liberal economists celebrated as the very emblem of personal freedom and political liberty—into a slave.[367] Workers in both cities therefore opposed the unregulated workday as a threat to their ability to participate fully in democratic life. In Berlin as in New York, the struggle for shorter hours was a means to reclaim political sovereignty and independence. This similarity contradicts Richard B. Stott's argument, according to which the legacy of early working-class republicanism evaporated in New York due to an influx of immigrant workers "to whom the language of 'virtue' and 'independence' had little meaning."[368] Neither can mid-nineteenth-century German working-class discourse be portrayed as hostile to or ignorant of republican ideals, nor did the producerist notion inherent in Wilentz' "artisan republicanism" simply vanish into thin air as an army of German immigrants began to replace the older native-born substrate of New York's working class. Immigrant no less than native-born workers in New York continued to distance themselves from the undemocratic and monarchical traditions and realities in Europe, yet they increasingly did so in order to show how far the American Republic had abandoned its core ideals. Analyzing the demand for a normal workday in 1877, New York's *Labor Standard* looked back at the previous years of struggle. The paper came to the conclusion that America's "free institutions are even now but nominal, because the rich control labor and all means of production, not the labourers, the creators of all wealth."[369] Although workers in New York City were free to express their opinion, join organizations, and—if they were adult men—vote, they saw their political freedom increasingly rendered meaningless by the unlimited power of unregulated markets. While workers in New York deeply cherished their republican institutions, they also became conscious of the system's limitation

366 Even when universal male suffrage was successively introduced at the national level, workers in Berlin remained heavily marginalized by Prussia's discriminatory three-class suffrage system.

367 Stanley, *From Bondage to Contract*, 89–91.

368 Stott, *Workers in the Metropolis*, 3.

369 "The Normal Workday," *Labor Standard*, 3 February 1877, 2.

to promote equality and participation. Workers in Berlin likewise struggled for their ideal of a free and democratic political system, and they regularly looked at the US for inspiration. But studying the US experience also made workers in Berlin aware that civic institutions alone would not guarantee democratic results. As much as activists in Berlin and New York thus hoped that the shorter workday would fulfill their desire for democratic participation, they understood that they also needed to address the obstacles that emerged from the broader system of rules and practices provided by society.

4. Society: Shorter Hours and the Struggle for Human Rights

"Free yourselves from the chains of a production regime that dehumanizes you to a common commodity."[370]
Ferdinand Lassalle, 1864

4.1. Commodification as Dehumanization

As the previous chapter has demonstrated, organized labor developed a rich arsenal of political ideas that provided local shorter-hour movements with the rhetorical weapons for the battle against commodification and unfettered markets. But resistance to the uncontrolled purchase of labor did not only draw upon notions of political freedom, republican virtue, and democratic participation. This chapter argues that shorter-hour activists also opposed the free exchange of labor power as a violation of what they regarded the historical legacy and moral grammar of their respective communities. When addressing their respective polities, shorter-hour activists argued that the unregulated commodification of labor constituted an attack on the selfhood of workers. In the political realm, the loss of selfhood and autonomy was associated with a lack of citizen status and equal political rights. In the social realm, however, the loss of selfhood was associated with a loss of *humanness* itself. Unlike the "artisan republicanism" that interpreted commodification as an attack on the autonomy of small producers (see Chapter 3), opposition to the dehumanizing effects of labor commodification drew on a legacy of humanist thought that focused on man's position in society rather than the polity. It is therefore not surprising that socialist intellectuals and reformers featured prominently among the voices that framed the shorter-hour demand as a protective shield against dehumanization.

As the above statement by Lassalle indicates, the belief that the commodification of labor resulted in the dehumanization of workers consti-

370 Lassalle, *Herr Bastiat-Schulze von Delitzsch*, 254. ("Rettet euch aus den Banden eines Produktionszustandes, der euch zur Waare entmenscht.")

tuted an important element in early social-democratic rhetoric. Shortly before his death in 1864, Lassalle explained in a polemic against Schulze-Delitzsch that this loss of humanness had nothing to do with a lack of humanity, although workers were seldom treated decently by their employers. Rather, what he meant here was that contemporary wage relations no longer qualified as social interaction among humans. As repressive as the life of peasants and workers had been in the medieval past, the fact that they were able to autonomously set their will to work bestowed earlier work relations with an irreducible human quality. The commodification of labor, however, dehumanized the sellers of labor to mere objects. As long as labor markets were governed exclusively by the law of supply and demand, workers were traded like any other non-human commodity. According to Lassalle, it was

> the employer's cold, impersonal view of the worker as a thing, a thing that is produced like any other commodity on a market that answers only to the general laws of production […], that specifies the dehumanized physiognomy of the *bourgeois* era.[371]

As Lassalle made abundantly clear, the objectification of the worker that resulted from his transformation into a commodity was not a side aspect of capitalist societies, but their core characteristic. Lassalle's critique of commodified labor was shared by many local socialists and labor reformers. Theodor Metzner, one of the founding figures of Berlin's ADAV section, published an open letter to the members of the rival BAV in which he argued that free-market apologists like Schulze-Delitzsch or Faucher failed to understand that workers did not simply question the general logic of supply and demand.[372] Rather, Metzner stressed, workers rejected the idea that their labor power could be reduced to this logic in the first place. In so doing, workers opposed the idea that they could be degraded to the status of a commodity. The objectification that underlay the commodification of labor,

371 Lassalle, *Herr Bastiat-Schulze von Delitzsch*, 190. ("Die kalte unpersönliche Beziehung des Unternehmers auf den Arbeiter als eine Sache, auf eine Sache, die wie jede andere Waare auf dem Markte nach dem Gesetz der Productionskosten erzeugt wird—daß ist es, das die durchaus specifische, durchaus entmenschte Physiognomie der bürgerlichen Periode bildet!")

372 See the Berlin membership list provided by Offermann, *Die erste deutsche Arbeiterpartei*, 150. Metzner represented the oppositional fraction of ADAV activists who were in contact to Liebknecht without officially breaking with the ADAV. In the course of the 1860s, Metzner moved further towards a Marxist perspective and eventually became one of the conveners of the Eisenach congress; cf. "Theodor Metzner †," *Der Wahre Jacob*, 9 September 1902, 3840.

Metzner concluded, was one of the prime causes of working-class resistance.[373]

Wilhelm Hasselmann, the notoriously hawkish editor of Berlin's *(Neuer) Social-Demokrat*, agreed. Hasselmann frequently used the pages of the ADAV organ to challenge the system of wage labor that transformed the worker into a common commodity. Unprotected from the cruel dictum of the market, commodified workers were forced to sell their labor power under the terms dictated by their employers. The misery of the wage worker was thus firmly woven into the capitalist fabric. He could only hope to be free, Hasselmann concluded, "once labor ceases to be a commodity."[374] According to Johann Jacoby—the prominent intellectual, radical democrat, and respected *1848er*—there were indeed a few employers who did not see their workers as market commodities like any other, bought at the cheapest price and exploited as thoroughly as possible.[375] Yet Jacoby, who would soon resign from the liberal Progress Party and join the Eisenacher SDAP, warned that the philanthropic views of a small number of employers would not gain general acceptance without legislative intervention.[376] Revealing his *Soziales Glaubensbekenntnis* (social creed) to the mostly working-class audience of Berlin's second electoral district, Jacoby insisted that if organized labor wanted to be protected from the commodifying pressures of the market, legislation to limit the length of a normal workday was necessary.[377]

On the other side of the intra-socialist divide, the Berlin-based editors of the *Social-Demokrat* insisted that the Lassalleans were the true defenders of a humanism that required the de-commodification of work. Wilhelm Eichhoff, a prominent journalist and friend of Marx who had just returned from his exile in England, argued at a workers' meeting in Berlin that Prussia needed to follow the tariff example of the US. The introduction of protective tariffs had helped the American economy fight off English competition and maintain relatively high wages. According to Eichhoff, the best way to in-

373 Th[eodor] M[etzner], "An die Mitglieder des Berliner Arbeiter-Vereins," *Der Social-Demokrat*, 22 January 1865, Supplement.

374 H.[asselmann], "Die Kathedersocialisten," *Neuer Social-Demokrat*, 21 July 1872, 1. ("[...] wenn die Arbeit aufhört, Waare zu sein.")

375 Johann Jacoby, "Das Ziel der Arbeiterbewegung: Rede des Abgeordneten Dr. Johann Jacoby vor seinen Wählern im zweiten Berliner Wahlbezirke am 20. Januar 1870," *Beilage zum Volksstaat*, 26 January 1870, 2.

376 For Jacoby's reason to join the social democrats, see "Lokales (Demokratischer Verein)," *Demokratische Zeitung*, 21 April 1872, 5.

377 Jacoby, "Das Ziel der Arbeiterbewegung," 2.

crease the price of labor—and therewith guarantee better wages—was to shield off international competition through protective tariffs.[378] This argument provoked the editors of the *Social-Demokrat* to intervene. Without naming Eichhoff, the paper firmly rejected this logic:

> Labor does not have to become more expensive—it shall be neither more expensive nor cheaper, since only commodities are expensive or cheap—but labor shall cease to be a commodity; instead it shall become the determining element in state and society.[379]

The paper continued that efforts to increase the price of labor were, as Lassalle had put it in his *Bastiat-Schulze*, nothing but "the futile struggle of the commodity to become human."[380] The *Social-politische Blätter* elaborated further on the critique offered by Lassalle. The system of free competition resulted in the commodification of human labor power. As a consequence, it deprived social relations of their inner human quality.[381] Working men thus needed to be protected from the free market—and the demand for shorter hours promised to provide this very protection by partially de-commodifying labor. This now was a logic that clearly resonated with shorter-hour activists in the US.

In New York City, the German-American *Arbeiter-Union* was confident that the shorter-hour movement would eventually be successful precisely

> because it struggles in the name of mankind against arbitrary institutions that reduce workers to mere things, zeroes in arithmetic problems, and which degrade human labor to a commodity under the rule of speculators.[382]

Lucien Sanial, the prominent French-born editor, apparently agreed. In the spring of 1874, his self-styled *Organ of the Labor Interest* covered an assembly that had met the previous night at Cooper Institute. The assembled work-

---

378 "Vereins-Theil: Berlin (Social-Demokratischer Arbeiter-Verein)," *Der Social-Demokrat*, 15 August 1866, 3–4.

379 "Vereins-Theil: Berlin," *Der Social-Demokrat*, 17 August 1866, 4. ("Die Arbeit muß nicht theuer werden—sie soll weder theuer noch wohlfeil sein—denn theuer und wohlfeil sind nur Waaren—die Arbeit soll aber aufhören, eine Waare zu sein, die Arbeit soll das Bestimmende in Staat und Gesellschaft werden.")

380 Ibid. ("[…] das vergebliche Streben der Waare, sich als Mensch zu gebärden.")

381 "Die Organisation der Arbeit," *Social-Politische Blätter*, 3 February 1873, 25.

382 "Die 'New York Times' und die Arbeiterbewegung," *Die Arbeiter-Union*, 4 June 1869, 2. ("[…] weil sie im Namen des 'Menschen' gegen willkürliche Einrichtungen kämpft, welche aus ihnen Sachen machen möchte, Nullen in ihrem Rechenexempel, und aus ihrer Arbeit eine Waare unter der Herrschaft der Speculanten.")

ers fiercely demanded that public and private employers respect the eight-hour laws passed in the late 1860s. In so doing, Sanial's *Toiler* stressed, these workers opposed the notion that their labor could be degraded to a common commodity that was subjected to the cruel law of supply and demand. In an emotional appeal, they demanded that labor be "considered only from the standpoint of humanity [...], and we insist that the greatest good for the greatest number should be the foundation of all legislation."[383] Wrapping their opposition to commodification in classical utilitarian rhetoric, New York City's eight-hour activists clearly understood how to appeal to the local movement for radical reform. The American *Social-Demokrat* likewise expressed moral contempt for the commodification of labor. Looking back at the rapid proliferation of wage labor, the organ of the New York City-based SDPNA argued that the system of commodified labor transformed humans into what they were not meant to be. It "degraded man into a mere object."[384] Criticizing the replacement of local strikers with other *Menschenwaare* (human commodities), the paper expressed the conviction that human beings could not be treated as commodities because they differed from one another in their essence.[385] The compound noun *Menschenwaare* used here displays an almost oxymoronic quality, as it evokes a feeling of repulsion by bringing together two concepts that are seemingly incompatible or whose combination seems immoral. Terms like *Menschenwaare* or the widely used *Menschenfleisch* (human flesh) or *Menschenhandel* (human trafficking) appealed directly to the moral grammar of fellow workers.[386] Rather than requiring deep political-economic insight, terms like these immediately conveyed the moral debauchery associated with the unregulated exchange of human labor. Readers or listeners simply *understood* that it was wrong.

Working-class Berlin and New York were equally quick to translate theoretical debate into everyday discourse. Highlighting the dehumanizing impact of commodification, organized workers regularly contrasted wage labor with either animals or machines. Berlin's organized shoemakers, for in-

383 "Cooper Institute: Working-Men Mass Meeting," *The Toiler*, 23 May 1874, 1.

384 "Die heutige Lohnarbeit und ihre Folgen," *Social-Demokrat* (New York), 20 December 1874, 1. ("[...] wie denn überhaupt [das Lohnsystem] dahin führt, den Menschen schließlich zu einer Sache herabzuwürdigen.")

385 "Arbeiter-Bewegung: New York," *Social-Demokrat* (New York), 28 November 1874, 2.

386 So it did in Germany; see "Ausland: Amerika [Warnung vor unüberlegter Auswanderung]," *Der Social-Demokrat*, 10 March 1866, 3. Towards the turn of the century, the term "trafficking" was increasingly used in the context of female prostitution; cf. Stanley, *From Bondage to Contract*, 218–263; Stanley, "Slave Emancipation and the Sovereign Market."

stance—which, like the local clothing trade in general, was prone to anti-Semitic simplifications—exclaimed angrily that Jewish speculation increasingly transformed petty masters into dependent wage workers. Those speculators who had supposedly never learned a trade themselves now degraded once-proud craft workers to the status of automata. Yet the local shoemakers were not willing to accept their fate quietly. Blood still ran through their veins, they thundered. They were not machines.[387] In New York City, German émigré Gustav Lyser came to a similar conclusion.[388] Free competition, he argued in the pages of the New York based *Social-Demokrat*, had transformed workers into bloodless objects:

> Even now, there exists no other bond between most people than "naked interest and cold cash payment," which dissolves the human dignity of the individual in exchange values.[389]

While machine analogies were supposed to illustrate the cold character of commodified labor, comparisons to animals served to reveal the vicious barbarism that unregulated wage labor entailed. In 1867, von Schweitzer, the newly elected ADAV president, published a humorous play titled *Ein Schlingel* (A Rascal) in the pages of the *Social-Demokrat*.[390] According to von Schweitzer, the play was not meant to be performed on stage, yet it nevertheless became part of the standard repertoire of folk theatre productions, especially in Berlin. The local section of the Lassallean carpenters' association, for instance, reported that it had performed the play during an informal local convention. At the ADAV's *Stiftungsfest* (foundation anniversary) that took place in Berlin in the summer of 1871, it was put on stage in front of

387 "Zur Arbeiterbewegung," *Demokratische Zeitung*, 30 October 1872, 3. A similar argument appeared in "Die Organisation der Arbeit," *Social-Politische Blätter*, 3 February 1873, 25.

388 Gustav Lyser was a prominent member of the SDAP in Braunschweig where he published satirical pieces and reports in social-democratic papers. According to Wilhelm Blos, Lyser was accused of having approached leaders of the ADAV in search for unity in the early 1870s. Following the publication of a letter by Lyser in which he expressed regret over the social-democratic trench warfare, he was forced to leave the party in 1873. The following year, he emigrated to the US. From here, he continued to contribute to various social-democratic papers; see Blos, *Denkwürdigkeiten eines Sozialdemokraten*, vol. 1, 124–139.

389 G.[ustav] L.[yser], "Die Heutige Lohnarbeit und ihre Folgen," *Social-Demokrat* (New York), 10 December 1874, 1. ("Bereits existirt zwischen den meisten Menschen kein anderes Band mehr, als das 'nackte Interesse, die gefühllose bare Zahlung,' welche selbst die persönliche Würde des Individuums in Tauschwerth auflöst.")

390 "Ein Schlingel," *Der Social-Demokrat*, 3 November 1867, 1–2; "Ein Schlingel (Fortsetzung)," *Der Social-Demokrat*, 6 November 1867, 1–2; "Ein Schlingel (Schluß)," *Der Social-Demokrat*, 10 November 1867, 1–2.

large working-class audiences. Apparently even workers abroad performed the play.[391] In the opening scene of said play, a stereotypical *Kommerzienrat* (Councilor of Commerce) summons a young worker by the name of Roth to his drawing room. Here the *Kommerzienrat* charges Roth with agitating among his workers and contributing to an unnamed socialist newspaper. Roth frankly admits the charges. Since the Councilor fails in his attempt to bribe Roth into ending his agitation, he tries to persuade the young worker with words. In a fatherly manner, the Councilor begins reasoning with him:

Councilor: Do you agree that labor is a commodity that is bought and sold on a market just like any other commodity?

Roth: Under present-day conditions, yes.

Councilor: Do you not agree that, if I have bought a commodity, I am entitled to use it as I wish?

Roth: Yes.

Councilor: So that if I have rented, for instance, a horse for a day, that is, if I have bought the right to use its power for a day, no one may prevent me from employing the horse for the entire day?

Roth: Yes.

Councilor (triumphant): Do you then not agree that, if I have bought a certain labor power on a market for a particular wage for eight days, it is only just that I may employ it for the entire eight days?

Roth: No, I do not.

Frustrated with Roth's refusal to follow his argumentation, the Councilor, now angry, asks:

What difference do you think there is between the nag and the worker? He who rented the horse's power is entitled to employ this power; he who rented the worker's power is equally entitled to employ this power.[392]

---

391 Cf. "Verbands-Theil: Allgemeiner Deutscher Zimmerer-Verein (Die Berliner Mitgliedschaft)," *Der Social-Demokrat*, 3 February 1869, 3; "Vereins-Theil (Für den Allg. Deutsch. Arb.-Verein): Berlin," *Neuer Social-Demokrat*, 21 July 1871, 2; Johann Baptist von Schweitzer, "Ein Schlingel," *Agitator*, 15 April 1870, 3.

392 "Commerzienrath: Geben Sie zu, daß die Arbeitskraft eine Waare ist, die sich wie jede andere Waare auf dem Markte kauft und verkauft?
Roth: Unter den heutigen Umständen, ja.

Yet Roth still begs to differ. Over the course of the discussion, to which a certain Dr. Fisch is brought in as "a man of science," the unruly young worker insists that human labor power cannot simply be equated with the power of a horse. Von Schweitzer's play here reveals several controversies that energized Berlin's social-democratic movement of the 1860s and early 1870s. On the one hand, the authoritarian yet somewhat dull *Kommerzienrat* represents a soulless class of employers who were utterly indifferent to the well-being of their workers. As references to self-help funds and workers' saving trusts indicate, the Councilor personifies liberal reformers such as Schulze-Delitzsch and the corresponding movement of the BAV. Second, the figure of the physician Dr. Fisch offers a critique of the magisterial attitude of Prussia's leading economists. Epitomizing prominent *laissez-faire* proponents like Faucher or Prince-Smith, Dr. Fisch stands for a science that is at the loyal service of capital. Together, the Councilor and Dr. Fisch represent a system that had as little regard for the rights and desires of wage workers as for the rights of animals—if not, as some suggested, less. At the annual ADAV convention of 1867, delegate Schneider from Berlin claimed that today even animals enjoyed better protection than the average wage worker. In a heated debate with the liberal guests to the convention, Schneider argued that the worker enjoyed a right to be protected from the burden of unregulated labor markets and devilishly long hours. But liberal Berlin proved to be more receptive to the hardship of animals than to the suffering of workers. As Schneider concluded, "associations were founded here in Berlin against the torture of animals; let there also be associations against the tor-

---

Commerziehrath: Sehen Sie nicht ein, daß, wenn ich eine Waare gekauft habe, ich berechtigt bin, sie beliebig zu verwenden?
Roth: Ja.
Commerzienrath: Daß also, wenn ich z.B. ein Pferd für einen Tag gemiethet, d.h. dessen Gebrauch für einen Tag gekauft habe, Niemand mir verwehren kann, den ganzen Tag über das Pferd zu benutzen?
Roth: Ja.
Commerzienrath (triumphierend): Sehen Sie also nicht ein, daß, wenn ich eine Arbeitskraft auf dem Markte um einen gewissen Lohn für acht Tage gekauft habe, es der Gerechtigkeit entspricht, daß ich sie die ganzen acht Tage über muß gebrauchen können?
Roth: Nein.
Commerzienrath: [...] Welcher Unterschied soll sein zwischen dem Gaul und dem Arbeiter? Wer das Pferd, d.h. seine Kräfte, gemiethet hat, der hat ein Recht auf Verwendung dieser Kräfte; wer den Arbeiter, d.h. seine Arbeitskräfte, gemiethet hat, hat gleicherweise ein Recht auf Verwendung dieser Arbeitskraft." Cited in von Schweitzer, "Der Schlingel," 132.

ture of humans."[393] Schneider's Eisenacher comrade, the construction worker H. Wendt, agreed. Speaking to the delegates of the nascent *Berliner Arbeiterbund*, he emphasized that animals surely enjoyed certain rights. Yet, Wendt ended, the protection of humans had to precede the protection of beasts.[394]

Organized workers in New York City used similar metaphors when protesting the dehumanization of workers that followed from the unchecked commodification of labor. In the debate between New York's *National Workman* and the *Dry Goods Reporter* referred to earlier, the business paper fiercely opposed the eight-hour demand as it strongly rejected any legislative intervention into the free labor market. In the eyes of *The National Workman*, the position of the *Dry Goods Reporter* reflected the inability of organized business to understand the deeper moral significance of their demand.[395] *The National Workman* argued that it was the inalienable right of every human being to develop his moral capacities as fully as possible. "Any obstacle to this development, whether imposed by custom or human laws, must be swept away as contrary to civilization and progress. Man," the paper concluded, "has a right to something more than mere animal existence."[396] The German-language counterpart of *The National Workman* agreed. As organ of the city central of German trade unions, the *Arbeiter-Union* likewise emphasized that the shorter-hour demand was a crucial tool in the struggle to restore humanness in the labor market. Early in 1869, the New York City-based paper covered a workers' meeting that had recently taken place in Berlin. Following a lengthy debate about the nature of free competition and the need to regulate the labor market, comrades in Berlin had passed a resolution that ended in a "bitter polemic against the liberal Manchester doctrine."[397] According to this resolution, unhindered competition—or the free labor market—had severely intensified the exploitation of labor and therewith ruined the health and well-being of the working class. And yet, the *bourgeoisie* did not grow tired of pretending that the unhindered commodification of labor power was a guarantor for workers' freedom. But if liberal freedom boiled down to haggling over how to buy labor power as cheaply as possible,

393 "Zweite Beilage," *Der Social-Demokrat*, 29 November 1867, 1.

394 "Lokales," *Demokratische Zeitung*, 21 November 1871, 5. For the Berliner Arbeiterbund, see Chapter 4.

395 The paper first appeared in October, 1866. Two months later, the Workingmen's Union made it its official organ; see "The National Workman: The Organ of the Workingmen's Union," *The National Workman*, 29 December 1866, 2.

396 "A Plea for the Eight-Hour System," *The National Workman*, 24 November 1866, 2.

397 Bernstein, *Die Geschichte der Berliner Arbeiterbewegung*, 182.

workers would inevitably come to the conclusion that this sort of freedom had nothing to offer for them. Instead, they would soon demand "democratic freedom, established on the equality of everything that bears a human face."[398]

The *Arbeiter-Union* warmly welcomed this resolution from the other side of the ocean. In its own words, it epitomized that "the worker is not supposed to be a beast of burden, but a respected human being."[399] And as a human being, the paper concluded, every worker enjoyed the natural right to rest and recover. Too often, Alexander Troup of New York's Typographical Union declared at a mass meeting in April 1869, capital seemed to forget that workers were also humans. When organized labor in New York City thus demanded the strict observance of the state's eight-hour law, it simply reminded employers and legislators of their shared humanness.[400] Analogies of unregulated wage labor and the (mis)use of animals were therefore often comic in nature. The *Volksstaat*, for instance, published a satirical proposal to Otto von Camphausen, the Prussian Minister of Finance in Berlin. Rumor had it, the paper stated, that in faraway Ceylon plantation workers had been replaced by gangs of cheap chimps. Suggesting to von Camphausen that this model would work in Prussia, too, the author argued that animals, unlike humans, do not oppose their commodification, since they lack any understanding of morality and justice. "No longer would the *bourgeois* have to fear demands for higher wages or shorter hours; and the honest chimp also has no idea of strikes."[401]

New York's English-speaking world of labor also interpreted fears about the dehumanizing effects of commodification as a violation of divine will. In a publication that appeared in 1867, labor reformer P.M. McGill argued that the shorter-hour movement was a struggle for not only republican rights, but also Christian values. Focusing on the urban experience of labor in places like New York City, McGill concluded that no human being could

---

398 "Ein Sociales Programm," *Die Arbeiter-Union*, 20 March 1869, 5. ("[...] die demokratische Freiheit, gegründet auf Gleichheit alles Dessen, was Menschengesicht trägt.")

399 "Gefahren für die Arbeiter: Eine Warnung," *Die Arbeiter-Union*, 5 December 1868, 3. ("Der Arbeiter soll kein Arbeitsthier sein, sondern als Mensch geachtet werden.")

400 "Die Massenversammlung am 16. April im Cooper-Institute," *Die Arbeiter-Union*, 24 April 1869, 4.

401 "Ein unmaßgeblicher Vorschlag an Se. Exzellenz Herrn Camphausen," *Der Volksstaat*, 28 February 1875, 1. ("Der Bourgeois hat künftig weder höhere Lohnforderungen noch Forderungen nach Verkürzung der Arbeitszeit zu fürchten; auch von Strikes hat der ehrliche Chimpanse keine Idee.")

ever be reduced to the status of a thing because this form of unfettered commodification betrayed what God wanted man to be.[402] Christian notions in support of shorter hours influenced working-class activists as radical as Robert Blissert. A prominent trade unionists and labor leader, Blissert had become an important voice in New York's shorter-hour movement by the early 1870s. Addressing a large workers' demonstration in New York in 1874, Blissert argued that men commit a sin if they disrespect the sacred principle that *by the sweat of your brow you will eat your bread.* The reason that urban workers were forced to put in excessively long workdays was that they worked in order to augment the wealth of their employers, who did not produce any value themselves. With surprising specificity, he predicted that if everyone did

> his fair share of work, the daily hours of toil required of each in the world would be reduced to three hours and forty-two minutes, instead of ten, twelve and eighteen hours as now imposed on some, while others did nothing but subsist on the sweat of the laborer.[403]

Yet the nexus of Christian belief and working time was rather ambiguous. After all, it had been Protestant notions of temperance and free agency that had helped legitimize long workdays in the first place, as E.P. Thompson shows with respect to the Methodist tradition.[404] Sean Wilentz similarly illustrates that, especially in urban places like New York City, Protestantism contributed enormously to the emergence of a middle-class worldview that tied aspects of personal thrift and salvation to the more down-to-earth challenges of long workdays. Awareness that time on earth was scarce and had to be used effectively helped legitimize the break with the irregular work rhythms of the preindustrial era and thus buttressed the proliferation of wage labor and the acceptance of long but regular working days.[405] Drawing on Thompson, Howard Rock argues that Protestant ideals as personified by the craftsman Benjamin Franklin fostered this new time consciousness among early republican artisans. Franklin famously lectured the American artisan to make diligent use of his time on earth and let no hour pass idly. But the same notion also helped reclaim authority over the use of working time. Rock argues that if artisans wanted to use time efficiently, they had to be in control

402 McGill, *The Wrongs and Rights of Labor*, 18.

403 "Philadelphia: Workingmen's Festival and Demonstration," *The Toiler*, 22 August 1874, 1.

404 Thompson, "Time, Work-Discipline, and Industrial Capitalism," 86–89.

405 Wilentz, *Chants Democratic*, 343–349.

of it in the first place.[406] In a similar vein, Teresa Murphy shows that religious devotion for the sake of individual salvation and moral integrity required that workers had time to study Scripture and perform or attend religious services.[407] As much as Protestant notions of time efficiency had thus helped enforce long standardized workdays, they also provided a discursive weapon in the struggle for shorter hours.

Workers in the predominantly Protestant capital of Germany, however, made no significant use of this weapon. This does not mean, however, that religion generally had little impact on them. Although the social-democratic leadership attacked any form of spirituality as an obstacle to social progress, it seems that religious ideas were in fact not so easily purged from popular consciousness.[408] The rank and file's frequent comparisons of Jesus and Lassalle demonstrate this very vividly. In April, 1873, for instance, the *Berliner Frauen- und Mädchenverein* (Association of Women and Girls of Berlin) organized a Good Friday celebration that reminded attendants that it was not only the "day of commemoration of Jesus' crucifixion," but also "the birthday of Ferdinand Lassalle, the pioneer and champion of human rights." It was the president of the association, Bertha Hahn, in particular who stressed the twofold character of this holiday in honor of "these two great men: Jesus of Nazareth and Ferdinand Lassalle, savior of the proletariat."[409] Though expressions of religious devotion could not be wiped out completely, they were increasingly restricted to family festivities and meetings of working-class women. By pushing popular religiosity to the supposedly female sphere, leading German social democrats hoped to keep the sphere of politics clear of what they saw as the *naïve* and *unscientific* passions of workers not yet fully conscious of their situation. According to Erhard Lucas, the leadership of the German workers' movement failed to understand the significance of spirituality for working-class identities. As a consequence, it resisted the integration of elements of Christian belief and liturgy into everyday politics. Thus, social democracy began replacing Protestant traditions in the urban centers of the North while increasingly estranging rural Protestant work-

406 Rock, "Independent Hours," 23.

407 Cf. Murphy, "Work, Leisure, and Moral Reform;" Brody, *In Labor's Cause*, 15–16.

408 "Unfehlbarkeit," *Social-Politische Blätter*, 30 November 1873, 233–234.

409 Höppner, "Berlin (Arbeiterfrauen- und Mädchenversammlung)," *Neuer Social-Demokrat*, 18 April 1873, 3. ("[…] dem Erinnerungstage der Kreuzigung Jesus von Nazareth und […] Geburtstage Ferdinand Lassalle's, des Denkers und Kämpfers für die Menschenrechte;" "[…] dieser beiden großen Männer: Jesus von Nazareth und Ferdinand Lassalle's, als Erlöser des Proletariats.")

ers and Catholic workers, especially in the Southern and Western parts of Germany. In Lucas's eyes, it was the strictly materialist understanding of human agency that alienated a large part of the German working class from the party.[410] At the same time, this materialist understanding was the reason that religious ideas were largely absent from the rationale for shorter hours in Berlin.

4.2. De-Commodification as Counter-Hegemony

As the foregoing has shown, socialist intellectuals and shorter-hour activists in Berlin and New York City opposed unregulated labor markets because they feared that the underlying phenomenon of commodification fostered the dehumanization of their respective social realms. In addition, they also drew on a critique of historical consciousness. In his chapter on "So-Called Primitive Accumulation," Marx had argued that the emergence of capitalism rested on the massive expropriation of peasants from the sixteenth century onwards. For centuries, peasants and artisans had to produce only enough to meet their own reproductive needs, as well as a certain quantum they owed to their feudal lord or master craftsman. The historical conditions of pre-capitalist accumulation had a direct effect on the length of the workday. In towns, craft guilds determined the beginning and end of the working day. In the countryside, sunrise and sunset did the same.

Yet when *primitive* gave way to *capitalist accumulation*, Marx argued, the length of the workday was no longer dependent on what was needed by producers, but on what was sought by the buyers of labor. Instead of a workday that was determined by the respective season of the year, the time of the day, the stock of food available, the size of the family, or the demands of lord and local custom, it was determined by capital's endless striving for surplus value.[411] Since surplus value was obtained by the appropriation of the unpaid surplus labor time of others, it followed that capitalists struggled to increase the time the worker labored for his employer rather than for himself. As Marx elaborated in Chapter 8 of the first volume of *Das Kapital*, this was the reason that the absolute length of the working day in a capitalist system could never be reduced to the minimum of time necessary to guarantee the repro-

410 Cf. Lucas, *Vom Scheitern der deutschen Arbeiterbewegung*, 89–131.
411 Marx, *Das Kapital* I, 741–769.

duction of labor—after all, this would mean that there would be no surplus labor time left during which labor produced surplus value that capital could appropriate.[412] Yet this was also the reason that the absolute length of the workday could actually decrease while the amount of surplus labor time increased. A general boost in productivity, for instance, meant that reproductive costs were met in a shorter period of time and a larger quantity of daily working time was allotted to capital. While now the minimal length of the working day was therefore determined by the intrinsic laws of the system itself, its maximum was set by both natural and social barriers. Even the most extensively exploited laborer could not work without rest. The physical and mental presuppositions of human life thus imposed a natural limit on the length of the workday. Yet the first half of the nineteenth century revealed that this natural limit was in fact astonishingly flexible. Experience demonstrated that the effective protection of their interest required organized workers to focus on the enforcement of social barriers instead.

Marx's analysis quickly found acceptance in Berlin's world of social-democratic thought. At the ADAV's annual convention in Berlin in 1867, Johann Baptist von Hofstetten gave a detailed presentation of his party's view on shorter hours. Without mentioning Marx—who therefore accused him of plagiarism—von Hofstetten reproduced his account step by step.[413] Like Marx, he eventually came to the conclusion that history had indeed proven natural barriers an illusion. Von Hofstetten thus urged his listeners to follow the example of their English and American comrades by enforcing a ten-hour normal workday, fixed by law and enforced through inspectors.[414] But not all in the audience agreed. As the second day of the general assembly was open to the general public, Nathan Schlesinger, a liberal guest to the convention, challenged von Hofstetten's statements by pointing towards the neglected interests of employers, which had to be taken into account as well. Schlesinger was widely known in Berlin as both an editor and a leader of the liberal workers' association, which brought him regular attacks from the

412 Says Marx: "But, on the basis of the capitalist method of production, necessary labour time cannot possibly constitute the whole of the working day. The working day cannot possibly be restricted to this minimum." Ibid., 231. See also Scharf, *Geschichte der Arbeitszeitverkürzung*, 28–47.

413 Marx, "Plagiarismus." See also Scharf, *Geschichte der Arbeitszeitverkürzung*, 127.

414 "General-Versammlung des Allg. Deutsch. Arbeiter-Vereins," *Der Social-Demokrat*, 29 November 1867, Supplement.

socialist press.[415] Interestingly, Schlesinger was the only non-member in the entire minutes introduced by his complete name—a fact that also holds true for similar meetings covered by the social-democratic press. Given the anti-Jewish tendencies that existed among organized labor, this was surely no coincidence. Rather, the mention of Schlesinger's first name Nathan here epitomizes the logic of discrimination from which Berlin's Jewish community suffered. Among a considerable fraction of the local workers' movement, being Jewish regularly translated into belonging to a different class of non-workers, as social-democratic speakers also stressed during this convention. In so doing, they fueled the belief that it was his Jewish background that made Schlesinger claim that labor needed to be employed like any other commodity. According to the ADAV minutes, Schlesinger argued that in a free-market society, all factors of production answered to the same logic of supply and demand. There was no way of protecting one while leaving the other unprotected. The struggle for shorter-hour legislation was thus doomed to fail. Having overrun his speaking time, Schlesinger was abruptly stopped by von Schweitzer. However, the following speaker, the "non-member Richter from Berlin," continued where Schlesinger was forced to stop.[416] According to Richter, the daily working time could not be determined by legislation without violating the rights of employers. Echoing almost literally von Schweitzer's fictive Councilor in the play *Ein Schlingel*, Richter concluded that if "labor power is a commodity, then I must be able to use this commodity as I wish."[417] Following an angry verbal exchange with their liberal guests, the latter were eventually evicted from the meeting. With the disturbers removed, the delegates passed the resolution proposed by von Hofstetten.

The ADAV's Eisenacher rivals followed a similar logic of shorter-hour demands. During the late 1860s and early 1870s, the economist and insurance officer Carl August Schramm had become a strong supporter of Berlin's small Eisenacher circle, and he repeatedly used the *Volksstaat* to popularize socialist economics.[418] By that time, the *Volksstaat* had come under

415 See, for instance, "Lokales (Nathan, der Würgengel)," *Demokratische Zeitung*, 2 July 1872, 2.

416 It is unlikely that the liberal Member of Parliament Eugen Richter would have attended a social-democratic convention.

417 "Zweite Beilage," *Der Social-Demokrat*, 29 November 1867, 1.

418 "Carl August Schramm an Wilhelm Liebknecht," 783, Footnote 1; Welskopp, *Das Banner der Brüderlichkeit*, 176. Schramm was not a follower of the ADAV, as a popular online encyclopedia suggests; see Wikipedia (ed.), "Carl August Schramm (Ökonom)." On the

criticism over its editorial focus. According to critics, the paper revealed a bias towards political analysis at the cost of socio-economic explanation. In a letter to August Geib, Liebknecht conceded that the paper had indeed devoted more attention to the theoretical and practical questions regarding the concept of a democratic state than to issues like wage labor or the origin of surplus value. Despite the paper's personal and ideological affinity with Marx, it was the *Social-Demokrat* rather than the *Volksstaat* that had popularized Marx's critique of political economy in the late 1860s.[419] In order to remedy this shortcoming, Liebknecht and Schramm agreed on a new series to promote an explicitly socialist perspective on economic issues. In an article that appeared in two installments on March 13 and 16, 1872, Schramm opened with a historical sketch of the "Condition of Workers in the Middle Ages." Stressing the importance of the commons or *Allmende*, Schramm suggested that this legal institution guaranteed every man and woman the right to collect wood and free access to the local pasture. Yet these rights were increasingly taken from peasants and artisans as they were forced from their land and robbed of their means of production. This development culminated in the late eighteenth and early nineteenth-century abolition of peonage, which granted the former bondsman legal freedom, but at the same time "threw him," as Schramm put it, "on the market as a common commodity." Lacking any means of production or subsistence, he had no choice but to offer his labor power on the market.[420]

Schramm's interpretation of the process of labor commodification was not merely an exercise in critical historiography. Rather, historical consciousness equipped the movement with a powerful legitimation for protective demands. At the annual ADAV meeting in 1868, delegate Wilhelm Frick gave a talk on the historical meaning of workday regulations. Under all historical regimes of accumulation, Frick argued, there had been some degree of restriction. Although the peasant or worker of the past enjoyed few rights, he was at least allowed to rest. But the great transformation of production that had occurred over the past century or so had pulled down all protective barriers. This was the reason that, wherever one looked, labor was forced to

contrary, Schramm was an early Eisenacher in Berlin; see, for instance, the public debate with Max Hirsch or his obituary; Schramm, *Mein offener Brief*; "Carl August Schramm," *Oesterreichische Revue*, 11 September 1905, 212–215.

419 See "Wilhelm Liebknecht an August Geib," 444–448.

420 C.[arl] A.[ugust] S.[chramm], "Arbeiter-Verhältnisse im Mittelalter," *Der Volksstaat*, 13 March 1872, 1; C.[arl] A.[ugust] S.[schramm], "Arbeiter-Verhältnisse im Mittelalter," *Der Volksstaat*, 16 March 1872, 3.

work barbarically long hours.[421] Yet the lesson history had to teach was that excessively long workdays were not an eternal feature of workers' collective destiny. In the past, Frick showed, the length of the workday had not been determined by the laws of supply and demand. This surely gave hope and inspiration for the future. Frick's analysis epitomized that, when contrasted to the past two thousand years of Western civilization, the system of commodified labor was a peculiar anomaly rather than a social norm.

Liberal economists saw things rather differently. Proponents of the free-market movement insisted that labor was meant to evolve naturally into a commodity like any other. This evolution not only fostered economic growth, but also guaranteed the freedom of labor. According to dominant liberal economics, efforts to intervene in this process were nothing but destructive violations of the supposedly natural law of supply and demand. This notion constituted a crucial element in the argumentation of the adversaries of the campaign for an eight-hour bill in New York State. *The Economist and Dry Goods Reporter*, the above-cited organ of the manufacturers and dry-goods trade in New York City, argued that shorter hours would inevitably result in lower wages. Since the income of many workers was extremely meagre as it was, a further wage reduction would threaten their very survival. Therefore, workers would be forced to disregard any hour legislation and work longer hours for higher pay. In so doing, the author reassured his brothers, the workman himself would render the law obsolete. Even if passed, the

> eight hours' law would stand upon the statute book as a memento of the folly of law-makers attempting to control the operation of those natural laws which inevitably determine the province of all classes in the community.[422]

The New York Times agreed wholeheartedly. In a free-market society, the length of the workday was a result of the law of supply and demand. If labor proved to be as productive on eight-hour shifts as it was on ten-hour shifts, the eight-hour day would naturally result from free negotiation. If it proved less productive—as the *Times* was sure it would—no law in the world could force upon capital and labor regulations that failed to respect the verdict of the market. In this case, the law was simply *silly*. "And," the paper concluded,

421 "An die Arbeiter Deutschlands," *Der Social-Demokrat*, 30 August 1868, 4.
422 "Objection to the Eight-Hour System," *The National Workman*, 24 November 1866, 1.

> our faith in the good sense and good citizenship of the mass of American mechanics forbids all fear that they will carry a mere idea, however delusively attractive, to undue lengths.[423]

But as the coming years showed, American mechanics did indeed rally behind this "delusively attractive" idea. Frustrated with persistent working-class resistance, one of the city's most influential business paper declared that by

> one of those perverse freaks which often deprive society of a much needed relief, the working classes have organized influential combinations for exacting unnaturally high wages, and, still worse, for curtailing the hours of labor.[424]

In the eyes of *Hunt's Merchants' Magazine*, the shorter-hour activists simply failed to understand that the market was governed by natural laws. What made the demand for eight-hour legislation so outrageous to New York's business world was that it dismissed the historical inevitability of free labor markets. The laws of supply and demand had supposedly evolved in an organic process whereby the great efficiency of allocating labor from where it was available to where it was sought resulted in the eventual replacement of labor markets controlled or regulated by guilds or other public restrictions. Thanks to the efficiency of the laws of supply and demand, the free market was thus bound to emerge naturally. Yet in the eyes of *The National Workman*, there was in fact nothing natural about this development. According to the organ of New York City's Workingmen's Union, the free labor market was the result of centuries of conflict, brutal force, and careful planning. It was not so much the free market as the movement for protection from this very market that evolved naturally, as an inevitable reaction to the pressures of the former. In the history of free wage labor, *The National Workman* concluded, the eight-hour demand emerged as a rational and morally sound response. The laboring classes clearly had the right to protect themselves from overwork. It was thus nothing but "natural" that attempts were made to publicly regulate the length of the workday.[425]

On the other side of the ocean, Berlin's *Social-Demokrat* came to a similar conclusion. According to the paper, it was commonly known that under the current system of economic organization, labor power was degraded to the

423 "The Eight-Hour Movement," *The New York Times*, 15 April 1866, 4.

424 Cited in Montgomery, *Beyond Equality*, 265.

425 "The Dry Goods Reporter and The National Workman," *The National Workman*, 29 December 1866, 2.

status of a commodity. Their liberal opponents now acted as if this system of organization was based on some eternal law, and as if anyone who rebelled against this law was an enemy of all the cultural achievements of mankind. "Nothing is more ridiculous," the paper concluded, "than this howl."[426] Following his election to the parliament of the North German Confederation, von Schweitzer prepared a bill concerning the "Protection of Labor." The bill provided protection against wage abuse and the Truck system, protection of children, and protection against overwork. In particular, Section 10 of the bill stated that large-scale factory labor was not to be employed for more than ten hours a day.[427] Defending the bill in parliament, von Schweitzer declared that

> under present-day conditions, [...] labor is a commodity that is offered on the market. The only difference between the dominant school of thought and our approach is that we find regrettable and reprehensible what others applaud and praise.[428]

Schramm agreed with von Schweitzer that there was nothing natural about the emergence of a free market for labor. Despite *laissez-faire* rhetoric, the commodification of labor was by no means a product of the natural play of supply and demand. Rather, local as well as national authorities used every power at their disposal—from legislation to pure physical force—to sup-

426 "Die Arbeitskraft als Waare," *Neuer Social-Demokrat*, 10 July 1874, 1. ("Die Grundlage der gegenwärtigen Gesellschaftsorganisation ist bekanntlich, daß die Arbeit oder, richtiger gesagt, die Arbeitskraft eine Waare ist, welche gekauft und verkauft wird. Dabei geberden sich die Gegner des Socialismus, als beruhe diese Gesellschaftseinrichtung auf einem ewigen Naturgesetze, als sei sie absolut nothwendig und als wolle ein Jeder, welcher sie bekämpft, alle Kulturerrungenschaften der Menschheit von Grund aus vernichten. Nichts ist aber Lächerlicher, als dieses Geschrei [...].")

427 "Gesetz zum Schutze der Arbeit gegen das Kapital," *Der Social-Demokrat*, 9 October 1867, 1–3. This bill was the first legislative attempt by the ADAV to regulate the length of the workday. Von Schweitzer's initiative failed due to lack of support. Even Bebel and Liebknecht opposed it because they did not want "to give credit to the Prussian parliamentary system;" see "Politischer Theil: Berlin," *Der Social-Demokrat*, 16 October 1867, 3. Criticized for his lack of support by his own followers, Bebel declared in front of the delegates of the Weavers' Day in Glauchau that he did not support the bill because it would have granted the Reich Chancellor sole authority over the selection of factory inspectors; see Deutsches Weber-Central-Comitee (ed.), *Ausführlicher Bericht*, 53–54.

428 "Wörtlicher Auszug aus dem amtlichen stenographischen Bericht über die 19. Sitzung des Norddeutschen Reichstages," *Der Social-Demokrat*, 18 October 1867, 1. ("Die Arbeit unter den heutigen Verhältnissen [...] ist eine Waare, die Arbeit geht auf den Markt und bietet sich aus. Der Unterschied zwischen der Auffassung der herrschenden Schule und der unsrigen ist nur, daß wir für bedauerlich und verwerflich halten, was Jene ganz natürlich finden, ja loben und preisen.")

port this mass process of dispossession and dislocation. It was therefore the inalienable right of wage workers to be protected from the free market. Said Schramm:

> Since the state has, as we have seen, assisted a small minority in exploiting the majority of its citizens, it is nothing but the state's right and responsibility to do everything in its power to reverse this century-old injustice. Yet here come the economic peddlers preaching the doctrine of *laissez-faire* [...]. But the hollowness and shallowness of *laissez-faire* is increasingly recognized. From all sides, even among the adversaries of socialism, academic voices arise that expose the perversity of this entire school of thought; and with certainty we see that Bastiatism and the Manchester party finally face bankruptcy.[429]

Rather than the free market, Schramm concluded, it was the movement for protection from this market that emerged as a natural consequence of the former. The voice of German-speaking trade unions in New York City implied that liberals' emphasis on the alleged naturalness of free markets only served to force the working class into accepting its fate. As the *Arbeiter-Union* declared,

> "supply and demand"—these are the two magic words, the "hocus-pocus" of national economics. If you succeed in convincing a destitute or suffering man that it is an inevitable law of nature that causes his pain, and that his suffering would only worsen if he tried to remedy it, he might calmly accept the unacceptable.[430]

---

429 S.[schramm], "Arbeiter-Verhältnisse Im Mittelalter," *Der Volksstaat*, 16 March 1872, 3. ("Hat der Staat, wie wir gezeigt, darauf hingearbeitet, die Mehrzahl seiner Bewohner zugunsten einer kleinen Minorität auszubeuten, so ist es nicht mehr als Recht und Pflicht desselben, nun durch alle ihm zu Gebote stehenden Mittel dahin zu wirken, daß das Jahrhunderte alte Unrecht wieder gut gemacht werde. Und da kommen nun die 'volkswirtschaftlichen Hausirburschen' [sic] und predigen uns die Lehre von der Nichteinmischung des Staates [...]! Aber die Hohlheit und Flachheit dieser Lehre wird immer mehr erkannt! Schon erheben sich von allen Seiten, auch aus den Reihen der Gegner der Socialisten, wissenschaftliche Stimmen, welche das Verderbliche dieser ganzen wirtschaftlichen Richtung darthun, und mit Zuversicht kann man schon jetzt behaupten: Das Basthiatthum und die ganze Manchesterpartei stehen vor dem Bankerott!") The term "Basthiatthum" refers to Frédéric Bastiat, who promoted the notion of a free and unrestricted market in France. Among German workers, it achieved popularity primarily through a polemic by Lassalle, in which the latter ridiculed the liberal reformer Schulze-Delitzsch. Following Lassalle's publication "Herr Bastiat Schulze von Delitzsch, der ökonomische Julian," the term "Bastiatthum" (or Bastiatism) became popular among German social-democrats.

430 "Nachfrage und Angebot," *Die Arbeiter-Union*, 20 February 1869, 4. ("'Angebot und Nachfrage'—das sind die beiden großen Zauberworte, der 'Hokuspokus,' womit die Na-

There was no doubt, the paper explained, that the theory of supply and demand as such was plausible. In a truly free market, supply and demand clearly determined one another. Yet there had never been such a perfectly free market. Rather, the modern market was dominated by powerful monopolies that enjoyed the protection of governments. The vast monopolies of production, land, and money that controlled the American market jeopardized the well-being and participation of hardworking men and women all over the US. The monopolization of Polanyi's *fictitious commodities*, in other words, enabled capital to dictate its terms to labor. In the eyes of the *Arbeiter-Union*, the myth of the free play of supply and demand only helped legitimize the hegemony of *bourgeois* thought. No market that emerged from conditions like these would ever yield equality and freedom for all. The struggle for legislative intervention into the supposedly free labor market was thus also seen as a challenge to dominant liberal ideology:

> We want to expose the hypocrisy of an economic school of thought that speaks of unchecked competition as a blessing for society, while at the same time it defends the monopolies and other privileged institutions that oppose any true meaning of free competition.[431]

Anticipating present-day demands for a "commoning" of both natural and social resources, the *Arbeiter-Union* stressed that it was the free-market movement rather than the movement for protection that had sinned against "the natural law that had made land, air, light, water, and the means of exchange the common property of all."[432] New York's *Toiler* agreed completely. The paper argued passionately that never in human history had there been a truly free market where prices and conditions for labor exchange responded entirely to the laws of supply and demand—nor would there ever be. Rather,

---

tionalökonomen Fünfe gerade machen. Wenn man einen Nothleidenden oder Schmerzensdulder überzeugt, daß ein unerbittliches Naturgesetz Schuld an seiner Noth und seinen Schmerzen ist, und daß es das Uebel verschlimmern heiße, wenn er dagegen ankämpfen wolle, so beruhigt er sich viel leichter und trägt das sonst Unerträgliche.")

431 "Concurrenz," *Die Arbeiter-Union*, 29 July 1869, 2. ("Wir wollten die Heuchelei der Nationalökonomen bloßstellen, welche von schrankenloser Concurrenz als einer unersetzlichen Wohlthat in einer Gesellschaft sprechen, bei welcher überall noch Monopole oder sonstige privilegirte Einrichtungen jede wahrhaft freie Concurrenz unmöglich machen.")

432 "Die 'New York Times' und die Arbeiterbewegung," *Die Arbeiter-Union*, 4 June 1869, 2. ("[…] so ist das eine Sünde gegen ein Naturgesetz, welches Land, Luft, Licht, Wasser und Tauschmittel zum gemeinsamen Eigenthum aller gemacht hat.") For more detailed discussions of the idea and historical practice of "commoning," see Federici, *Revolution at Point Zero*, 138–148; Linebaugh, *The Magna Carta Manifesto*.

the "politico-economic dogma of supply and demand" was installed by a ruling class that clearly understood its implication. While employers regularly interfered with the so-called free market, they had made it an untouchable sanctuary vis-à-vis the suppliers of labor.[433] Berlin's and New York's shorter-hour movements thus emphasized the inconsistency of liberal thought. Even if unregulated labor markets *were* the natural result of an organic process, they asked rhetorically, would that make the effort to regulate their effect for the benefit of all *unnatural*? Addressing a workers' meeting at Berlin's *Alhambra* in 1865, von Schweitzer invited the audience to think of a river that regularly flooded a valley. If the people of the valley decided to build a dam to protect their livelihoods, and if one of them opposed the idea based on the fact that it was a natural law that made the river flood their homes and fields once in a while, would the majority then not respond: "To hell with you and your natural law!"[434]

4.3. Chapter Conclusion

This chapter has shown that shorter-hour activists in Berlin and New York opposed the unchecked commodification of labor power as a menace to their common understanding of humanness. Their struggle for a normal workday was fueled by the notion that labor required protection from a free market because the latter threatened the very essence of man. In particular, organized workers in Berlin and New York resisted what Nick Haslam describes as a binary strategy of dehumanization. According to Haslam, dehumanization regularly occurs in either "animalistic" or "mechanistic" forms. While animalistic analogies detect a flaw in what is usually regarded a culturally acquired group of features that characterize "human uniqueness"—such as civility or refinement—mechanistic dehumanization usually refers to a particular lack in the supposedly primordial set of features that characterize

433 "Supply and Demand," *The Toiler*, 22 August 1874, 2.

434 "Vereins-Theil: Berlin," *Der Social-Demokrat*, 17 October 1865, 3. ("Denken Sie sich, eine Gegend würde durch einen Fluß überschwemmt werden, und die Bewohner dieser Gegend würden einen Damm machen, der einem Einzelnen nicht zusagt, und der deshalb einwendete, man müsse dem Fluß seinen durch das Naturgesetz vorgeschriebenen Lauf lassen. 'Hol' dich der Teufel mit deinem Naturgesetz!'—würden doch die anderen sagen, denen die Überschwemmung die Felder wegschwemmte, und ruhig ihren Damm machen.")

"human nature"—such as agency or emotional responsiveness. Whereas the former tends to dehumanize others as wild, the latter sees them as cold. Haslam argues that these forms of dehumanization play an important role in various group conflicts, including race-, disability-, and gender-based discrimination.[435]

But as the foregoing has shown, the strategy of dehumanization could also be used reversely as a protective shield in industrial conflict. Rather than dehumanizing a racialized or gendered other, wage workers in Berlin and New York argued that they themselves suffered from the dehumanization of a socio-economic system. By stressing that dehumanization resulted from the unfettered commodification of their labor power, working-class discourse could hope to win sympathy far beyond the strict boundaries of their class. The social rationale of the shorter-hour movement thereby promoted a proto-theory of dehumanization that understood the free market as the central agent in this process. In Haslam's terms, the local workers' movements rejected what they regarded the mechanistic objectification that followed from the metamorphosis of labor into a commodity. Commodification was perceived as a vile conversion of autonomous beings into mere objects. Workers thus struggled against the free market, which transformed human labor into automata—just as they would later fight against the monotony and soullessness of factory labor.[436] The normal workday promised to reverse this transformation by restoring human agency. The movement for shorter hours maintained that, unlike inanimate machines, workers would not simply toil for as long as some invisible law required. In addition to protesting against mechanistic objectification, organized workers also opposed what they regarded as an animalistic attribution that likewise resulted from the commodification of their labor power. Images of exploited animals that were utilized for barbarically long hours thereby served as both drama and satire in working-class discourse. The idea that a supposedly natural law could force workers to toil for up to 16 hours a day like a submissive beast was so outrageous that it even seemed surreal. And yet it was happening everywhere around them. Workers in Berlin and New York City shared the conviction that no morally decent society would allow this dehumanization of labor. A joint mass meeting of English- and German-speaking workers at New York's Cooper Institute thus reached a simple conclusion. The unreg-

435 Haslam, "Dehumanization."

436 See Pollard, "Factory Discipline," 257–258.

ulated workday brought "shame on any notion of civilization."[437] Workers were neither animals nor things. They were not for sale.

Yet, as we have seen in this chapter, the struggle for shorter hours was not only a means to restore human agency in social relations. It also was a wedge that could be driven deep into the ideology of free markets. Liberal discussions about the naturalness of labor markets epitomized the hegemonic position of *laissez-faire* thought. By giving the free market an aura of historical inevitability, liberal discourse was able to discredit any resistance as absurd. For if the free market really was the product of an organic process that was bound to happen, opposition not only was futile, but also, as the *Times* put it, "silly."[438] Against this backdrop, the legal reduction of the daily hours of work was seen as a first step towards withdrawing labor from the iron grip of the market, thereby undermining the power of dominant economic theory. According to Marx, this was in fact the true meaning of the struggle. Emphasizing the transnational significance of the English Ten-Hour Law, Marx used his IWA inaugural address in 1864 to show that the passage of the bill in 1847 was the first time that a working-class movement prevailed over dominant ideology. The struggle for shorter hours was so crucial because it

> intervened in the great antagonism between the blind rule of the law of supply and demand, the political economy of the bourgeoisie, and the principle of the social regulation of production, the political economy of the working class. And for that reason the Ten Hours Act was not merely a great political advance, it was at the same time the victory of a principle. For the first time in the clear light of day the political economy of the bourgeoisie suffered defeat at the hands of the political economy of the working class.[439]

The movement for a shorter workday drew heavily on the notion that the unhindered commodification of labor threatened social cohesion and violated workers' inalienable rights. Rather than the result of natural or organic evolution, the free market was thereby seen as the political project of a liberal movement that acted simultaneously on the legislative and ideological fronts. And the shorter-hour demand was perceived as a counter-movement for protection that had emerged as a logical response to this free-market movement. After all, shorter-hour activists inferred, they could not simply stand

437 "Die Arbeiter-Massenversammlung am 23. März 1869," *Die Arbeiter-Union*, 27 March 1869, 5.

438 "The Eight-Hour Movement," *The New York Times*, 15 April 1866, 4.

439 Marx, *Two Speeches*, 14.

back and watch the free market cause havoc in their communities. This idea now is precisely what Karl Polanyi characterized as a central element of the "double movement." Although the liberal movement of the nineteenth century emphasized that the unfettered market was the result of a natural process, Polanyi stresses that it actually required the concerted action of capital and state to forge it. According to Polanyi, there

> was nothing natural about laissez-faire; free markets could never have come into being merely by allowing things to take their course. [… Rather], laissez-faire itself was enforced by the state.[440]

While Polanyi portrayed the free market as the result of both private and public intervention, he argued that the opposing movement for protection emerged as an unplanned yet immanently logical reaction by those who suffered under the commodification of life. By the late 1860s, organized labor had reached a very similar concept of a double movement—including surprisingly similar terminology. In a short review of Friedrich Albert Lange's influential *Die Arbeiterfrage in ihrer Bedeutung für Gegenwart und Zukunft*, Berlin's *Social-Demokrat* stated in 1865 that

> two large and fundamental movements oppose each other; one argues: Leave all to itself, only make sure that the last barriers to economic freedom fall and everything will turn out fine. The other one states: The foundation of our present-day economy is flawed. The mere *negative* reduction of free-trade barriers will not help; what is needed instead is a *positive* re-organization of the entire economy.[441]

The paper offered a theory of social contestation that differed markedly from Marxist notions of class struggle. Rather than exploitation, it was the lack of protection from the free market that determined conflict in society. According to this approach, society was not torn apart by a battle between a propertied class on the one side and a propertyless class on the other, but by two opposing movements that struggled for and against the commodification of labor, land, and money. The fight for shorter hours that organized

440 Polanyi, *The Great Transformation*, 145.

441 "Literarisches," *Der Social-Demokrat*, 8 March 1865, 4. ("Zwei große, fundamental von einander verschiedene Richtungen stehen einander gegenüber; die eine meint: Laß alles im Wesentlichen beim Alten, sorgt nur dafür, daß die letzten Schranken der freien wirtschaftlichen Bewegung fallen und Alles wird gut sein. Die andere meint: Die Grundlagen der jetzigen wirthschaftlichen Bewegung tauge nichts. Nicht das blos Negative der Wegräumung aller Schranken kann helfen; eine durchgreifende positive Organisation der wirthschaftlichen Bewegung thut noth.")

labor waged in Berlin and New York City thus qualifies as a Polanyian "protective movement" par excellence. Shorter-hour activists hoped that the normal workday would offer protection from the unchecked hegemony of the market. They were certain that it would enforce political equality, promote human dignity, and challenge the power of dominant ideology. Yet, as the subsequent chapter will show, they also saw it as a central pillar in the formulation of their very own economics. The following analysis of the economic arguments advanced by shorter-hour activists thereby reveals a striking discursive shift. In the social and political realms discussed so far, the notion of de-commodification constituted an important reservoir for shorter-hour arguments. Arguments that referred directly to the economy, however, often stood in stark contrast to de-commodification. The acceptance of the category of commodified labor in fact provided crucial leverage in labor conflicts. This was the reason that, while the notion of de-commodification featured prominently in socialist theory and political debate, the young trade-union movement increasingly refrained from opposing the commodification of labor. Analyzing the economic arguments brought forward by Berlin's and New York's shorter-hour movements, the following chapter thus pays particular attention to the tension between social-democratic and trade-union discourse.

5. Economy: Shorter Hours and the Struggle for Redistribution

"Whether you work by the piece or by the day,
reducing the hours increases the pay."[442]
Mary Steward

5.1. The Political Economy of Shorter Hours

During the fierce campaign for the first general eight-hour bill in the state, New York's *Economist and Dry Goods Reporter* continuously attacked the shorter-hour movement as a menace to working-class interests. According to the local business paper, producers in the US had to compete with foreign manufacturers that were not restricted by "the folly of eight hour legislation." If American employees worked fewer hours a day, American industry would suffer a severe competitive disadvantage compared with European industry. In order to remain in the market, manufacturers would be forced to sell cheaper despite the productivity differential. The resulting fall in profits would surely be passed on to their employees. In the end, the paper concluded, shorter hours would inevitably depress wages.[443] This view, highly characteristic of New York City's business world, was challenged by one of the most distinctive voices of postbellum American labor. Over the course of the 1860s, the Bostonian Ira Steward rose to prominence as a central figure in the development of a political economy of eight-hours.[444] According to Steward, the introduction of an eight-hour law was the best way to accus-

442 As Cashman states, this "popular jingle [is often] attributed to [Ira Steward's] wife;" see Cashman, *America in the Gilded Age*, 104. Cashman here draws on Roediger, who provides a source from the Labor Standard of 1877; see Roediger, "Ira Steward," 418. Other sources credit Steward himself; see "Our Common Interest," *Cigar Makers' Official Journal*, 10 March 1878, 1.

443 "The Dry Goods Reporter and The National Workman," *The National Workman*, 29 December 1866, 2.

444 Douglas, "Ira Steward," 534.

tom the American worker to the taste for a better life. From eight hours, he taught, there was no going back. In contrast to liberal warnings that shorter hours would result in shrinking wages, Steward argued that they would have the opposite effect. A working class used to working no more than eight hours would soon demand a greater share of the wealth it produced. Said Steward:

> The truth is, as a rule, that men who labor excessively are robbed of all ambitions to ask for anything more than will satisfy their bodily necessities, while those who labor moderately have time to cultivate tastes and create wants in addition to mere physical comforts.[445]

The eight-hour workday, Steward reasoned, would give the oppressed and exploited the free time necessary to become aware of their oppression. They would request higher compensation for the new lifestyles they were gradually adopting. Higher wages would in turn help promote technical innovation, which would free manual labor from long hours of physical toil. This would then further refine the habits of the working class, which would eventually demand further hour reductions and better pay until the whole system of wage labor would fall and "the capitalist and laborer were one."[446] Following Steward's death, his disciple George Gunton published a comprehensive yet surprisingly business-friendly account of what Commons and Andrews regarded as "the first philosophy springing from the American labor movement."[447] Gunton defined his teacher's theory as the "idea that the standard of living is the basis of wages, and that social opportunity, or more leisure for the masses, are expressed in less hours of labor." Shorter hours were thus seen as "the natural means for increasing wages and promoting progress."[448] Like many of his fellow workingmen, Steward did hope to see a future where every laborer was his own capitalist and received the "full fruits of his labor." Yet the abolition of the wage system here served as a distant utopia rather than an immediate objective. In Steward's political-economic theory of eight hours, what mattered was the idea that the shorter workday would have a positive impact upon the average costs of reproduction and,

---

445 Steward, "A Reduction of Hours," 285.

446 Ibid., 287. See also Steward's unfinished manuscripts "On Hours" and "The Political Economy of Eight Hours or The Science of Human Progress" at the Wisconsin Historical Society, "Ira Stewards Papers," U.S. Mss 9 A, Box 2, Folder 1.

447 Commons and Andrews, "Introduction to Volumes IX and X," 24.

448 Gunton, *Wealth and Progress*, vi. Gunton was later criticized by labor historians for drawing a much more business-friendly picture than Steward; see Douglas, "Ira Steward," 534.

thus, wages. In contrast to the liberal wage-fund doctrine, Steward suggested that wages were not dependent on the actual number of workers relative to a fixed capital fund.[449] Rather, the level of wages was the result of the respective standard of living in any given society. Steward therewith also opposed the idea that the level of wages was the result of capital reinvestments that had become possible thanks to employers' abstention from personal consumption.[450]

As Steward's brother in mind, George E. McNeill, put it in a collection of arguments in defense of shorter hours, wages rested exclusively "upon the habits of thought and feeling, customs and manners of the masses."[451] This notion had a tremendous impact on the local shorter-hour movement. In 1874, a reader of New York's *Toiler* sent an angry letter to the paper arguing that what determined the conditions of labor, including the daily hours of work, was the standard of customs and habits among the suppliers of labor.[452] Following a critical rejoinder by a certain Dr. Kinget, the editors of the *Toiler* rallied to the defense of the anonymous reader. If they wanted to increase their economic participation, organized workers were well advised to concentrate on boosting the standard of living in their communities.[453] And the most promising way to do this, the editors stressed, was to enforce a reduction in the daily hours of labor. A few years earlier, the veteran abolitionist and social reformer Wendell Phillips had come to a similar conclusion. Phillips invited his audience to picture an average American worker:

> There is an American, bred in the public schools, with the right to vote and an idea of having a house to himself, of having his children go to school, of reading a newspaper, going to a lecture, having a book to read and a certain class of clothing as good as his neighbor. He makes an easy chair. In a year or two, there comes a German, fresh from Hamburg. He can make just as good an easy chair, exactly, and he never has had a dream of having a newspaper; he has never thought of having the same class of clothes as the American; he never has opened a book; he has had no ambition that his wife and children should live in a certain sort of comfort; one room, with no ornament, satisfies him. [...] The consequence is, he will work for half the wages that the American will. Let him live here five years. Let him get his ideas lifted to the level of American civilization. Let him be ashamed not to read a

449 Montgomery, *Beyond Equality*, 253–260.

450 In Lassallean literature in particular, this idea was ridiculed as the "millionaire's hardship wage" or "Entbehrungslohn." For a characteristic polemic, see von Schweitzer's *Schlingel*.

451 McNeill, *Argument on the Hours of Labor*, 9.

452 "Supply and Demand," *The Toiler*, 22 August 1874, 2.

453 "Supply and Demand," *The Toiler*, 5 September 1874, 4.

newspaper; let him be ashamed not to have his boys go to school as well dressed as his neighbor's; let him, too, have the ambition to go to a public meeting, attend an entertainment, amuse himself at a concert; cultivate himself as his neighbor does, and he will not work for those lower wages; he demands a higher level.[454]

On the one hand, Phillips here fueled the sort of exceptionalism that characterized the American radical reform movement of the 1860s and 1870s. In Phillips' eyes, the republican institutions and liberal heritage of the US provided a potential for freedom and equality unmatched by any other society. Here in the US, even a submissive soul like the German immigrant worker would eventually prosper. Yet the fictive worker from Hamburg who did not dream of civic rights and a decent life for himself and his family was clearly the product of Phillips' imagination. Thus, the statement testifies to Phillips's ignorance of working-class life in Europe in general and in Hamburg—another urban hotspot of social-democratic thought and activism—in particular.[455] On the other hand, however, Phillip's analogy epitomizes how widespread the idea had become that the standard of living determined the level of wages. Shorter-hour activists in the US were certain that the reduction of the workday would enable workers to refine their lifestyles and enforce better compensation.

At first sight, all this was nonsense from an orthodox Lassallean perspective. As Lassalle had explained in his famous "Open Reply" of 1863, the iron law of wages provided

that the average wage will always be reduced to that level which a given people habitually requires for subsistence. [...] It cannot rise above this level for long—for if it did, the workers' less deprived situation would necessary lead to an increase in the working-class population, which would then result in an oversupply of labor, which would eventually reduce the wage to the earlier level or below. Yet the wage also cannot fall below that level for long—after all, this would lead to emigration, a decrease in marriages, and a decline in births, which would lead to a reduction in the

454 "The Eight-Hour Movement: Wendell Phillips' Advice to the Working Men," *The New York Times*, 24 May 1870, 2.

455 For a comprehensive account similar to Bernstein's history of the movement in Berlin, see the two-volume work by Laufenberg, *Geschichte der Arbeiterbewegung in Hamburg*. For more recent studies, see Kutz-Bauer, *Arbeiterschaft*; Ullrich, *Die Hamburger Arbeiterbewegung*. Richard J. Evans has greatly deepened our understanding of working-class life in nineteenth-century Hamburg; see Evans, *Kneipengespräche*; Evans, *Death in Hamburg*.

number of available workers, which would eventually reduce the supply of labor and therewith elevate the wage to the earlier level.[456]

In a system of free competition, wages were therefore bound to fall to subsistence levels irrespective of working-class desires or habits. As we have seen in Chapter 1, this was the reason for the ADAV's uneasiness with strikes and trade unionism in the first place—for if trade unionism was futile, workers would do better to concentrate on politics instead. Yet in fact Steward's approach was surprisingly compatible with Lassallean perspectives on shorter hours. In a parliamentary debate about the amendment of the Trade Regulation Act of the North German Confederation, the new Member of Parliament, von Schweitzer, demanded the introduction of a normal working day. As a crucial economic rationale for his demand, von Schweitzer stated:

According to today's laws of value and labor value, the level of wages is generally low because the present-day standard of living does not allow new wants or habits to emerge among workers. If it were possible for workers to develop new wants, then the wage would rise to meet these wants. [...] Allow that each day the worker has a little time for himself and he will cultivate new wants, he will become accustomed to the new standard, and soon the entire working class will find new vigor to demand that the wage increase accordingly.[457]

456 See Jenaczek, *Ferdinand Lassalle*, 181. ("Das eherne ökonomische Gesetz, welches unter den heutigen Verhältnissen, unter der Herrschaft von Angebot und Nachfrage nach Arbeit, den Arbeitslohn bestimmt, ist dieses: daß der durchschnittliche Arbeitslohn immer auf den notwendigen Lebensunterhalt reduziert bleibt, der in einem Volke gewohnheitsgemäß zur Fristung der Existenz und zur Fortpflanzung erforderlich ist. [...]. Er kann sich nicht dauernd über diesen Durchschnitt erheben—denn sonst entstände durch die leichtere, bessere Lage der Arbeiter eine Vermehrung der Arbeiterehen und der Arbeiterfortpflanzung, eine Vermehrung der Arbeiterbevölkerung und somit des Angebots von Händen, welche den Arbeitslohn wieder auf und unter seinen früheren Stand herabdrücken würde. Der Arbeitslohn kann auch nicht dauernd tief unter diesen notwendigen Lebensunterhalt fallen, denn dann entstehen—Auswanderung, Ehelosigkeit, Enthaltung von Kindererzeugung und endlich eine durch das Elend erzeugte Verminderung der Arbeiterzahl, welche somit das Angebot von Arbeiterhänden noch verringert und den Arbeitslohn daher wieder auf den früheren Stand zurückbringt.")

457 "Aus dem Reichstag des Norddeutschen Bundes," *Der Social-Demokrat*, 21 March 1869, 3. ("Nach dem heutigen Werthgesetze und insbesondere Lohnwerthgesetze ist der Lohn darum ständig auf so niederer Höhe, weil nach der jetzigen Lage der Arbeiterklasse überhaupt nur die nothwendigen Lebensbedürfnisse in den Arbeitern aufkommen können. Wenn es möglich ist, daß höhere Bedürfnisse in den Arbeitern aufkommen können, dann wird auch der Lohn steigen müssen. [...E]rmöglichen Sie es, daß der Arbeiter jeden Tag eine längere Zeit frei hat, dann entstehen neue Bedürfnisse in ihm, er gewöhnt sich an

We do not know whether von Schweitzer was familiar with Ira Steward's theory of eight hours, but Steward could not have put it better. Demonstrating a rather flexible interpretation of Lassallean doctrine, von Schweitzer here declared openly that wage levels were determined not by an iron law, but by the costs of reproduction.[458] If organized labor were able to increase the costs of reproduction, wages could increase too. In an almost exact replica of the *Toiler*'s analysis cited above, the Berlin-based *Social-politische Blätter* declared that there was nothing

> more decisive in triggering new wants in man, yes, nothing that makes the emergence of wants and their gratification downright irrefutable, as when man has plenty of free time.[459]

The normal workday was the perfect means through which to accustom workers to higher lifestyles, and thus to increase the costs of reproduction. Unlike strikes for higher wages, many Lassalleans saw strikes for shorter hours as a means through which to improve the material conditions of working people. Hasenclever and Hasselmann's *Social-politische Blätter* thus concluded that shorter hours would automatically increase the daily wage because the working class would cultivate new and better tastes once they had been freed from the dulling and exhausting reality of long workdays.[460] Yet it was not only Lassalleans, but also local Eisenachers who subscribed to this very formula. According to labor leaders like Theodor Metzner, there could be no doubt about the accuracy of the law

> according to which—as science has demonstrated—the worker's wage always stands on the lowest level that the worker habitually requires to secure reproduction.[461]

---

neue Bedürfnisse, und dann findet die Arbeiterklasse in sich auch die nachhaltige Kraft, zu verlangen, daß demgemäß der Lohn erhöht werde.")

458 Welskopp argues that Lassalle's iron law of wages increasingly became a propagandistic tool largely void of analytical meaning. Both ADAV and SDAP members referred to the law in order to organize working-class support rather than to influence discourse; see Welskopp, *Das Banner der Brüderlichkeit*, 559–560.

459 "Die Verkürzung der Arbeitszeit," *Social-Politische Blätter*, 31 March 1874, 45. ("[…] was mehr die Bedürfnisse im Menschen hervorruft, ja das Aufkommen von Bedürfnissen und deren Befriedigung unabweisbar macht, als wenn der Mensch viel freie Zeit hat.")

460 "Der gesetzlich festgestellte Normalarbeitstag," *Social-Politische Blätter*, 7 February 1874, 3; "Die Verkürzung der Arbeitszeit," *Social-Politische Blätter*, 31 March 1874, 45.

461 "Lokales (Die Internationale Manufakturarbeiterschaft)," *Demokratische Zeitung*, 2 March 1872, 3. ("[…] nach welchem—wie wissenschaftlich nachgewiesen—der Lohn des Arbeiters stets auf der niedrigsten Stufe der jeweiligen Lebensbedürfnisse steht, deren derselbe gewohnheitsmäßig zur Fortpflanzung und Existenzsicherung bedarf.")

As the Lassallean-turned-Eisenacher emphasized, the normal workday had the potential to reverse this trend precisely by increasing what workers "habitually required." The slogan that "Whether you work by the piece or by the day, reducing the hours increases the pay" had indeed won acceptance on both sides of the Atlantic.[462] In so doing, it equipped the emerging trade-union movement with a powerful rationale for their struggle to shorten the workday.

5.2. The Decline of the Concept of Commodification

By the beginning of the 1870s, organized labor in New York City had been fighting for shorter-hour legislation for years. Yet, as mentioned before, the eight-hour laws that had been passed between 1866 and 1868 at the municipal, state, and federal levels all suffered from the special agreement clause that was either inscribed directly into the bill or assumed to exist by courts. Not even the city or state themselves were complying with existing laws, as public agencies openly demonstrated by employing or subcontracting workers at various construction sites for ten hours rather than eight. Organized workers in New York were so disappointed by the end of the decade that they concluded that, as William Jessup put it, "it were better the Law did not exist at all."[463] Only the brownstone cutters and plasterers of New York City were working eight-hour shifts, and the latter were soon forced back to ten hours when their employers used the business slump in the winter of 1869/1870 for their advantage.[464] A survey published by the Workingmen's Assembly of New York State showed that the majority of the trades in New York City did indeed work at least ten hours a day.[465]

Fueled by widespread frustration over the ineffectiveness of legislation, workers once more turned their energies from political to economic action. And it was the city's construction workers who spearheaded the emerging struggle. Second only to the printing trade, the building sector had witnes-

462 "Our Common Interest," *Cigar Makers' Official Journal*, 10 March 1878, 1.

463 *Proceedings of the Sixth Annual Session of the Workingmen's Assembly*, 4.

464 *Proceedings of the Seventh Annual Session of the Workingmen's Assembly*, 17.

465 *Proceedings of the Sixth Annual Session of the Workingmen's Assembly*, 15–16, 25–26. This survey calls into question Roediger and Foner's conclusion that there had been a general shift to eight hours in New York City in the aftermath of the Civil War; see Foner and Roediger, *Our Own Time*, 101.

sed some of the earliest instances of trade-union activity in New York City. As early as 1830, local carpenters had been able to enforce a ten-hour workday.[466] From these successes, the city's construction workers drew inspiration and strategic direction when the shorter-hour struggle regathered pace in the late 1860s. Following lengthy negotiations between New York's master masons and the local sections of the Bricklayers' Union, more than two thousand unionized bricklayers walked out on June 22, 1868 in order to enforce an eight-hour workday—without reductions in wage if possible, with wage cuts if necessary.[467] *The New York Times* was furious. Not only did the striking bricklayers violate the state's conspiracy laws by hindering those willing to work for ten hours from doing so, they had also brought construction in the city to a halt. According to the paper, the bricklayers' strike therewith deepened the housing crisis and fostered the further increase of working-class rents—a charge that was also made against the striking bricklayers of Berlin.[468] The bricklayers of New York City saw things differently, yet they, too, disagreed on the prospect of the strike. Many workers feared that they possessed neither the power nor the resources to sustain a prolonged strike with uncertain ends. Nor were all of them prepared to offer their employers wage cuts in exchange for shorter hours. As much as trade-union leaders preached that such wage losses would quickly be regained once the shorter workday was established, workers feared the very idea of lower wages. The German-speaking bricklayers in particular had serious reservations, and their local union No. 12 split over the strike question. Their English-speaking colleagues were not in agreement either, yet two-thirds of their unionized members eventually walked out. In order to prepare for a tough winter—during which, as the president of the bricklayers' union of New York City warned, capital would try to starve out the strikers—the bricklayers appealed for support to all organized workers in the country. In their eyes, this was not the struggle of a local trade, but of the entire American working class.[469] What thus made this conflict so important was that, as Irwin Yellowitz has put it in a detailed account of the strike, it "became the major test case for the viability of the demand for eight hours."[470]

---

466 Galenson, *The United Brotherhood of Carpenters*, 6.

467 Bates, *Bricklayers' Century of Craftsmanship*, 29; Burrows and Wallace, *Gotham*, 987–988; "Strike of the Bricklayers," *The New York Times*, 23 June 1868, 5.

468 "The Bricklayers' Strike," *The New York Times*, 2 August 1868, 4.

469 "Vereinsleben," *Die Arbeiter-Union*, 26 September 1868, 6.

470 Yellowitz, "Eight Hours and the Bricklayers' Strike," 85.

No wonder the eyes of organized workers across the country were fixed on the striking bricklayers of New York City. If the local bricklayers were able to win eight hours by striking, many in the movement hoped, they would be able to do so, too. If they were defeated, the entire eight-hour movement would come to a halt. Thus the Workingmen's Union rallied behind the bricklayers and urged the striking workers to stick to the eight-hour demand at all costs.[471] Over the course of the strike, the city central not only organized rallies in moral support of the bricklayers, but also raised funds for the strikers. Jessup and other representatives of the Workingmen's Union tirelessly toured the region and promoted the bricklayers' cause. And they did so rather successfully.[472] The Workingmen's Union received funds from both local groups, such as New York's painters, who "contributed handsomely to the bricklayers' strike," and places upstate or out of state, such as the bricklayers of Albany or Philadelphia, which each sent 1,000 Dollars in support of the bricklayers in New York City.[473] In addition, unions outside of New York City helped find employment for those striking workers willing to leave the city. According to the bricklayers' union, roughly a thousand members left New York City during the strike.[474]

Blessed with widespread support, New York's bricklayers were soon able to announce that more and more employers were giving in to their demand in the early weeks of the strike. From the very beginning of their strike, the local bricklayers stressed that shorter hours would directly improve productivity. Those bricklayers who had been able to secure the eight-hour day heralded that they were now laying 1,800 bricks a day compared to the 1,000 bricks they had laid on ten-hour shifts.[475] Speaking in defense of the striking bricklayers in the city, Mr. Whelan of New York's Typographical Union No. 6 announced that it was no wonder that workers proved more productive under the eight-hour system, now that they were able to rest and recover in the well-deserved peace of their homes.[476] Especially among the skilled

471 "The Workingmen's Union," *The New York Times*, 15 August 1868, 8.

472 Yellowitz argues that the amount of money received by the striking bricklayers should not be overestimated; see Yellowitz, "Eight Hours and the Bricklayers' Strike," 90–92. Yet neither should it be underestimated. Though not the first of its kind, the fundraising campaign proved highly popular among local workers, and it increased mobilization far beyond the actual amount of financial contributions.

473 "The Workingmen's Union," *The New York Times*, 19 September 1868, 8.

474 Yellowitz, "Eight Hours and the Bricklayers' Strike," 88.

475 Ibid., 92.

476 "Vereinsleben," *Die Arbeiter-Union*, 26 September 1868, 6.

trades, the argument that productivity would actually increase with shorter hours was an essential element of trade-union discourse at the time.[477] Contrary to claims by employers, the New York City-based *Socialist* was sure that the "reduction of the hours of labor to eight per day would not decrease the present productive power."[478] The workshops or trades that had already introduced a reduction of hours showed that, far from jeopardizing productivity, the shorter workday had actually made them more productive than before. Workers on eight-hour shifts were more relaxed and more willing to perform their labor with diligence and care. Based on this observation, the paper promoted the shorter workday primarily as an expression of economic rationality. Therewith, it was in line with ideas promoted by the local building trades. In the eyes of many construction workers, the shorter workday promised a rationalization of production that also catered to the interests of employers. Rather than stretching the workday during nine months of employment and enforcing idleness during the sluggish winter months, the continuous employment of labor for eight hours over the entire year would guarantee steady production and a more rational usage of time. The notion of de-commodification, however, was strikingly absent from this logic. Trade unionists in fact appealed directly to employers' commercial sense by arguing that shorter hours would allow them to use the commodity that workers provided more efficiently. From this perspective, the shortening of the workday was a promising investment rather than a political right or moral obligation.

Despite initial success, the bricklayers' strike revealed that trade unions in New York faced difficulties that stemmed directly from the diversity of labor in the city. Not only did workers from abroad bring different traditions and political ideologies, they also often lacked basic language skills that impeded closer co-operation. While labor reformers and socialist professionals like Friedrich A. Sorge and Adolph Strasser quickly championed the new language, many rank-and-file trade unionists simply did not understand their fellow native-born workers. Yet the local unions knew that co-operation was vital. When, for instance, the large employer Steinway & Sons fired a worker who had dared to organize support among the workforce for the bricklayers' eight-hour strike, the German Piano Workers' Union of New York City assembled both German and English-speaking workers in protest. In order to facilitate exchange and joint action, the union provided trans-

477 Cf. Schmiede, "Die Entwicklung der Arbeitszeit in Deutschland," 73–74.

478 "The Eight Hour Question," *The Socialist*, 15 April 1876, 3.

lators to help bridge the language gap.[479] The pages of the *Arbeiter-Union* likewise testify to efforts at bilingual co-operation. Time and again, the paper translated and thereby made accessible key US labor documents to a local German-speaking audience.[480] Despite the commitment by German and English-speaking labor, however, the bricklayers' strike showed the first signs of failure. When, towards the end of the year, the bricklayers' union announced that the majority of its men were working eight hours, organized employers ridiculed this number and stressed that the majority of the city's bricklayers in fact worked ten hours. As winter dragged on, even the union was forced to concede that most bricklayers were back on ten-hour shifts. The slump that followed Jay Gould's infamous adventure in gold in the fall of 1869 finally sealed the fate of the bricklayers' eight-hour struggle. With the exception of Brooklyn, where two unions succeeded in winning an eight-hour day, New York's bricklayers had proven unable to enforce the eight-hour day through collective action.[481] For the next three years, trade unions in New York City and beyond abstained from organizing shorter-hour strikes. Instead, they returned to political campaigns, a road that largely ended in electoral disaster.[482] But with the renewed economic boom of 1871 and early 1872, trade conflicts once more presented themselves as a promising avenue towards shorter hours. And local construction workers once more stood at the forefront in this fresh round of battle.

The housepainters of Brooklyn were among the first to strike for eight hours in April 1872. They were soon followed by construction workers all over the metropolitan area. Protesting that contractors violated the federal eight-hour law at a public work site in the city, New York's bricklayers even saw President Grant side with them when he passed an executive proclamation in 1872 reminding officials of the existing federal law.[483] As a close reading of their papers and announcements shows, the local construction workers employed a rationale that openly adopted the logic of the market as

479 "Vereinsleben," *Die Arbeiter-Union*, 12 September 1868, 5. The city's pianoforte makers, for instance, had already been translating important documents and debates in antebellum New York; see Stott, *Workers in the Metropolis*, 157.

480 See, for instance, Sylvis's speech, which the paper was *happy to translate*: "Zinsfuß und Arbeit," *Die Arbeiter-Union*, 14 November 1868, 4.

481 Bates, *Bricklayers' Century of Craftsmanship*, 38.

482 For ward-to-ward statistics of the election of 1869, see "Das Wahlergebniß für die Arbeiter-Partei," *Die Arbeiter-Union*, 3 November 1869, 2. See also Burrows and Wallace, *Gotham*, 988; Yellowitz, "Eight Hours and the Bricklayers' Strike," 93–96.

483 Montgomery, *Beyond Equality*, 328–329.

a weapon in industrial conflict. Due to decades of domestic and international migration, the urban labor market witnessed a dramatic oversupply of skilled construction workers. The legislative reduction of daily hours, these distressed workers argued, was simply a much-needed restriction in the supply of the commodity of labor. This notion also resonated with other trades. As the *Labor Standard* put it more broadly, the "worker's capital is his time and labor force; he must be economical with regard to both."[484] By accepting that labor power constituted a commodity, organized workers increasingly struggled to control the market for this peculiar article of trade. In contrast to the bricklayers' strike of 1868, this time workers in other sectors did not leave it at signs of solidarity. A devastated *New York Times* observed that the

> movements of the various trade societies indicate that it is the intention of all trades to follow the plan of those engaged in the different branches of building, and demand eight hour's [sic] as a day's labor.[485]

The paper predicted that the strikers would soon realize that a shorter workday would only decrease their already meager incomes. Surely they would quickly abandon the idea. Yet the *Times* was seriously mistaken. As summer approached, the city's iron and metal workers, the piano, coach, and sewing-machine makers, and many other urban trades struck for eight hours.[486] Under the auspices of the North American Eight Hour League, which held daily meetings in New York in the summer of 1872, local leagues were founded in various sectors. While the Building Trades League united the mostly English-speaking construction workers, the Furniture Workers' Eight Hour League was comprised exclusively of German workers. Others, such as the Metal Workers' Eight Hour League, had mixed memberships.[487] In the summer of 1872, the international gaze of organized labor was once more fixed on New York. Following the city's stone masons, plasterers, and painters, the carpenters swiftly won the eight-hour day on May 20 and 21, 1872. From New York, the demand and strategies—such as the carpenters'

484 "The Normal Workday," *Cigar Makers' Official Journal*, March 1877, 2.

485 "The Working Men: Additional Particulars about the Strike in this City; The Post-Office Men, Longshoremen, Pattern-Makers, Wheelwrights, Blacksmiths and Others Demand the Eight-Hour System," *The New York Times*, 23 May 1872, 5.

486 "Other Strikes: The Iron and Metal Workers' League; The Sewing-Machine Men; The Piano-Makers; The Marble-Polishers; Coach-Makers; Card. Journeymen Barbers," *The New York Times*, 19 June 1872, 8.

487 Montgomery, *Beyond Equality*, 328.

tactic of visiting shops in large, organized squads in order to ensure the efficacy of the strike—travelled the country. Day after day, local unions announced that employers in their sector had succumbed and accepted their demand. For a few weeks, it looked as if New York's eight-hour movement had finally been able to enforce the shorter workday.[488] Discussing local successes, an exceptionally optimistic New York City-based correspondent exclaimed in the pages of the German *Volksstaat* that "the Eight-Hour Day Movement has grown considerably, and it scores victory after victory."[489] Yet the larger employers in the city in particular stood their ground. Backed by the *Times* and *Tribune*, employers like Singer's Sewing Machine Company and the piano manufacturer Steinway & Sons became local strongholds of the ten-hour system. In an early example of business-location rhetoric, William Steinway declared that a reduction of daily hours would necessarily make his pianos more expensive and therewith less competitive on domestic and international markets. If ever enforced, the eight-hour system would thus inevitably drive industry out of New York City to places where, as he put it, labor remained free.[490] As a consequence, eight-hour confrontations escalated during the summer into the largest industrial conflict New York had witnessed so far, pitting the record number of "a hundred thousand workers from fifty-two crafts [...] against a newly unified manufacturing elite supported by most of the city's bourgeoisie."[491] Yet organized labor proved less and less able to defend previous gains, let alone make new ones. Friedrich A. Sorge thus wrote in a letter to Liebknecht that the local eight-hour movement was indeed enormous now, but he feared that the inertia of the German workers in particular jeopardized the success of the movement. "The way it stands now," Sorge ended, "I am afraid of the outcome."[492] And his fear was not unfounded. As the summer of 1872 progressed, more and more employers regained strength, while workers found it difficult to fight an increasingly hostile police united with their determined bosses. One last gasp of resistance emerged at the gas works when, in the spring of the fol-

488 "The Strikes: General Concessions of the Eight-Hour System," *The New York Times*, 21 May 1872, 8.

489 "Aus Amerika: New York, 22. Mai," *Der Volksstaat*, 15 June 1872, 1. ("Die Achtstundenbewegung ist gewachsen und verzeichnet Siege auf Siege.")

490 See "Article 3–No Title," *The New York Times*, 30 May 1872, 4. See also Montgomery, *Beyond Equality*, 329; Roediger and Foner, *Our Own Time*, 114.

491 Burrows and Wallace, *Gotham*, 1012.

492 "F. A. Sorge and Wilhelm Liebknecht," 422–423. ("So wie es jetzt steht, fürchte ich für die Folgen.")

lowing year, workers struck for eight hours, temporarily leaving Lower Manhattan in the dark.[493] Yet it was no more than an epilog in a long and heated battle. Despite impressive unity and initial gains, New York's eight-hour movement had proven unable to enforce the eight-hour workday by striking.

At first sight, workers in Berlin were more successful in enforcing hour reductions by strike. Not unlike the American Civil War ten years earlier, the Franco-Prussian war had put a serious strain on organized labor in Berlin. Nationalist euphoria, coupled with substantial conscription rates, had thinned out the ranks of organized labor and decreased the appeal of social-democratic agitation.[494] Yet with the war won and working-class veterans back home, the *Gründerzeit* years of 1871 and 1872 brought not only enormous economic growth, but also a wave of labor resistance against long hours of work. Given the quickly rising demand for private and administrative housing in the capital of the nascent empire, it was not surprising that here, too, the construction workers spearheaded the revival of trade unionism.[495] Already in the summer of 1868, local carpenters had launched the *Verein der Zimmerleute* (Carpenters' Association), which later that year joined the Lassallean *Arbeiterschaftsverband*, the umbrella organization of trade unions dominated by the generally union-hostile ADAV. In so doing, the Berlin-based Carpenters' Association contributed to not only the expansion of the ADAV in the capital, but also the centralization of their trade, which culminated in the formation of the *Allgemeiner Deutscher Zimmererverein* (General German Carpenters' Association).[496] In addition, the carpenters became a role model for other trades. In particular, they had a decisive impact on the formation of the *Allgemeiner Deutscher Maurerverein* (General German Bricklayers' Association), which was established in Berlin in January 1869. Neither the war nor the incoherent trade-union policy of the locally dominant ADAV could break the organizational ties of Berlin's carpenters and bricklayers. As in

493 "A City in the Shadow: The Gasmen's Strike Begun," *New York Tribune*, 7 April 1873, 4; "The Gas Companies' Workmen: Preparations for a Strike Cause of the Trouble," *The New York Times*, 25 March 1873, 8; "Collapse of the Gas-Workers' Strike," *The New York Times*, 18 April 1873, 4.

494 Renzsch, "Einleitung," xiv.

495 The following draws primarily on Renzsch, who has provided one of the richest studies of organized labor in Berlin during the early 1870s. Renzsch suggests that until 1878, construction workers probably had the most successful social-democratic trade unions in Berlin; see Renzsch, *Handwerker und Lohnarbeiter*, 68. For an overview of the bricklayers' movement of Berlin between 1869 and 1878, see Paeplow, *Zur Geschichte der deutschen Bauarbeiterbewegung*, 238–298.

496 Renzsch, *Handwerker und Lohnarbeiter*, 50–51.

New York City, it was the latter who first entered the struggle for shorter hours in the aftermath of the Franco-Prussian War. In mid-June 1871, several thousand bricklayers attended an impressive mass meeting that resolved that from now on they would work no more than ten hours. Since Berlin's employers in the building sector, who had recently launched the so-called *Baubude* as a local organization representing their interests, rejected the bricklayers' demand, the latter decided to walk out.[497] In the pages of their official organ, the *Neuer Social-Demokrat*, the striking bricklayers pointed out that in the past, strikes had usually been the result of struggles about wages or against repressive factory statues. But as Paul Grottkau, the new president of the General Bricklayers' Association, emphasized in a letter to its members, the struggle for shorter hours now for the first time even preceded the wage question itself.[498] The *Neuer Social-Demokrat* thus urged its readers to do what they could to support the bricklayers' struggle and help prevent the migration of bricklayers to Berlin.[499] Over the coming weeks, more and more employers signed the agreement that fixed ten hours as the absolute length of a normal workday. In order to increase the pressure on those employers who had not accepted their demand (as well as on those who had accepted it but showed little commitment in enforcing it), Berlin's bricklayers announced a general walkout on all masters. That the city's bricklayers were able to sustain a prolonged strike was credited to the solidarity and support of the local carpenters, painters, and other organized workers who collected funds for their striking comrades.[500] Even workers as far away as Bel-

497 The exact number of bricklayers on strike is uncertain. While the *Neuer Social-Demokrat* claimed that 8,000 bricklayers had walked out, Machtan suggests that it had been no more than 3,500; see "Verbands-Theil: Allgemeiner Deutscher Maurer-Verein. Berlin," *Neuer Social-Demokrat*, 16 July 1871, 3; "Aufruf an die Maurer sowie sämtliche Arbeiter Deutschlands," *Neuer Social-Demokrat*, 28 July 1871, 4; Machtan, *Streiks und Aussperrungen*, 80. Though they lagged somewhat behind, it was the organized joiners of Berlin who gave a crucial impulse for the foundation of the national *Allgemeiner Tischler und Schreiner-Verein* in October 1872; see lm., "Lokales (Die Tischlergesellen)," *Demokratische Zeitung*, 24 September 1872, 3; w., "Lokales (Tischler-Kongreß, Dienstag, Dritter Tag)," *Demokratische Zeitung*, 9 October 1872, 2–3.

498 Paeplow, *Zur Geschichte der deutschen Bauarbeiterbewegung*, 244–245.

499 "Verbands-Theil (Für den Allg. Deutsch. Arbeiter-Unterstützungsverband): Berlin," *Neuer Social-Demokrat*, 19 July 1871, 3.

500 "Verbands-Theil (Für den Allg. Deutsch. Arbeiter-Unterstützungsverband): Berlin," *Neuer Social-Demokrat*, 21 July 1871, 3; "Verbands-Theil (Für den Allg. Deutsch. Arbeiter-Unterstützungsverband): Berlin (Der Strike)," *Neuer Social-Demokrat*, 30 July 1871, 3.

gium and England organized support committees on behalf of the striking bricklayers and sent donations to Berlin.[501]

As the local building masters soon learned, the shorter-hour strike proved highly contagious. At a large convention in August 1871, Berlin's joiners (*Tischler*) resolved that they would no longer work for employers who resisted their demand for a cut from twelve to nine and a half hours.[502] In response to the masters' dismissal, several thousand joiners followed the bricklayers and declared that they would boycott every employer who did not agree to their demand.[503] By August 1871, two of the most populous trades in construction were on a shorter-hour strike that threatened to paralyze Berlin's booming building sector. About 200 employers quickly agreed to the joiners' demand. Roughly nine weeks after the start of the strike and following the exodus of more than 2,000 mostly young joiners, most of the joiners who had remained in Berlin worked shorter hours.[504] By that time, the bricklayers had already declared that their strike had ended successfully after six weeks of struggle. The impressive number of roughly three thousand bricklayers had left Berlin in the course of the strike, and the vast majority of the remaining bricklayers had won the ten-hour workday together with a wage increase.[505] Next came the organized carpenters of Berlin, who, having supported the striking bricklayers and joiners for months, now themselves engaged in shorter-hour struggles in the autumn of 1871.[506] For

---

501 Lange, *Berlin zur Zeit Bebels*, 160.

502 "Verbands-Theil (Für den Allg. Deutsch. Arbeiter-Unterstützungsverband): Berlin (Tischlerversammlung)," *Neuer Social-Demokrat*, 30 July 1871, 3. It is not always clear whether this included the construction carpenters (Bautischler). While the *Neuer Social-Demokrat* spoke of the joiners (*Tischler*) only, Renzsch and Bernstein refer to the construction carpenters (*Bautischler*) instead; see Bernstein, *Die Geschichte der Berliner Arbeiterbewegung*, 232–234; Renzsch, *Handwerker und Lohnarbeiter*, 58.

503 Machtan, *Streiks und Aussperrungen*, 95; "Aufruf an die Tischler sowie sämtliche Arbeiter Deutschlands," *Neuer Social-Demokrat*, 23 August 1871, 3; "Verbands-Theil (Für den Allg. Deutsch. Arbeiter-Unterstützungs-Verband): Berlin (Strike der Tischler)," *Neuer Social-Demokrat*, 23 August 1871, 3.

504 Cf. Machtan, *Streiks und Aussperrungen*, 95. See also "Verbands-Theil (Für den Allg. Deutsch. Arbeiter-Unterstützungsverband): Der Strike der Tischler Berlins," *Neuer Social-Demokrat*, 25 August 1871, 3.

505 Machtan, *Streiks und Aussperrungen*, 83–84; "Verbands-Theil (Für den Allg. Deutsch. Arbeiter-Unterstützungsverband): Allgemeiner Deutscher Maurer-Verein," *Neuer Social-Demokrat*, 30 August 1871, 3–4; "Verbands-Theil (Für den Allg. Deutsch. Arbeiter-Unterstützungsverband): Berlin (Siegreiches Ende des Strikes)," *Neuer Social-Demokrat*, 30 August 1871, 4; Renzsch, *Handwerker und Lohnarbeiter*, 55–56.

506 Bringmann, *Geschichte der deutschen Zimmerer-Bewegung*, vol. 2, 58.

months, the local carpenters bargained with their masters. With no solution in sight, negotiations turned into open conflict in the spring of 1872. Local masters and construction companies locked out Berlin's carpenters who refused to work for more than ten hours. Given the building boom of the *Gründerzeit*, most employers were unable to uphold the lock-out for long.[507] By summer 1872, the majority of Berlin's organized construction workers had successfully enforced a general reduction of their workdays, accompanied by a modest rise in wages.[508]

Stating the reasons that in their eyes justified the strike for a shorter workday, Berlin's bricklayers declared that it was an established fact in economics that the wage was dependent on supply and demand. As long as the wage system lasted—as it seemed it would for some time—workers had to face the unbreakable law of supply and demand. Rather than fighting it, trade unions had to control it.[509] The bricklayers' analysis resonated with other construction workers. On July 32, 1871, the local carpenter Otto Kapell, an active member of the carpenters' association and the brother of later Reichstag deputy August, addressed a large shorter-hour rally at the *Alcazar*, one of Berlin's prominent working-class venues. According to Kapell, the first speaker to address the convention, labor was indeed a commodity. As such, it was subject to the laws of supply and demand. The normal working day would result in a falling supply of labor, which would automatically increase the price that employers were forced to pay. Rather than rejecting the commodification of labor, Kapell accepted the inherent market logic and tried to use it to the advantage of sellers.[510] Though unwanted, support came from the emerging *Kathedersozialisten*. Lujo Brentano, for instance, proposed that a shorter workday would clearly yield more rested and, therefore, more productive workers. Put differently, Brentano and his fellows likewise insisted that the normal workday would boost productivity.[511] As in New York, striking construction workers in Berlin openly accepted the categories of a market-mediated exchange for labor. And, again similarly to construction workers on the other side of the Atlantic, they implicitly promoted the notion that shorter hours would allow a more efficient utilization of their labor

507 Renzsch, *Handwerker und Lohnarbeiter*, 58–61.

508 Rößler, "Zur Lage der Berliner Arbeiter," 205–206.

509 "Aufruf an die Maurer sowie sämtliche Arbeiter Deutschlands," *Neuer Social-Demokrat*, 28 July 1871, 4.

510 "Vereins-Theil (Für den Allg. Deutsch. Arb.-Verein)," *Neuer Social-Demokrat*, 26 July 1871, 3.

511 Wolff, *Der 8-Stunden-Tag*, 16–18.

power. When Berlin's joiners resolved in early 1873 to put all their energies into enforcing the eight-hour day, they did so by demanding an end to breakfast and afternoon tea breaks. For decades, workers had struggled against employers' attacks on breaks and the resulting intensification of work. Here, now, we have a local union of construction workers that openly demanded the abolition of breaks in exchange for a more efficient utilization of labor power—that is, four hours in the morning and four hours in the afternoon.[512] When the masters dismissed the resolution, the local joiners replied that they would adhere firmly to the eight-hour demand since, as they put it, "under current social conditions, every worker has both the right and the obligation to sell his labor power as expensively as possible."[513] Berlin's varnisher helpers (*Lackierergehilfen*) agreed. They too informed their employers that they wished to shorten their workday "through the discontinuation of all breakfast, lunch, and supper breaks."[514] The varnishers' demand indicates that construction workers not only accepted time-oriented work, but also tried to use this new time rationality in order to control the length of their workday.[515] These workers understood that their trades no longer answered to the bygone rhythm of artisanal production. At least among some employers, this new time consciousness fell on sympathetic ears. Berlin's association of master joiners (*Tischlermeister*), for instance, explained in the early 1870s that they did not oppose the shorter-hour demand per se, as long as it was introduced generally.[516] A more intensive (and less extensive) exploitation of labor power promised an overall increase in productivity and, eventually, in surplus value. Large employers in the metal industry, like Borsig and Schwartzkopff, likewise understood that a shorter workday would not necessarily harm their interests. As a commission of prominent machine-building employers declared that same year, metal manufacturers did not see

512 f., "Lokales (Eine äußerst zahlreich besuchte Tischlerversammlung)," *Demokratische Zeitung*, 30 January 1873, 3.

513 W., "Lokales (Die Tischlergesellen Berlins)," *Demokratische Zeitung*, 13 March 1873, 3. ("[…] unter den heutigen gesellschaftlichen Verhältnissen ein jeder Arbeiter die Pflicht und das Recht hat, seine Arbeitskraft so theuer wie möglich zu verwerthen.")

514 f., "Lokales (Die Lackierergehilfen)," *Demokratische Zeitung*, 2 February 1873, 3. ("[…] mit Wegfall aller Frühstücks-, Mittags- und Vesperzeit.")

515 Renzsch, *Handwerker und Lohnarbeiter*, 56.

516 "Lokales (Die Tischlermeister und Gesellen)," *Demokratische Zeitung*, 25 July 1872, 2.

the ten-hour demand of their workers as a threat to productivity and growth.[517]

Inspired by the initial successes of Berlin's organized construction workers, hardly a week passed without a local union declaring that it was following suit. In October and November of 1871 alone, Berlin's typesetters and shoe, box, basket, and watch makers all joined the strike movement for shorter hours, followed by the local purse makers and upholsterers at the beginning of the next year.[518] When the latter convened in Berlin in the summer of 1872 for the first German Upholsterers' Congress, delegate Neubauer stressed that a legislative introduction of shorter hours would "increase the demand for labor, which would result in higher wages."[519] Organized skilled workers like Neubauer clearly accepted the logic that a restriction in the supply of the commodity they offered would necessarily lead to higher wages—not because shorter hours would improve working-class habits, as Steward and von Schweitzer suggested, but simply because it would curtail the supply of labor. In their eyes, it was the market rather than the level of consumption that determined their income. Equipped with new confidence, the building trades grew ever more daring. In March and July 1872, many of the city's local paper hangers (*Tapezierer*), upholsterers (*Sattler*), and plasterers (*Verputzer*) were able to enforce the introduction of a nine-hour normal workday.[520] Over the course of spring 1873, various trades outside the building sector were likewise able to enforce a nine-hour workday until, in May, the local construction carpenters (*Bautischler*) and several groups of joiners won the first eight-hour day in the history of Berlin.[521] Belying the warnings of their opponents, they crowned their success with wage raises between 25 and 33.3 percent.[522]

517 "Lokales (Der Berliner Maschinenbauarbeiter-Verein)," *Demokratische Zeitung*, 16 July 1872, 3.

518 Machtan, *Streiks und Aussperrungen*, 99, 117, 121, 141, 147.

519 "Lokales (Der erste Deutsche Sattler-Kongreß)," *Demokratische Zeitung*, 3 July 1872, Supplement, 5. ("[…] erhöhe sich die Nachfrage nach Arbeitskräften, wodurch der Lohn steige.")

520 Machtan, *Streiks und Aussperrungen*, 159, 227; "Lokales (Sattler-Verein)," *Demokratische Zeitung*, 9 March 1872, 3; "Lokales (Sämtliche Arbeitgeber der Tapezierer Berlins)," *Demokratische Zeitung*, 1 March 1872, 3; "Lokales (Zum Strike der Sattler)," *Demokratische Zeitung*, 21 March 1872, 3.

521 Machtan, *Streiks und Aussperrungen*, 320–321.

522 Bernstein, *Die Geschichte der Berliner Arbeiterbewegung*, 268; Rößler, "Zur Lage der Berliner Arbeiter," 208.

Heightened activity among organized workers in Berlin at the same time fueled the desire for greater centralization. Following the initiative by Paul Grottkau, the *Verein der Akkordträger und Bauarbeiter* (Association of Piece-work Porters and Construction Workers) took a first step by bringing together all branches of the local building trades. At the same time, delegates from 17 trade unions and representatives of the two competing social-democratic currents convened and announced that they would join their forces in a city-wide association.[523] On November 19 and 20, 1871, 139 delegates representing almost 14,000 local workers from 23 different trades launched the *Berliner Arbeiterbund*.[524] Though members of the local ADAV branch and the building trades (except the bricklayers, who remained independent from the *Arbeiterbund*) were overrepresented, this city central epitomized the desire for closer co-operation. Despite often violent intra-socialist clashes at local venues and the editorial war that was being waged at the time, the minutes of the founding congress reveal that a fair minority of Eisenachers sat side by side with their Lassallean rivals.[525] In the official declaration of the *Arbeiterbund*, the introduction of a nine-hour normal work-day for all workers in Berlin appeared as the association's first demand, even before the enforcement of higher wages.[526] Whereas Berlin's crafts and trades had fought earlier workday struggles in a largely isolated manner, the *Arbeiterbund* marked the first citywide movement for the universal shortage of daily hours—and it radicalized the struggle by demanding nine hours rather than ten. Similar to the Workingmen's Union and the *Arbeiter-Union* of New York City, Berlin now possessed a powerful umbrella association of various trade unions that were united in their determination to enforce a normal workday.

Yet while workers in Berlin were able to obtain their gains through the winter, for the time being they proved as unable as their comrades in New York to enforce a permanent reduction of hours in any of the urban trades. Lacking enforceable legislation and facing a phalanx of determined bosses and a hostile press, workers in both cities discovered that seasonal booms facilitated the enforcement of shorter hours, but slack seasons regularly allowed employers to force them back on longer shifts. This trend intensified

---

523 "Verbands-Theil: Berlin (Der erste Schritt zur Einigung)," *Neuer Social-Demokrat*, 8 October 1871, 3; "Verbands-Theil: Berlin (Gründung eines Vereins der Akkordträger und Bauarbeiter)," *Neuer Social-Demokrat*, 8 October 1871, 3; "Lokales: Ein Verein der Akkordträger und Bauarbeiter," *Demokratische Zeitung*, 10 October 1871, 5.

524 "Lokales," *Demokratische Zeitung*, 21 November 1871, 5.

525 "Der Berliner Arbeiterbund," *Neuer Social-Demokrat*, 22 November 1871, 3.

526 "Berliner Arbeiterbund," *Neuer Social-Demokrat*, 24 November 1871, 3.

dramatically when the first signs of what would become the worst economic crisis of the century hit the urban economies of Berlin and New York. Beginning in mid-May 1873, the working-class papers of Berlin kept a watchful eye on the stock-market crash in Vienna. Social democrats were especially fearful that the crisis in Austria would spread to the German Empire. As early as June, 1873, August Kapell, who belonged to the paid staff of the *Arbeiterbund*, argued that Berlin's building sector was facing a severe economic crisis. According to the later Member of Parliament, the construction masters of Berlin were already rejoicing over that fact that

> due to the widespread idleness of bricklayers and carpenters, there now exists an oversupply of labor power based on which the wage masters will reduce the wage and increase working time.[527]

The social-democratic press of Berlin urged workers to prevent this. Hasselmann loudly demanded that "by all means the normal workday has to be defended."[528] Therewith the course for the coming months was set. From now on, organized labor in Berlin was waging a defensive battle.[529] Less than a week after Hasselmann's postulation, the *Neuer Social-Demokrat* was already referring to a "*Berliner Krise*" that resulted in several spectacular business crashes in the city.[530] In issue after issue, the local carpenters, bricklayers, and joiners published warnings about employers in Berlin who demanded a return to the longer workday. Many of the strikes that had been underway when the crisis hit Berlin were lost. The causal relationship between the beginning of the crisis and the inability to win hour demands was so obvious that a worker named Bruno Scholz simply declared that the recent hour strike by Berlin's weavers was lost because "the crisis began before the strike had ended."[531]

---

527 August Kapell, "Verbands-Theil: Berlin (Krise)," *Neuer Social-Demokrat*, 15 June 1873, 3. ("[…] daß nun durch die Brodlosigkeit der Maurer- und Zimmererleute ein übermäßiges Angebot von Arbeitskräften entstehen würde, in Folge dessen dann die Herren den Lohn heruntersetzen und die Arbeitszeit verlängern könnten.")

528 H.[asselmann], "Die Arbeiter und die Geschäftsstockung," *Neuer Social-Demokrat*, 20 July 1873, 1. ("Daher muß unter allen Umständen der Normalarbeitstag festgehalten werden.")

529 From the autumn of 1873 onwards, strikes in Berlin were almost exclusively directed against employers who tried to re-enforce longer shifts and lower wages; see Machtan, *Streiks und Aussperrungen*, 368–369, 371, 374, 376.

530 "Die Berliner Krise," *Neuer Social-Demokrat*, 25 July 1873, 2.

531 Bruno Scholz, "Verbands-Theil: Berlin (Ende des Strikes der Weber)," *Neuer Social-Demokrat*, 13 August 1873, 4.

The crisis spread from Vienna and Berlin to other European cities before crossing the Atlantic in the form of bank failures, credit crunches, and a spectacular decline of interest in US railroad bonds. The depression hit New York City on September 18, 1873, where it quickly expanded from Wall Street to the urban real-estate market. The rapid devaluation of land and property values virtually brought construction to a halt in New York. As a consequence, many local construction workers filled the ranks of the unemployed, soon followed by other trades that experienced a cataclysmic economic downturn.[532] But organized workers did not stand idly by. Towards the end of 1873, New York City witnessed one of the largest workers' conventions in months. Thousands occupied the great hall of Cooper Institute, and many more filled the surrounding streets. Faced with massive unemployment, New York's working classes demanded not only immediate help from city authorities, but also a rigorous observance of the eight-hour law. In their eyes, the current practice of stretching the workday only deepened the crisis for workers.[533] The rise in unemployment dramatically underscored the notion that it was especially important to distribute work among more men when demand for labor was low. The enforcement of eight-hour workdays was thus seen as a crucial step in fighting joblessness.[534] According to the carpenters of New York City, it was thus "a crime against labor and mankind if, given the current crisis, workers still put in more than ten hours [...]."[535] Speaking on behalf of the Central Committee of the Trade Union of Furniture Workers, Carl Speyer reasoned that the current crisis that cap-

532 Barreyre, "The Politics of Economic Crisis;" Burrows and Wallace, *Gotham*, 1020–1025; Glasner, "Crisis of 1873."

533 "Die Arbeiterbewegung," *Arbeiter-Zeitung*, 20 December 1873, 2.

534 As Yellowitz stresses, the argument that shorter hours would remedy the oversupply of labor and divide work more evenly among workers contradicted the argument that shorter hours would increase productivity. A rise in productivity meant that less work time was needed to produce as much as or more than under longer shifts. The idea that shorter hours would remedy unemployment was therefore implicitly based on the notion that no increase in productivity would occur. However, this contradiction was virtually absent from contemporary working-class analysis. See Yellowitz, "Eight Hours and the Bricklayers' Strike," 80–82.

535 "Vereins-Angelegenheiten," *Arbeiter-Zeitung*, 9 August 1873, 4. ("[...] daß es ein Verbrechen an der Gesammt-Arbeiterklasse und jeder Menschlichkeit zuwider ist, wenn Arbeiter bei gegenwärtiger Geschäftslosigkeit noch mehr den 10 Stunden arbeiten [...].") The same notion also informed the slogan that Manhattan-raised Samuel Gompers later carved into stone. Said Gompers, "so long as there is one who seeks employment and cannot find it, the hours of labor are too long." Cited in Roediger, *The Movement for a Shorter Working Day*, 7.

italist speculation had imposed on labor testified to the tremendous significance of the eight-hour struggle. This demand, Speyer heralded from New York to all locals of the union, had to precede all other demands.[536] The organized cigar makers did not need to be told twice. In their official organ, they rallied behind the programmatic call that "Shorter Hours would furnish Employment for All."[537] Thus, in addition to the economic argument that shorter hours would increase productivity and wages, workers in Berlin and New York City also argued that it would distribute employment more evenly. This view rested on the notion that the supply of labor needed to be especially restricted in times of shrinking demand. In no way, however, did it challenge the law of supply and demand itself. Analyzing the impact of the crisis, New York's *Labor Standard* thus concluded that a "normal workday of even eight hours would go far to give employment to all and to render the now unemployed able to produce their own livelihood."[538] The idea that shorter hours would end the unemployment crisis was closely linked to hopes for increasing consumer demand. The *Arbeiter-Zeitung* of New York argued in 1873 that

> our sluggish present-day economy should convince any opponent of organized labor that the latter had been right when it demanded the shorter workday. If there were demand for goods or, more precisely, if there was not such an oversupply of commodities on the market, then manufacturers would employ their workers and the latter would be able to demand these products as purchasers.[539]

New York's prominent cigar maker and trade unionist Adolph Strasser merged this idea with the hope for increased employment discussed above. In the pages of the *Cigar Makers' Official Journal*, he argued that if employers hold in stock more goods than they can sell,

536 "Vereins-Angelegenheiten," *Arbeiter-Zeitung*, 8 November 1873, 4.

537 "Shorter Hours Would Furnish Employment for All," *Cigar Makers' Official Journal*, January 1877, 1.

538 "The Normal Workday," *Labor Standard*, 3 February 1877, 2.

539 "An die Leser!" *Arbeiter-Zeitung*, 15 February 1873, 1. ("[...] unsere jetzige geschäftslose Zeit liefert den Gegnern der Arbeitersache den Beweis, daß die Arbeiter Recht hatten, wenn sie den Arbeitstag verkürzt haben wollten. Wenn Nachfrage nach Waaren vorhanden wäre oder besser nicht zu viele Waaren auf dem Markte wären, würden doch die Fabrikanten ihre Arbeiter beschäftigen und dann wären die Arbeiter im Stande, als große Mehrzahl der Käufer auch kaufen zu können.")

> then let us curtail production by the introduction and rigorous enforcement of the eight hour law. It is most absurd to tolerate that while a portion of the trade is working 10, 12, 16, and 18 hours per day, the others are tramping over the country in search of employment.[540]

The proto-Keynesian nexus of shorter hours and aggregate demand was also an important element in Steward's analysis.[541] Yet the approaches by Strasser and Steward also differed in at least one respect. Steward had argued that working-class demand would rise as a result of the refined lifestyles that workers were adopting thanks to an increase in leisure time. Steward therewith ascribed a very active role in the struggle to organized labor. Despite the business-friendly twist that his "wayward disciple" George Gunton later added to his approach, Steward was not, as Roediger emphasizes, genuinely interested in increasing aggregate demand as a stabilizing factor in production, but in promoting class consciousness and "decreas[ing] the rate of exploitation."[542] Strasser, in contrast, argued that overproduction was the result of underconsumption, which could easily be remedied if the oversupply of labor were reduced by introducing shorter hours. Rather than hoping for a working class that actively enforced better compensation, Strasser assumed that consumer demand would automatically increase once the shorter workday had boosted overall employment. His was a demand to better regulate the market for labor, not to abolish it.

5.3. Chapter Conclusion

Whether in nineteenth-century Berlin or New York, socialist thinkers and labor reformers agreed that the level of wages was determined by the respective habits of workers. In their eyes, the shorter workday was the best means through which to cultivate working-class habits and, therewith, increase wages. Timothy Messer-Kruse stresses convincingly that this idea opened the door wide to racist interpretations. It was no coincidence that Ira Steward, for instance, struggled for shorter hours while fighting the influx of Chinese workers. Often foaming with rage, Steward and other reformers exclaimed that the Chinese were content with a diet of a bowl of rice a day

540 A.[dolph] S.[trasser], "An Explanation," *Cigar Makers' Official Journal*, October 1876, 3.
541 Montgomery, *Beyond Equality*, 257.
542 Roediger, "Ira Steward," 412–414.

and an occasional rat. According to these voices, their Chinese fellows lacked both cultural refinement and a comparable standard of living. In the light of Steward's theory of shorter hours, the supposedly low costs of reproduction of Chinese labor became a serious obstacle to the movement for shorter hours. After all, if Chinese workers lacked a desire for leisure time and consumption, they also lacked an incentive to struggle for better pay and shorter hours, which supposedly undermined the shorter-hour demand of white European and native-born workers, who stylized themselves as exceptional in regards to not only wants and desires, but also courage and defiance.[543] Yet such racist ideas were not limited to the nativist scene of organized labor, nor were they actually endemic to the US. On July 17, 1869, the *Arbeiter-Union* of New York City published an article that had originally appeared in the German *Social-Demokrat*. In this article, the paper from Berlin argued that the importation of Chinese labor had ruined wages and prolonged the workday for white Europeans in the US. As if the latter enjoyed a birth right of migration while the former clearly did not, the *Social-Demokrat* characterized Chinese workers as a threat to the well-being of all class-conscious white workers. After all, the paper stated, the modest Chinese worker happily survived on what was a starvation wage for civilized Europeans.[544] As long as there were workers who accepted the excessively long workdays that followed from unregulated markets, labor would not be free. Organized labor on both sides of the Atlantic in fact agreed that there were "Enough Chinamen Already" in the US.[545]

Yet the analysis of the economic rationale not only reveals a disturbingly racist undertone in American and German working-class discourse, it also testifies to a striking shift away from the pattern established in the previous chapters. While socialist intellectuals and labor reformers argued that wages depended on the respective habits and desires of the working classes, many of the organized construction workers we have met in this chapter interpreted the actual level of wages as the mathematical result of supply and demand. Resistance against commodification thus mattered little in local trade-union discourse. Struggling for shorter hours as a means through which to increase wages, productivity, and employment, Berlin's and New York's trade-union movements found no inspiration from arguments for de-com-

543 Messer-Kruse, "Eight Hours, Greenbacks and 'Chinamen,'" 147–148.

544 "Das eherne Lohngesetz: Aus dem Berliner 'Social-Demokrat,'" *Die Arbeiter-Union*, 17 July 1869, 4.

545 "Schon Chinesen genug," *Die Arbeiter-Union*, 23 July 1869, 2.

modification. The local construction workers, who represented a leading trade of the urban industry, had largely accepted commodification by the early 1870s. While reformers and socialist thinkers continued to emphasize the political and moral benefits of a shorter workday, organized construction workers increasingly concentrated on the normal workday as a way to improve the bargaining power of labor. These workers in fact used the logic of market exchange to legitimate demands to restrict and control the output of the commodity of labor power.[546]

There were several reasons why the notion of de-commodification increasingly lost its appeal among the skilled construction workers of Berlin in the early 1870s. The latter featured a relatively high degree of unionization at a time when the economic organization of German labor still lagged far behind the political movement of parties and associations.[547] For a short time in the late 1860s and early 1870s, the city's organized construction workers were thus able to launch independent campaigns and enforce their demands while maintaining a relative autonomy from the political arm of the movement. Berlin's construction workers experienced little technical innovation, and machines played a minor role in their trades. In 1875, there were, for instance, fewer than 50 circular saws in the entire city, a fact that clearly shows that the great mass of carpenters and joiners continued to work without mechanical support.[548]

What did change, however, was the internal organization of their trades. By the early 1870s, houses in Berlin were no longer built on order, but for the market. They thus became transformed from objects of utility to havens for speculative capital that promised substantial returns. The resulting pressure of the market accelerated the differentiation of the trade as well as the rationalization of production. Unlike many of the mass trades in which masters and journeymen continued to toil side by side or in which small, contracted masters often suffered as much as their employees from the pressure of large retailers and merchants, Berlin's construction workers were clearly separated from their masters.[549] Over the course of the 1850s and 1860s, masters either sank into the ranks of workers themselves or, trained at one

546 See also Stanley, *From Bondage to Contract*, 81.

547 For the weakness of German trade unionism in the early movement, see Welskopp, *Das Banner der Brüderlichkeit*, 255–290.

548 Bezirksleitung (ed.), *Geschichte der revolutionären Berliner Arbeiterbewegung*, 176.

549 This distinction has also been observed in other cities. See, for instance, Lenger's study of changing work realities in mid-nineteenth-century Düsseldorf; Lenger, *Zwischen Kleinbürgertum und Proletariat*, 36–64.

of the new *Baugewerkschulen* (construction colleges), they developed into building contractors or architects.[550] As a consequence, fewer and fewer construction masters performed manual labor themselves. Instead, they increasingly focused on planning and supervision.[551] Construction companies also grew considerably in size, employing an ever greater number of individual workers.[552] This development not only reinforced class barriers, but also resulted in turning the city's construction workers into one of the first group of wage workers to use their new socio-economic position as a weapon in industrial conflict.[553]

The situation was no different in New York. During the mass strikes that the city's building trades staged in the late 1860s and early 1870s, urban construction workers regularly addressed their employers as "so-called masters." What seems rather trivial at first in fact testifies to a major industrial transformation that had already begun to revolutionize work relations in American cities in the first third of the nineteenth century.[554] By the 1860s, urban construction workers no longer recognized their masters as part of a community of producers. They knew that the advancement from journeyman to master, once a regular feature of the skilled crafts, was blocked for them. Clearly separated from their former masters, these workers had largely adapted to the fact that working conditions were determined by the market.[555] Like their comrades in Berlin, New York's construction workers were heavily unionized in organizations that featured a strong degree of autonomy; they possessed resources to sustain mass strikes; they were embedded in local and national networks of intra- and inter-trade solidarity and support; and they understood very well that in economic boom times, such as the construction spree that began in the late 1860s, their bosses suffered greatly if they decided to withhold labor power. Even more so than in Berlin, New York's building sector was dominated by large companies and con-

550 Wiedfeldt, *Statistische Studien zur Entwicklungsgeschichte der Berliner Industrie*, 278–284.

551 Renzsch, *Handwerker und Lohnarbeiter*, 19.

552 Although Rößler is right to stress that Berlin's machine-building companies were larger than the city's construction companies, the latter were nevertheless much larger than construction companies in the rest of the country; see Rößler, "Zur Lage der Berliner Arbeiter," 106; Renzsch, *Handwerker und Lohnarbeiter*, 46–47. Bringmann provides a detailed overview of the changes in carpentry, see Bringmann, *Geschichte der deutschen Zimmerer-Bewegung*, vol. 1, 94–127.

553 Welskopp, *Das Banner der Brüderlichkeit*, 284–285.

554 Laurie, *Artisans into Workers*, 15–46.

555 For the experience of American carpenters, see Brody, *In Labor's Cause*, 29–35.

tractors that often employed huge numbers of workers. Well-organized mass strikes therefore put enormous pressure on New York's contractors, which feared defaulting on existing projects.[556] In Berlin, fear of contract penalties made smaller construction businesses in particular likely to accept demands, which gave Berlin's construction workers a relatively strong bargaining position. This was, as Renzsch stresses, the reason that architects and building contractors were hit so hard by the shorter-hour strikes of the early 1870s.[557]

In sum, it was the interplay of collectively shared experiences of permanent wage labor, a comparatively strong degree of unionization, a relative (yet, in Berlin, short-lived) autonomy of local unions, a prolonged economic boom in the respective industrial sector, and the ability to put pressure on masters who feared default and contract penalties which made the notion of de-commodification unattractive for urban construction workers in their struggles for shorter hours. Berlin and New York's bricklayers, joiners, and carpenters had reason to hope that the rational utilization of their labor power would entail the prospect of better socio-economic participation. Such expectations indeed made it easier to accept the profound transformation of everyday work. As a consequence, these workers formulated demands with explicit reference to the parameters of the market, thereby adapting to the emerging economy of time.[558] Unlike the English case E. P. Thompson describes, in the metropolitan economies of nineteenth-century Berlin and New York, it was the little mechanized building trades that first developed a new time consciousness.[559] Indeed, mechanized factory labor in these cities was a *laggard* in this respect.[560] Accepting that their labor power was bought and sold for particular intervals of time, urban construction workers struggled to limit the legal maximum of these intervals by appealing to a strictly economistic rationale. Ideas about self-employment or producerist notions of independence resonated less and less with workers who were embedded in a heavily synchronized and closely coordinated production process. As a consequence, resistance to the commodification of labor quickly retreated in these trades. Organized construction workers thus an-

556 For an overview of New York's building sector, see Burrows and Wallace, *Gotham*, 929–931. For the transformation of bricklaying as a leading trade in the building sector, see Bates, *Bricklayers' Century of Craftsmanship*, 5–9.

557 Renzsch, *Handwerker und Lohnarbeiter*, 61.

558 Ibid., 19–20.

559 Roediger stresses that in the US, this transformation had already begun in the second quarter of the century; see Roediger, *The Movement for a Shorter Working Day*, 19–20.

560 Brody, *In Labor's Cause*, 33.

ticipated a development that other trades soon caught up with. In 1878, the official organ of the social-democratic trade-union movement in Germany, the *Pionier*, stated that it did not oppose the commodification of labor in general. Rather, the paper argued that negotiations about the conditions under which labor would sell its power needed to be collectivized and standardized. Workers, in other words, had to be given a say in the buying and selling of labor power.[561] The paper's position on wage labor epitomizes a general shift that was characteristic of trade-unionist thought towards the end of the decade, and indeed well beyond. The time when the phenomenon of commodification was met with angry rejection was coming to an end. Increasingly, workers in cities like Berlin and New York accepted that a particular socio-economic entity—a publicly owned corporation or a centrally administered productive association, for instance—might buy their labor power as long as, on the one hand, the market for the labor they offered was embedded in a system of social protection and, on the other, they benefited from the surplus value they produced. The more the division of labor, the separation of master and worker, and, thus, the proletarianization of an urban industrial workforce progressed, the less the notion of commodification was met with resistance. In E.P. Thompson's famous words, organized labor in Berlin and New York was learning to "fight back with the categories introduced by its employers."[562] The struggle against commodification that had been linked to an idealized nexus of self-employment, political freedom, and social cohesion gradually passed into history.

Yet the early to mid-1870s witnessed more than a retreat of the concept of commodification. As the Long Depression deepened, the shorter-hour movement slowly made room for other objectives. Despite the conviction that shorter hours would remedy joblessness, demands like unemployment benefits, rent caps, and public-works programs increasingly pushed the shorter-hour struggle to the back stage of working-class conflict. The pages of *The New York Times* illustrate this shift vividly. Following a virtual absence of shorter-hour coverage during the Civil War, reports on eight-hour activity surged in the immediate postwar years. This development climaxed in 1872. The following year already witnessed a sharp decline until, in 1875, *The New York Times* published two articles covering eight-hour questions—*in the entire year*. On a single day in May, 1872, the same paper had published three times

561 "Die beste Form des Lohnverhältnisses," *Pionier*, 10 May 1878, 1.

562 Thompson, "Time, Work-Discipline, and Industrial Capitalism," 86.

as many articles on the various local trades on eight-hour strike.[563] In contrast to what Roediger suggests for the US as a whole, this indicates that, by the mid-1870s, the eight-hour movement was dead in New York.[564] Whatever was left of the city's crisis-ridden organized-labor scene focused all its energies on the fight against unemployment.

Before concluding this study of mid-nineteenth-century shorter-hour struggles, however, the following chapter draws attention to an aspect omitted so far. As we have seen, shorter-hour activists on both sides of the Atlantic strived for a firm response from state and society to protect workers from the power of the market. Yet, as a considerable segment of the urban workforce soon learned, protection could be a doubled-edged sword. In the summer of 1872, a broad petition campaign requested the first German Reichstag to pass normal workday legislation, a ban on Sunday work, and better protection for young and female workers. In accordance with dominant *laissez-faire* theory, the Committee on Petitions understood the unrestricted selling of labor power to be the precious right of any adult man. When it came to women, however, the committee noted that it was

> self-evident that the health of the female population is of particular importance for healthy progeny and the thriving of the nation. Due to its frail nature, the female body requires greater protection, and society needs to think of her in her capacity as a future mother. [...] Moreover, the married woman has to fulfill a social and moral duty of the deepest significance as the mother of the home. Explicitly for the woman then—*home time, nighttime peace, and Sunday rest!*[565]

563 "The Wheelwrights and Blacksmiths," *The New York Times*, 23 May 1872, 5; "The Show-Case Makers," *The New York Times*, 23 May 1872, 5; "The Cabinet-Makers, Wood-Carvers and Upholsterers," *The New York Times*, 23 May 1872, 5; "The German Painters," *The New York Times*, 23 May 1872, 5; "A New Claim from the Men Employed on the Post-Office Building," *The New York Times*, 23 May 1872, 5; "The Working Men: Additional Particulars about the Strike in this City," *The New York Times*, 23 May 1872, 5.

564 Roediger, *The Movement for a Shorter Working Day*, 7.

565 GStA PK, I. HA Rep. 120 BB VII, 3, Nr. 2, Bd. 1, 1872–1876: "Sechzehnter Bericht der Kommission für Petitionen, Deutscher Reichstag, 1. Legislaturperiode, III Session 1872," 1–15, Record Numbers 18–25. ("Was die Frauen betrifft, so spricht es für sich selbst, wie die gesunde Beschaffenheit der weiblichen Bevölkerung von der größten Wichtigkeit für die gesunde Nachkommenschaft und für das gedeihliche Fortleben des Volkes ist. Der weibliche Körper verlangt seiner zarteren Beschaffenheit wegen größere Schonung, und die Gesellschaft muss in jeder Arbeiterin die zukünftige Mutter sehen [...]. Die verheiratete Frau hat überdies in ihrer Stellung als Hausmutter soziale und moralische Aufgaben von tiefer Bedeutung zu erfüllen. Vornehmlich also der Frau—Feierabend, Nachtruhe, Sonntagsruhe!")

6. Gender: Shorter Hours and the Protection of Female Labor

"Man may enjoy his eight hour law relief, but it will be found still true that 'Women's work is never done.'"[566]
Parker Pillsbury

"[Women's protection] presupposes that the current mode of production ends where female workers are nothing but commodities."[567]
Wilhelm Hasselmann

6.1. Women's Work

As Chapters 3 and 4 of this book have shown, organized male workers in Berlin and New York fought for shorter workdays as a means to promote political rights and correct the moral compass of their respective communities. Workers were thereby united in the belief that, as both individuals and a class, they enjoyed the inalienable right to be protected from the unchecked power of the market. At its heart, the shorter-hour movement was a struggle for freedom and protection waged by autonomous subjects. As this chapter will show, the struggle for the reduction of women's hours, however, drew on a strikingly different rationale. Women were regarded as particularly worthy of protection from the market, yet the justification for female protection varied considerably from protective struggles by and for men. Before analyzing this dissimilarity, the following pages will provide a short overview of female labor in mid-nineteenth-century Berlin and New York.

Generally speaking, women in Germany and the US worked in domestic services, a few professions, farming, as well as manual and unwaged reproductive labor. Often, these forms of work overlapped as employment in services and manufacturing did not free women from their familial duties. During the first half of the century, wage labor had usually been a temporary

566 P.[arker] P.[illsbury], "Largest Store in the World," *The Revolution*, 3 September 1868, 137.

567 "Vereins-Theil: Berlin (Mitgliederversammlung)," *Neuer Social-Democrat*, 11 February 1872, 2. ("[Der Schutz der Frauen] setze voraus, daß die heutige Produktionsweise aufhöre, wo die Arbeiterin eine Waare sei.")

experience for most women in New York City. Young women entered the paid labor force for only a few years, until they married and established families of their own. Once married, women usually left formal employment, only to be introduced to non-waged care work or auxiliary labor in home workshops, an assistance that likewise was not compensated for directly through wages.[568] Thus female wage workers had long been predominantly young and single. Stanley Nadel has shown that as late as the beginning of the second half of the century, 75 to 80 percent of New York's German-born female wage workers were under the age of 30.[569] Yet, as a lengthy article series on "Our Working Classes" that appeared in *The New York Times* in early 1869 indicated, more and more women were unable (or unwilling) to find men to support them. The *Times* estimated that there were no fewer than 75,000 single or widowed women in New York City who relied exclusively on their own labor.[570] At the same time, wage labor also began to increase among young girls and married women. The fact that they either still lived with their families or had established families of their own allowed employers to pay wages far below subsistence. After all, female wage labor was seen merely as an additional contribution to the family wage. Employers also favored female workers with families because their familial duties supposedly made them more submissive workers. As a consequence of these developments, urban female labor increased rapidly over the course of the century. According to the US Census of 1870, there were 78,000 gainfully employed women in New York City (excluding the combined number of 5,000 female teachers, lodge keepers, and traders or sales persons, the only significant groups outside the manual-labor and service sectors).[571] Despite the growth of female labor, women were largely concentrated in three sectors in the dynamic postbellum economy. As David Montgomery puts it, the "kitchen, the great textile mill, and the sweatshop […] were the sponges soaking up the women in the labor force."[572] Since New York City lacked "the great textile mills" that characterized industrial life in New England, it was thus "the kitchen," or domestic service, and "the sweatshop," or the sewing trade, that gave work to the city's women. Together with the more

568 Stott, *Workers in the Metropolis*, 103.

569 Nadel, *Little Germany*, 75.

570 "Our Working Classes," *The New York Times*, 17 March 1869, 12.

571 "Selected Occupations, with Age and Sex, and Nativity."

572 Montgomery, *Beyond Equality*, 35.

than 5,000 laundresses, the roughly 42,000 women working in domestic services comprised the largest group. Female servants were usually young and unmarried since their service was hardly compatible with familial duties. Most of them were girls in their teens and early twenties.[573] Irish immigrants supplied half of all domestic servants in the city, followed by Americans and Germans, who provided an additional third and tenth respectively.[574] In addition to domestic service, about 30,000 women in New York City were employed in manufacturing, most of them as seamstresses, milliners, and dress and mantua makers.[575] As Susan Stansell rightly notes, the actual number of female manual workers was surely much higher. Yet, due to widespread outwork, statistics for the 1860s and 1870s generally underrepresent women in the labor force.[576] Thus, in addition to those officially recorded as employed, there were a vast number of unwaged or fictitiously self-employed women who worked in home production. This was especially true for the needle trade, which absorbed the vast majority of female manual labor.

In New York City, the tailoring trade had changed profoundly during the first half of the century.[577] Prior to the 1820s, tailors had worked almost exclusively in men's clothing, which required fitting and skill. Women's clothing, in contrast, had been the business of wives or domestic servants. The rise of ready-made clothing increasingly blurred this division. Ready-made workshops originated from the production of unfitted rough clothing for soldiers and slaves, usually referred to simply as "slop." Initially, slop workshops gave employment to journeymen in the slack season. As the century

---

573 Daul, *Die Frauen-Arbeit*, 34–35.

574 "Selected Occupations, with Age and Sex, and Nativity." Apparently, the ratio of domestic servants had changed profoundly between 1855 and 1870. Stansell states that three-quarters of all servants had been Irish in 1855, and only four percent had been native-born. The Irish had thus lost considerably to the Americans over the course of fifteen years.

575 "Selected Occupations, with Age and Sex, and Nativity."

576 Stansell, *City of Women*, 108, Footnote 13. Given her criticism of the figures provided for working women, it is surprising that Stansell apparently accepts the data for men employed by manufacturers in New York City; see ibid., 108. The figure of approximately 65,000 men listed in the 1860 census as employed in manufacturing seems far too low; see *Manufactures of the United States in 1860*. Only ten years later, the census of 1870 already lists about 115,000 working men employed in manufacturing alone; see "Selected Occupations, with Age and Sex, and Nativity."

577 The following is based on the very helpful account in Stansell, *City of Women*, 106–115. See also Weatherford, *Foreign and Female*, 112–126.

matured, however, ready-mades were less and less confined to clothing for slaves and soldiers. Traditional bespoke tailoring performed by independent artisans was being pushed back by ready-mades for men and, increasingly, women. The growth of an urban ready-made sector entailed new employment possibilities for women, who were soon regarded as unwelcome competitors by male tailors struggling for independence and control. But, in fact, women competed with men primarily in the outwork sector.[578] Individual tailors and large retailers both gave out work to an army of contracted workers, who performed their work in small shops or at home.[579] These female outworkers usually produced some intermediate product that was then finished in centralized or indoor production. Stansell illustrates the hierarchical complexity of the trade by highlighting that it regularly involved "a jabber or merchant, a master tailor, his inside workers, one or even two levels of subcontractors, and their outworkers."[580] The women who performed the outwork came from very diverse backgrounds. Unmarried daughters living on their own comprised the largest group, followed by daughters who still lived within male-headed families. In addition, there were substantial percentages of early widowed women who headed households of their own and supported children or relatives.[581] In addition to outwork, women also worked together with their children under the supervision of a skilled husband in so-called family workshops. These family or home workshops either produced independently or were contracted workers, often both. Finally, it was especially New York's young and single women who found employment in centralized production facilities outside their homes. Interestingly, these indoor workshops transferred the familial hierarchies of home production to the shop floor. Even though women here worked with unacquainted men,

578 Especially for readers less familiar with Anglo-American terminology, the concepts of indoor and outdoor or outwork might be somewhat confusing. "Outwork" refers to work that was "given out" by retailers or contractors. It was usually performed at home or in decentralized production facilities that were overseen by contractors and middlemen rather than the manufacturers themselves. Just as "outdoor relief" was the umbrella term for the material assistance that was given to poor recipients directly rather than in return for labor in work- or almshouses, outwork was determined by the fact that workers did not go to a particular production facility (a workshop or factory), where they were concentrated with fellow workers. Work in such a production facility was usually categorized as "indoor work," the harbinger of centralized industrial production.

579 Burrows and Wallace, *Gotham*, 742–743; Ernst, *Immigrant Life in New York City*, 17–18.

580 Stansell, *City of Women*, 109. For the spread of sweated labor in general, see Laurie, *Artisans into Workers*, 39–41.

581 Brody, *In Labor's Cause*, 22; Stansell, *City of Women*, 115.

their labor was regarded as the less skilled and, therefore legitimately, worse-paid labor of daughters or wives.[582] On top of this gendered employment discrimination, the sewing women of New York also suffered from the peculiarities that characterized their trade in general. The clothing sector was determined by a bi-annual wave of busy and slack seasons, and during the latter the apparel was sitting in stores, waiting to be bought.[583] Together with the growing dependence on long credit chains, this made the sewing trade highly vulnerable to economic crises. For sewing women in outwork in particular, these factors resulted in intense competition, low and unstable wages, and the alternation between long hours during high season and phases of un- or underemployment during the slack season. This tendency was exacerbated by the proliferation of sewing machines around mid-century, which further depressed the already meager piece-rates, especially for seamstresses in outwork. The latter saw no other remedy than to increase their hours. There are no reliable statistics showing how many hours needlewomen usually worked in New York City during the 1860s and early 1870s. Even a survey on hours and wages by New York's Workingmen's Assembly only provided numbers for men, not for women.[584] Yet by mid-century, the overwork of the city's "sewing woman" had become proverbial as writers and philanthropists regularly expressed concern over the devilishly long hours that urban seamstresses were forced to put in.[585] According to their estimate, it was not uncommon in the 1860s for women to sew between twelve and sixteen, sometimes even eighteen hours a day.[586] For these women, life was nothing but toil. Yet the transformation of their trade not only deteriorated working conditions for women, it also hampered the organization of collective resistance across the divisionary lines of ethnicity, gender, and employment position. Heavily atomized, urban female labor thus encountered serious obstacles in the path to independent trade unionism.

---

582 Stansell, *City of Women*, 116–117.

583 Stott, *Workers in the Metropolis*, 115–120.

584 *Proceedings of the Sixth Annual Session of the Workingmen's Assembly*, 25–26.

585 Stott, *Workers in the Metropolis*, 107. Stansell indicates that the image of the poor and vulnerable "sewing woman" differed markedly from the stereotypical "factory girl." While the former was seen as a burdened victim worthy of protection, the latter was seen as a morally compromised symbol of female self-assertion; see Stansell, *City of Wom-en*, 125–129.

586 Daul, *Die Frauen-Arbeit*, vol. 1, 81. See also Ernst, *Immigrant Life in New York City*, 68; Janiewski, "Making Common Cause," 781. The workday of domestic servants was no less demanding; see Burrows and Wallace, *Gotham*, 744.

On the other side of the Atlantic, female labor also expanded rapidly over the course of the century. The 1875 census returns showed that there were about 150,000 economically active women in the German capital. Here, too, the actual number of working women was surely higher, given the fact that women who assisted their husbands in family workshops were recorded as unproductive dependents.[587] As in New York City, women in Berlin were largely confined to the clothing and domestic-service sectors. More than a third of all working women, or about 59,000, were employed as maids, cooks, personal waiters, or similar occupations in the domestic-service sector. According to Jürgen Kocka, domestic service was changing rapidly across Prussia into a predominantly urban phenomenon as *bourgeois* demand increasingly replaced employment by the aristocracy and church. At the time of the foundation of the German Empire, almost a fifth of all households in Berlin employed domestic servants, most of whom were girls and women.[588] Günter Richter stresses that of the more than 75,000 Berliners who were employed in the personal-service sector in 1875, three-fourths were unmarried women.[589] In Berlin as in New York, female servants encountered serious obstacles in the path of trade unionizing due to their heavy isolation. The group of domestic servants was followed by about 40,000 female Berliners working in clothing and cleaning. The roughly 9,000 common laborers and 17,000 non-specified female workers most likely also belonged to the clothing trades, given that outwork entailed a great deal of irregular labor.[590] As was the case in New York, the actual number of sewing women was probably even higher, since widespread home production was not covered by the survey.[591]

The transformation of Berlin’s sewing trade also bears striking similarities to developments in New York. Already at the beginning of the century, Berlin’s journeymen tailors and so-called “patent masters” had begun

587 Rößler, “Zur Lage der Berliner Arbeiter,” 31–34. See also Schmitt, *Der Arbeiterinnenschutz*, 12; Schmitt, “‘All These Forms of Women’s Work.’”

588 Kocka, *Arbeitsverhältnisse und Arbeiterexistenzen*, 121, 123.

589 Richter, “Zwischen Revolution und Reichsgründung,” 660.

590 Magistrat der Stadt Berlin (ed.), *Bericht über die Gemeinde-Verwaltung der Stadt Berlin*, 55–56. Similarly to New York, the remaining sixth predominantly worked as teachers, nurses, traders, or restaurant keepers.

591 Wiedfeldt, *Statistische Studien zur Entwicklungsgeschichte der Berliner Industrie*, 196.

to work independently from masters.[592] This change resulted in dramatic overstaffing, intense competition, and the expansion of home production, which increasingly included wives and children. While, as we have seen in Chapter 5, urban construction workers had been transformed into permanent wage laborers, other trades in fact witnessed a proliferation of fictitious or real self-employment. Rößler indicates that between 1871 and 1875, the ratio of self-employed to employed workers in Berlin actually increased.[593] This trend was especially salient in the clothing sector. As in New York, the transformation of the sewing trade was fueled by the rise of ready-mades production, which took Berlin by storm thanks to a quickly expanding labor supply. As early as the 1840s, apparel production for domestic—and, beginning in the 1860s, foreign—markets started replacing bespoke tailoring. Often, formerly independent masters became heavily dependent on contractors, who determined everything from the size and number of orders to the quality of the product. Ready-made workshops grew quickly in size, yet even by the mid-1870s workshops in the clothing sector on average employed no more than 20 workers.[594] Rather than indoor work, it was the explosion of outwork that was responsible for the enormous increase in female labor in the clothing sector. This development eventually paved the way for the emergence of the notorious sweatshop or *Schwitz-System* that came to characterize the garment industries in Berlin and New York City in the second half of the nineteenth century.[595] The sector of women's wear was the first to experience the extensive introduction of sweated work. Here, so-called *Zwischenmeister*, or intermediary masters, received orders together with templates and fabrics from large ready-mades stores. If the *Zwischenmeister* did not employ tailors himself, he contracted so-called *Schwitzmeister*, or sweaters, who either organized production in closely monitored workshops (the sweatshops) or subcontracted orders to home producers.[596] Often, the boundary between workshop, sweatshop, and home production was fluid, as workers tended to bring pieces back from work to finish them at home

592 The following discussion draws on Renzsch, *Handwerker und Lohnarbeiter*, 70–80. Patent masters were masters who possessed a trade patent but had neither finished an apprenticeship nor joined a guild; see ibid., 70, Footnote 6.

593 Rößler, "Zur Lage der Berliner Arbeiter," 38. As Rößler stresses, this change also reflects the statisticians' changing understanding of self-employment.

594 Ibid., 106.

595 Renzsch, *Handwerker und Lohnarbeiter*, 70–73.

596 Wiedfeldt, *Statistische Studien zur Entwicklungsgeschichte der Berliner Industrie*, 202–206.

or changed back and forth between workshop and home production.[597] Among contracted women in particular, it was not uncommon to subcontract pieces to other women in the busy months.[598] For the majority of Berlin's seamstresses, rationalization meant not only an increasing division of labor, but also disastrously low wages and workdays that lasted from twelve to 15 hours.[599] Merging indoor work and outwork could easily prolong the workday to 18 hours.[600]

The memoirs of Ottilie Baader, who later became a prominent member of Berlin's social-democratic women's movement, allow a rare insight into the everyday lives of the needlewomen of Berlin. Born during the turbulent times of the democratic revolutions that swept across Europe in the late 1840s, Baader grew up in a working-class family in Frankfurt (Oder). As a young girl, Baader occasionally assisted her mother, a seamstress who died young of tuberculosis. During these early childhood days, she learned the stiches that later supported her as a young woman. Together with her siblings and widowed father, Baader moved to Berlin in the early 1860s. Given the few trades that actually employed women at that time, it was not surprising that, following a very short and uncompensated learning period that substituted for the apprenticeship of young men, Baader became a seamstress herself.[601] Her recollections of the following years, which she spent in a small workshop in what today is the border of Kreuzberg, reads like a quintessential description of the fate of a needlewoman in Berlin during the 1860s:

> In order to earn a little extra, I took home cuffs to back-stitch them at night. [...] How often did poor little me fall asleep while working, how badly did my back hurt! After all, I had already worked twelve hours, from eight to eight, with a short break for lunch.[602]

597 This flexibility has also been observed for the French case; see Boxer, "Protective Legislation and Home Industry," 52.

598 Renzsch, *Handwerker und Lohnarbeiter*, 74–75.

599 Otto-Peters, *Das Recht der Frauen auf Erwerb*, 21.

600 Ibid., 25; Renzsch, *Handwerker und Lohnarbeiter*, 77–79.

601 Such "learning periods" were also common for young seamstresses in New York City; see Stansell, *City of Women*, 118.

602 Baader, *Ein Steiniger Weg*, 8–9. ("Um noch etwas nebenbei zu verdienen, nahm ich abends Manschetten zum Durchsteppen mit nach Hause. [...] Wie oft mögen mir jungem Ding da wohl die Augen zugefallen sein, wie mag mir der Rücken geschmerzt haben! Zwölf Stunden Arbeitszeit hatte man immer schon hinter sich, von morgens acht bis abends acht, mit kurzer Mittagspause.")

Towards the mid-1860s, Baader learned to use the sewing machines that had recently begun transforming the needle trade in Berlin. Consequently, her next job was at a larger factory that employed about a hundred female workers who operated the machines that produced collars and sleeves for ready-made male clothing. As in New York, the sewing machine facilitated the standardized production of different parts of ready-made clothing and thus further boosted female outwork. Like many of her sewing sisters, Baader invested the little money she had, bought her own sewing machine, and joined the ranks of the thousands of contracted seamstress who worked from home. While this freed her from the tight rhythm of the workshop, it also deprived her of the boundaries set by the shopfloor clock. As a consequence, her workday expanded enormously. From the artisanal workshop to the mechanized indoor work of ready-mades to the outwork of contracted labor, Baader had went through virtually all positions that characterized women's manual labor in cities like Berlin and New York in the 1860s and early 1870s. Given the low wages and notoriously long hours, Baader would surely have agreed with *The New York Times* when it concluded that "the needle is the worst instrument with which women can dig their way in the world."[603]

As the foregoing has shown, female labor in Berlin and New York shared important characteristics. In both cities, women were confined to the domestic-service and clothing sectors. The latter featured a broad proliferation of outwork in which women usually worked as contracted laborers on piece rates. Female wage labor was common primarily among servants and seamstresses in indoor production. As a consequence of restricted employment opportunities and hierarchical chains of production, working women were heavily segregated and isolated, a fact that worsened their position in the labor market and their ability to organize collectively in order to enforce demands. The period under consideration thus witnessed little female proletarian organizing. It was not before the 1880s that independent associations of working women (re)emerged in Berlin and New York.[604] Middle-class feminist associations that acted on behalf of working women, however, mushroomed in the 1860s and early 1870s. Given the heavy concentration

603 "Our Working Classes," *The New York Times*, 17 March 1869, 12.

604 Berger, *Die zwanzigjährige Arbeiterrinnen-Bewegung Berlins*; Burrows and Wallace, *Gotham*, 802; Evans, *The Feminists*, 159–160; Losseff-Tillmanns, *Frauenemanzipation und Gewerkschaften*, 66–87; Twellmann, *Die deutsche Frauenbewegung*, 166–172. For social-democratic feminist perspectives towards the closing decades of the nineteenth century, see Schmitt, *Der Arbeiterinnenschutz*, 62–79.

of working women in a few trades, these early associations first and foremost strived to broaden employment opportunities for women. As Virginia Penny stressed in the preface to her widely acclaimed overview of female labor in the US that appeared in 1863, the single most destructive obstacle to female wage labor was the belief that women were not made for competitive labor markets.[605] What Penny and other feminist thus struggled for was the unrestricted opening of the labor market to women, so that "they need not be crowded into one or two employments."[606] One of the earliest war-time efforts to organize working women in New York City was made in late November, 1863, with the foundation of the Working Women's Protective Union. Rather than pushing for labor reform, the association strived to help women find employment in the city and protect them from "fraud and impositions of unscrupulous employers."[607] Backed by the city's reform-friendly circles, the local women's movement tirelessly struggled against any obstacle to free female wage labor. Herein, the *Times* declared, lay the only road to success for the working women of New York. The latter had to reduce their numbers in the couple of trades to which they had hitherto been restricted. Since they could not simply vanish into thin air, they needed to be distributed more evenly among the various urban trades.[608] New York's women soon found further editorial support. On January 8, 1868, the first issue of the feminist weekly *The Revolution* appeared in the city. Edited by the prominent suffragists Susan B. Anthony, Elizabeth Cady Stanton, and Parker Pillsbury, the paper solemnly promised to advocate for the freedom of female labor and defend the interests of working women.[609] Women's rights activists and reformers all across the country in fact saw equal access to the free labor market as a crucial precondition for increasing female wages, and thus also for tackling prostitution.[610]

Across the Atlantic, early feminists looked enviously at New York. In the summer of 1868, *The Revolution* published a letter it had received from Berlin. According to the author, the Prussian women's movement lagged behind its American equivalent due to massive state repression. Prussia not only disenfranchised women, but also outlawed any political participation by women.

---

605 Penny, *The Employments of Women*, iv–xii.

606 "Working Women," *The Revolution*, 1 October 1868, 200.

607 Working Women's Protective Union (ed.), *About the Working Women of New York*, 16.

608 "The Work of Women: A Suggestion for Their Benefit," *The New York Times*, 26 November 1863, 4.

609 "The Revolution Will Advocate," *The Revolution*, 8 January 1868, 1.

610 Stanley, *From Bondage to Contract*, 229–232.

As the infamous Paragraph 8 of the Law of Association determined, women were banned from all organizations and meetings that discussed issues of a political nature. Berlin's police regularly removed women from audiences if they dared to appear at political gatherings—as they did, for instance, in 1868 when the local workers' movement debated the frauds of a wool manufacturer who had wetted the wool he gave out to female workers and later, when the wool had dried and become lighter, claimed that the women had misappropriated raw material.[611] Because of this repression, the author of the letter that appeared in *The Revolution* stressed, women in Prussia followed the progress of their sisters in the US with all the more interest. The letter was signed by Louise Otto-Peters, one of the most distinctive voices of first-wave feminism in Germany.[612] Though based in Leipzig, Otto-Peters regularly appeared in Berlin, where her *Gesellschaft für arbeitende Frauen* (Society for Working Women) promoted the expansion of wage work among the city's female working class.[613] So did the local *Verein zur Förderung der Erwerbsfähigkeit des weiblichen Geschlechts* (Association for the Advancement of Employability of the Female Sex). Established under the influence of the *Centralverein für das Wohl der arbeitenden Klassen* (Central Association for the Welfare of the Working Classes) by Wilhelm Adolf Lette in 1866, the association opposed the political emancipation of women, yet it advocated an opening of employment for women.[614] In the same year that the "*Lette Verein*" (as the association came to be known) was established, Otto-Peters published *Das Recht der Frauen auf Erwerb* (The Right of Women to Employment). Much like Virginia Penny's contribution in the US, Otto-Peter's book called for an end to employment restrictions for women.[615] Also in 1866, the first issue of her bimonthly *Neue Bahnen* appeared as the organ of the recently founded *Allge-*

611 Bernstein, *Die Geschichte der Berliner Arbeiterbewegung*, 164; "Politischer Theil: Berlin," *Der Social-Demokrat*, 29 January 1868, 1; "Politischer Theil: Berlin," *Der Social-Demokrat*, 5 February 1868, 1–2.

612 Louise Otto-Peters, "Letter from Germany," *The Revolution*, 6 August 1868, 77.

613 Otto-Peters also contributed to the foundation of Berlin's first working women's association in 1869; see Zetkin, *Zur Geschichte der proletarischen Frauenbewegung*, 41.

614 "Berliner Lokalzeitung (Der Verein zur Förderung der Erwerbsfähigkeit des weiblichen Geschlechts)," *Der Social-Demokrat*, 2 March 1866, 4; "Blicke in die Runde," *Neue Bahnen* 1 (5), 1866, 38. For the early years of the "Lette Verein," see Obschernitzki, *"Der Frau ihre Arbeit,"* 1–43. The *Centralverein für das Wohl der arbeitenden Klassen* had been founded in 1844 as a liberal response to the growing destitution of the nascent working class. Over the course of the century, it rose to prominence as an advocate of social reform and education; see Reulecke, "Die Vereinsbewegung für das Wohl der arbeitenden Klassen."

615 Otto-Peters, *Das Recht der Frauen auf Erwerb*.

meiner Deutscher Frauenverein (General German Women's Association, ADF). As the paper made clear, it did not intend to transform *bourgeois* society, "but only to open an avenue for free labor."[616] Yet Otto-Peters also strove to put legislators under pressure. On behalf of the ADF, she submitted a petition to the parliament of the North German Confederation requesting that it "end the discrimination against women that stills exists with respect to free movement, free marriage, and free trade."[617] Rather than asking for protective measures, the prominent feminist pressed for the unrestricted commodification of female labor. According to Otto-Peters, the unhindered "renting out" of labor power spared women the experience of cut-throat competition in a few trades.[618] As such, she was in line with the majority of Berlin's liberal movement. Otto Michaelis, for instance, argued that working women simply contributed to a family wage that was composed of more than just one wage earner. In his eyes, any restriction on female labor deprived women of lawful and morally uncompromising ways to find buyers for the labor power they provided. Legislative intervention, in other words, would only push women into sectors or work arrangements that were difficult to surveil and control.[619]

6.2. Protecting Female Labor

In the eyes of the social-democratic movement, however, approaches like these were nothing but employers' ill-concealed attempts to make life miserable for working men. Two years after the publication of von Schweitzer's play *Ein Schlingel*, the ADAV president published a sequel that likewise be-

616 J. H., "Was Ist Arbeit," *Neue Bahnen* 1 (2), 1866, 10. ("[…] sondern nur 'der Arbeit eine Gasse' zu machen.")

617 GStA PK, I. HA Rep. 120 A, I, 1, Nr. 56: "Die beim Reichstage des Norddeutschen Bundes eingegangenen Petitionen," 1867–1873; here: "Reichstag des Norddeutschen Bundes, 1. Legislatur-Periode, Sitzungs-Periode 1867, drittes Verzeichnis der beim Reichstage des Norddeutschen Bundes eingegangenen, an die Petitions-Kommission abgegebenen Petitionen," Record Number 4. ("[…] die hier und da vorkommende Benachtheiligung der Frauen bei Fragen wie: Freizügigkeit, Orts- und Heimathsberechtigung, sowie Gewerbefreiheit, aufhören zu lassen.")

618 Otto-Peters, *Das Recht der Frauen auf Erwerb*, 20.

619 "Vereins-Theil: Berlin (Volkswirthschaftliche Gesellschaft)," *Der Social-Demokrat*, 17 December 1865, 4. Moritz Müller expressed similar views in liberal workers' associations; see Müller, *Vortrag über die Frauenfrage*.

came part of the standard repertoire of amateur theatre productions. The play introduces Anna, the sister of worker Roth, whom we have already met as the lead character in *Ein Schlingel.* Due to the massive introduction of sewing machines, Anna has recently lost employment as a seamstress. The Councilor now summons Anna to his office where, again with loyal support from Dr. Fisch, he lectures the young woman that any restriction on female labor constitutes an inexcusable violation of her right to sell her labor power as she pleases. According to the Councilor:

> The emancipation of the female sex from the marginalization it currently suffers is the holy objective of the great liberal party. But words alone do not suffice—things need to be done. A female association will be founded in order to promote the freedom of labor and, thereby, the expansion of the female labor market. [...] You, my young lady, will be president of this association.[620]

Obviously, the fictive example here alludes to the recently established Association for the Advancement of Employability of the Female Sex, which von Schweitzer hoped to expose as a menace to working-class interests. Von Schweitzer's play epitomizes the ADAV approach towards working women—and, in fact, towards women in general. Roth's sister Anna is portrayed as a good yet simple-hearted young woman who owes her superficial socialist knowledge to her brother. Despite a rather intuitive internalization of her brother's principles, Anna eventually accepts the Councilor's proposal to preside over the new association. At this moment, Anna's brother appears on the scene. Once again, worker Roth successfully challenges his former employer. Roth argues that the commodification of female labor is not an act of *bourgeois* philanthropy. Rather, the growing supply of labor power that has resulted from the employment of working women constitutes an organized attack on male wages and, therewith, on familial cohesion and working-class standards of living.[621]

Like von Schweitzer's first play, *Eine Gans* drew upon very real debates that raged among workers in Berlin—a city that, even in the eyes of organized labor abroad, suffered particularly badly from the increase of wage

620 Johann Baptist von Schweitzer, "Eine Gans (Fortsetzung)," *Agitator*, 4 June 1870, 1. ("Die Befreiung des weiblichen Geschlechts aus der Zurücksetzung, unter der es leidet, ist das heilige Ziel der großen liberalen Partei. Aber Worte genügen nicht—Thaten müssen geschehen. Ein weiblicher Verein wird gegründet werden, der die volle Freiheit der Arbeit und daher auch die Erweiterung des weiblichen Arbeitsmarktes erstrebt. [...] Sie, mein Fräulein, werden die Vorsteherin dieses Vereins sein.")

621 Johann Baptist von Schweitzer, "Eine Gans (Schluß)," *Agitator*, 2 July 1870, 4.

work among women. As far away as Vienna, social democrats expressed concern over the spread of female labor in Berlin, where, according to the Austrian workers' paper *Gleichheit*, every year more and more women were thrust onto the free labor market.[622] Berlin's organized workers despised the free market for female labor and the commodification it entailed. As the following shows, they struggled fiercely against the unregulated length of the female workday as a core symptom of unfettered commodification. And the *Neuer Social-Demokrat* spearheaded this struggle. The Berlin-based paper continuously stressed that long hours of factory work ruined women's sense of morality and harmed their health. Depressed, neglected, and isolated, many of the young female workers died before their 25th birthday. Yet, the paper exclaimed:

> What does today's mode of production care? Her place in the factory will soon be filled; thanks to free trade, liberal manufacturers have no difficulties in finding a replacement for human commodities.[623]

Perceptive to the workers' desire for debate, the ADAV organized a public lecture in Berlin at which Reinhold Schlingmann, editor of Lassallean publications and founding member of the local ADAV branch, tore apart the liberal take on female labor. According to Schlingmann, it was not surprising that the free-marketeers were eager to push women into the market. Pretending to promote the liberty and equality of women, what employers were really interested in was increasing wage competition between male and female workers.[624] To the dismay of the feminist *Neue Bahnen* that covered the event, Schlingmann interpreted female labor simply as an organized attack on male wages.[625] In the eyes of Schlingmann and his fellow social democrats, the unregulated commodification of women's labor power depressed wages and increased hours for working men. Based on this understanding, the ADAV decided to act. Addressing the "citizens, craftsmen, and

622 "Sozialpolitische Rundschau: Über die Frauenarbeit in Berlin," *Gleichheit* (Vienna), 28 August 1875, 3.

623 D., "Die Entbehrung des Weibes unter der Herrschaft des Kapitals," *Neuer Social-Demokrat*, 1 December 1872, 2. ("Was schadet's auch der heutigen Produktionsweise! Ihre Stelle in der Fabrik ist bald ausgefüllt, mit Hilfe der Freizügigkeit verstehen es die liberalen Fabrikanten, sich die Waare 'Mensch' nach Blieben kommen zu lassen.")

624 "Social-Demokratische Partei-Versammlung in Berlin," *Der Social-Demokrat*, 17 January 1866, 3. Since Berlin's local ADAV chapter was banned at the time, the Lassallean press regularly referred to "all social-democratic workers of Berlin," and it usually convened under the name "Social-demokratische Partei-Versammlungen."

625 "Blicke in die Runde," *Neue Bahnen* 1 (2), 1866, 14–15.

workers of Berlin," the Lassalleans published a leaflet in the run-up to the first Reichstag election in 1871. If elected, the local ADAV candidate promised to fight in parliament for the "introduction of a normal working day as well as the abolition of female, child, and Sunday work."[626] In contrast to the interpretation by Clara Zetkin, who later came to the Lassalleans' defense, the ADAV in fact adhered to the legislative restriction of female labor for as long as it existed.[627]

Schlingmann's talk clearly had an impact on working-class Berlin. In a letter to the editors of the *Social-Demokrat*, a typesetter S. from Berlin agreed that the *bourgeois* assertion—according to which the commodification of women's work would actually promote female emancipation—was clearly nonsense. The current system of wage labor was based, as he put it, on "the law of supply and demand that equated the propertyless worker with a commodity that capital could exploit."[628] What capital required was a constant supply of cheap labor to which it had unrestricted access via the free market. The expanding commodification of new segments of society—such as women or children—was not a movement for emancipation, but a struggle to increase the pool of available labor and, the author feared, to increase competition among those who had to offer their labor for sale. Given the fact that female labor was especially prevalent in their trade, the ready-made tailors of Berlin protested loudly against the employment of women. When they convened in early 1873, they declared that the increase in female employment had depressed their incomes and stretched their workdays to as much as 18 hours a day.[629] In the eyes of these male tailors, something had to be done. This view was underscored by a worker who, in another letter to the *Social-Demokrat*, addressed the liberal movement directly:

626 Bernstein, *Die Geschichte der Berliner Arbeiterbewegung*, 219.

627 See, for instance, the party program that the ADAV published prior to the Reichstag elections of 1874, the year before its fusion with the SDAP. In the program, the Lassalleans display a firm commitment to the abolition of female labor; see "Programm der deutschen Arbeiter für die nächsten Reichstags-Wahlen," *Neuer Social-Demokrat*, 3 December 1873, Supplement, 5–6. For Zetkin's defence, see Zetkin, *Zur Geschichte der proletarischen Frauenbewegung*, 54–55.

628 "Einsendung von Arbeitern: Ueber Frauenarbeit (Aus Berlin)," *Der Social-Demokrat*, 29 March 1866, 4. ("Es ist einfach das Gesetz von Angebot und Nachfrage, welches den besitzlosen Arbeiter der Waare gleichstellt und ihn ausbeutet im Interesse des Capitals […].")

629 W., "Lokales (Sämtliche Konfektionsschneider Berlins)," *Demokratische Zeitung*, 26 February 1873, 3.

You want to make our women independent, to allow them to provide for themselves through their own work, and indeed it sounds rather promising, the word 'emancipate.' But take your emancipation elsewhere, to circles where women, deprived of their human dignity as articles of exchange for miserable peddlers [...] or as 'pretty purses,' are called angels yet are treated as things.[630]

Organized workers strongly rejected the objectification of women that resulted from the unregulated commodification of their labor power. But working-class discourse merely replaced one objectification with another. As we have seen in the previous chapters, working men possessed a wide repertoire of arguments to challenge working conditions determined entirely by market demands. To organized workers, the system of unregulated wage labor threatened their autonomy as independent producers of value, jeopardized their position as self-governing citizens, undermined their ideal of masculinity, and perverted their notion of dignity. By putting the male producer at the center of arguments for shorter workdays, working men gained subjectivity. The demand to regulate and restrict female labor, in contrast, denied women this very subjectivity. Women were not seen as economically active subjects in possession of certain rights or privileges that followed from their labor. Rather, they were regarded as a structural obstacle that jeopardized the rights and privileges of working men. The foregoing examples thereby illustrate the prevalence of the belief in a male-centered family wage. At the ADAV annual convention in Berlin in 1867, delegate Wilhelm Bracke criticized liberal economics, which pretended that the proliferation of women's wage labor benefited the working-class family as a whole. Rather than increasing the average wage rate, the spread of female employment in fact decreased the male wage. Bracke, who would soon take his views on female labor to the newly established SDAP, concluded that where male labor had once been enough to support a family, now both husband and wife had to work for the same wage—if not for less. In the following open discussion, Berlin's ADAV member Schumann reminded his audience what the abstract argument of competition meant in real life. During a recent walk-out in the city, the striking workers were easily replaced by women. Ac-

630 "Einsendungen von Arbeitern: Über Frauenarbeit (Aus Hamburg)," *Der Social-Demokrat*, 11 July 1866, 2. ("Ihr wollt unsere Frauen selbstständig machen, ihnen durch Arbeit ermöglichen [...], sich ihren Unterhalt selbst zu erwerben, und es hört sich auch ganz gut an, das Wort: 'Emancipiren,' aber geht mit Eurer Emancipation wo anders hin, in Kreise, wo die Frauen als Tauschwaare elender Krämer [...] oder nur als 'schöne Geldbörse' all ihrer Menschenwürde entkleidet—Engel genannt und als Sachen behandelt werden.")

cording to Schumann, the female competitors gladly accepted the conditions against which the men protested. The overwhelming majority of delegates who addressed the question of women's work agreed that once wage labor had been abolished, the plight of working women would end as well. In the meantime, however, they demanded special legislation for the restriction of female wage labor.[631] In their eyes, such a restriction would end the cut-throat wage competition to which working men were subject.

Unlike the local Lassalleans, the rivaling Eisenacher faction had a reputation for supporting female wage labor. When Louise Otto-Peters discussed the relationship between feminism and social-democracy in Germany, she lamented the fact that among organized workers there was only one party

> that welcomes our approach, which has offered us a hand here and there, and which has committed itself to opening new employments to women; while the other workers' party opposes our endeavor to expand the market for female labor and acts on the maxim: "Away with female labor!"[632]

At first glance, both the SDAP and the Internationalist trade-union movement did indeed appear to display a genuine commitment to the equality of male and female labor. Some of their unions even opened their doors to female memberships, for instance the *Internationale Gewerksgenossenschaft der Manufaktur-, Fabrik- und Handarbeiter beiderlei Geschlechts* (International Union of Manufacture, Factory, and Manual Workers of both sexes) in Saxony. According to Clara Zetkin, the organized weavers likewise showed that the Eisenachers firmly supported female equality. Assembled for the Weaver's Day of 1871, they passed a resolution that demanded free access for wom-

631 "Generalversammlung des Allgemeinen Deutschen Arbeitervereins," *Der Social-Demokrat*, 29 November 1867, Supplement, 1–4. The source refers to a speaker "Schuhmann," who was most likely the locally prominent ADAV agitator Schumann; see Welskopp, *Das Banner der Brüderlichkeit*, 559.

632 Louise Otto-Peters, "Menschenwürdiges Dasein für Alle," *Neue Bahnen* 3 (16), 1868, 122. Given that the future Eisenachers had not yet seceded from the liberal workers' association, Otto-Peters here referred to the VDAV in general. ("[...] welche unsere Bestrebungen freundlich aufgenommen, uns hier und da die Hand dazu geboten hat, und selbst mit bemüht ist, die Frauen in neue Erwerbsgebiete einzuführen, indes die andere Partei der Arbeiter das Losungswort ausspricht: 'Fort mit der Frauenarbeit!' und unsere Versuche, den Markt für die Frauenarbeit zu vergrößern, verwirft.")

en to trade unions.[633] Yet as the full minutes of the Weavers' Day of 1871 demonstrate, the delegates were actually in bitter disagreement. Although the convention eventually did pass the resolution referred to by Zetkin, the representatives from Berlin stood out as leading opponents of free female labor. The Berlin delegates Uhlmann and Scholz both insisted that the commodification of female labor had put male wages under serious pressure and, therefore, needed to be contained.[634] Despite the abovementioned reputation for female equality, many of the rank-and-file Eisenachers in fact shared the ADAV's view on female wage work. Like their Lassallean rivals, they too criticized the *bourgeois* strategy to sell the exploitation of female labor as an act of emancipation. Even Liebknecht's *Volksstaat* argued that only a socialist state of the future could guarantee the true emancipation of women. In today's society, the paper reasoned, the emancipation of women was nothing but an empty phrase. A woman's labor power

> faces the capitalist as a common commodity that habitually requires but little cost for its reproduction. The *bourgeois* seeks the commodity of female labor power only because it is cheaper, because it always will be cheaper, than male labor power. Rather than humanism or pity for the sad and unprotected position of working women, it is his business interest that makes him seek female labor.[635]

Ideas like these quickly found their way into the political demands of the small Eisenacher circle in Berlin. Although the Eisenachers presented themselves as the female-friendly social-democratic alternative, their political program belied their claims. Yet rather than openly demanding an end to female wage labor (as did the ADAV), the local Eisenachers struggled for both universal protective legislation and legislation that applied only to women. As its statutes demonstrate, Berlin's *Demokratischer Arbeiterverein* advocated for the "legislative restriction of daily work hours [...] for all workers," but "all workers" apparently did not include working women. After all, the second

---

633 Zetkin, "Die Anfänge der proletarischen Frauenbewegung," 67. A revised and extended version of this argument appeared in Zetkin, *Zur Geschichte der proletarischen Frauenbewegung*, 86–108.

634 Deutsches Weber-Central-Comitee (ed.), *Ausführlicher Bericht*, 50.

635 "Der Staat und die Frauenarbeit," *Der Volksstaat*, 8 February 1872, 2. ("[...] steht dem Kapitalisten gegenüber nur als Waare, aber als eine billige Waare, die nach Gewohnheit und Herkommen nur geringer Produktionskosten bedarf zu ihrer Wiederherstellung. Weil die Waare weibliche Arbeitskraft billiger ist, stets billiger ist als die männliche, darum sucht sie der Bourgeois. Also nicht die Humanität, nicht das Mitleid mit der traurigen hülflosen Lage unserer Frauen ist es, die ihn veranlaßt, sich ihrer anzunehmen, sondern einzig und ausschließlich das Geschäftsinteresse.")

article of the statutes explicitly demanded a separate hour regulation for working women.[636] This declaration by the *Demokratischer Arbeiterverein* casts doubt on the analysis by Zetkin, who, in a rare discussion of early proletarian feminism, argued that the Eisenachers fought for a normal workday for "all wage slaves," irrespective of their sex.[637] Quite to the contrary, the *Demokratischer Arbeiterverein* testifies to the growing tensions between universal demands to regulate the workday on the one hand and demands for the special protection of women on the other. If Berlin's Eisenachers really had endorsed gender-blind normal workday legislation, there would have been no need for special legislation for working women. Here, too, the different rationalities underlying the demand for shorter male and female workdays explain the Eisenachers' double strategy. Followers of the local SDAP knew that their struggle for a normal workday for men—a struggle that drew on an emancipatory logic of political equality and economic transformation—was fiercely resisted by liberals and conservatives alike. Since the demand for shorter hours for working women, in contrast, drew on a paternalistic strategy of differentiation and protection rather than equality and emancipation, the *Demokratischer Arbeiterverein* could trust that it would find support among conservatives like the aforementioned *Kathedersozialisten*, who feared that moral decay and social destabilization would result from female wage work. Despite their prominent critique of *laissez-faire* liberalism, Germany's *Kathedersozialisten* opposed the demand for universal normal workday legislation. This did not stop them, however, from endorsing better protections for working women. When they convened in 1872, they dismissed workday legislation for men but passed a resolution demanding the introduction of legislative hour restrictions for female and child labor.[638] The Eisenachers' strategy to make separate demands for *all* workers on the one hand and for women only on the other hand was owed to the expectation that even if a universal demand failed due to parliamentary resistance, the gendered bill might still have a chance of passing.[639]

The foregoing has shown that, much like the ADAV, many rank-and-file members of Berlin's *Demokratischer Arbeiterverein* deplored the unchecked commodification of female labor. Like their Lassallean rivals, they too

---

636 "Ein sociales Programm," *Die Arbeiter-Union*, 20 March 1869, 4–5.

637 Zetkin, *Die Anfänge der proletarischen Frauenbewegung*, 64–66.

638 "Die Eisenacher Maus," *Neuer Social-Demokrat*, 13 October 1872, 1–2.

639 The unified SAP later followed the same strategy; see Braun, *Gewerbeordnung und Geschlechtertrennung*, 84–85, 94.

wished to see women protected from the long hours that the free labor market entailed. Though to different extremes, both strategies were fueled by the desire to restrict female labor as a means to reduce wage competition for working men.[640] But Berlin's male workers did not merely dread female competition as a threat to the male-centered family wage. Speaking in front of an ADAV convention in Berlin, Wilhelm Hasselmann argued that the saddest aspect of the women's question was that "not only on the labor market, but quite in general, women and girls are considered commodities."[641] Hasselmann here introduced a striking twist to the de-commodification debate. According to him, working women needed special protection against the commodification of their labor power, but they also needed special protection against the commodification of their *bodies*. According to mainstream social-democratic analysis, the female proletariat suffered a double abuse at the hands of the *bourgeoisie*. As if it were not enough that the ruling classes kept their fathers, brothers, and husbands in constant poverty, they also exploited the destitute and defenseless daughters for the pleasures of their rich and idle sons. Hasselmann suggested that if women were protected from the labor market, protection from the sex market would follow: De-commodifying female labor power would automatically entail the de-commodification of female bodies. Put differently, if women were no longer forced to offer their labor for a wage, they could return to the protected sphere of the home. Said Hasselmann:

> Legislation thus has to attend first to the better protection of those women who work in factories, as is slowly happening in England. Only once women return to their true calling can we really speak of emancipation. And this presupposes that the current mode of production, in which female workers are commodities, will end.[642]

End the commodification of female labor and you will end the commodification of female sexuality. The two forms of commodification here appear as equally immoral practices that needed to be addressed not by the socialist

640 See also Welskopp, *Das Banner der Brüderlichkeit*, 730–731.

641 "Vereins-Theil: Berlin (Mitgliederversammlung)," *Neuer Social-Demokrat*, 11 February 1872, 2. ("[…] Frauen und Mädchen nicht bloß auf dem Arbeitsmarkt, sondern überhaupt als Waare betrachtet werden.")

642 "Vereins-Theil: Berlin (Mitgliederversammlung)," *Neuer Social-Demokrat*, 11 February 1872, 2. ("Die Gesetzgebung müsse sich also zunächst damit beschäftigen, den Frauen, in Betreff der Fabrikarbeit Schutz zu gewähren, wie es z.B. auch in England langsam angebahnt wird. Denn dann erst, wenn das Weib seinem Berufe zurückgegeben sei, könne von einer Emancipation die Rede sein. Und dies setze voraus, daß die heutige Produktionsweise aufhöre, wo die Arbeiterin eine Waare sei.")

state of the future, but by the capitalist state of the present. As Kathrin Braun suggests, the equation of female wage labor and prostitution allowed social democrats to oppose commodification on moral grounds while revealing male anxieties over the increasing loss of patriarchal hegemony.[643] Most of the speakers who followed Hasselmann emphatically endorsed his talk. But there was one solitary voice of opposition. Mr. Jörissen, who was introduced as a "writer" in order to emphasize his non-worker status, argued that in today's mode of production the woman was the real slave. To the organized worker of Berlin, this "writer" was no stranger. Jörissen regularly appeared at local conventions where, as the social-democratic media put it, he proposed his "radical-*bourgeois*" or "anarchist" views.[644] At the meeting referred to above, Jörissen argued that pushing women back into the home, where they would enjoy the fruits of their husbands' labor, was in fact the best way to guarantee the dependence and suppression of the female sex. Even if women were not made for wage work, to offer their labor power as a commodity in exchange for a wage not only spared them the experience of prostitution, but also fostered their emancipation from male dependence. As long as the current system of free wage labor was in place, the commodification of labor offered women an avenue towards greater equality and emancipation.[645] Yet Jörissen's ideas were met with fierce opposition from the working-class Berliners assembled here. To them, the commodification of female labor was just as morally compromising as the commodification of the female body.[646] Female wage labor and prostitution were merely two sides of the same coin.

The equation of female labor commodification with the commodification of the female body tied in with growing concerns regarding the mobility of working women. Addressing the ADAV delegates to the annual convention of 1867 in Berlin, Bracke argued that, given their physical and mental peculiarities, women could not be dehumanized to the level of tools. Their inner constitution, their health, their entire being (*Wesen*) suffered under the commodification that was inherent in wage labor. Despite unconcealed male opposition to female labor, the struggle to protect working women from the

643 See also Braun, *Gewerbeordnung und Geschlechtertrennung*, 69–70.

644 See, for instance, w., "Lokales (Der Sozialdemokratische Arbeiterverein)," *Demokratische Zeitung*, 1 September 1872, 3.

645 "Vereins-Theil: Berlin (Mitgliederversammlung)," *Neuer Social-Demokrat*, February 14, 1872, 3.

646 Braun comes to a similar conclusion; see Braun, *Gewerbeordnung und Geschlechtertrennung*, 67–74.

free market was thereby depicted as a right that followed directly from women's true nature. Schlingmann thus came to the conclusion that the unprotected commodification of female labor was in fact a violation of the natural rights of women. Quoting Jules Simon, he argued that "if there is anything that nature has taught us with clarity, it is that women were made to be protected."[647] Social democrats, Bracke seconded, did not oppose female work *per se*. Rather, they wished to see women work in the sphere for which they were "made:"

> Liberal economics want freedom in all respects. We also want the greatest possible freedom; but unrestrained freedom makes the weak servants of the strong. We say: Away with female labor! But give the worker the full fruits of his labor and he will be able to satisfy the wants of his family; and give women the sort of labor they are made for.[648]

But free female wage labor threatened more than the position of the male family head; it supposedly also threatened the very survival of the proletarian family. Rather than promoting a system of public child care, as social democrats would do a generation later, the ADAV insisted that the protection of family life could only stem from a return of working women to their allegedly natural sphere.[649]

Ideas about the presumed right of women to be protected from unchecked commodification also resonated with German-Americans in New York. A vivid example of the dynamic transfer of ideas that connected working-class movements across wide distances was the decision of the *Arbeiter-Zeitung* of New York City, the organ of the German-speaking IWA sections in the US, to reprint an article on female labor that had recently appeared in the *Volksstaat*. Despite the paper's self-declared commitment to gender equality, the *Arbeiter-Zeitung* accepted the author's analysis, according to which it was not surprising that employers rejoiced over the further com-

647 "Ueber Frauenarbeit und Arbeiterfrauen: Vortrag des Herrn R. Schlingmann," *Der Social-Demokrat*, 20 January 1866, 3.

648 "General-Versammlung des Allg. Deutsch. Arbeiter-Vereins," *Der Social-Demokrat*, 29 November 1867, Supplement. ("Die liberale Oeconomie will in allen Stücken die volle Freiheit. Auch wir wollen die größtmögliche Freiheit in jeder Hinsicht; aber bei voller Freiheit sind die Schwachen doch wieder die Knechte der Stärkeren. Wir sagen: fort mit der Frauenarbeit; aber geben Sie dem Arbeiter den vollen Ertrag seiner Arbeit, dann kann er alleine die Bedürfnisse der Familie befriedigen, und geben sie den Frauen die Arbeiten, die ihrer Eigenthümlichkeit angemessen sind.")

649 "Die Frauenarbeit in den Fabriken und die Auflösung der Familie," *Social-Politische Blätter*, 9 April 1873, 76–77.

modification of female labor power. After all, the weaker sex was far more submissive, and it regularly contented itself with worse working conditions and lower wages than those of men. Female labor thus depressed male wages and brought misery to working-class households. And this was in fact exactly what capital wanted for the proletarian family:

> To the *bourgeois*, the proletarian "family" is nothing but an institution that serves to breed new workers for the exploitative passion of the capitalist lord and to thrust as much human meat on the labor market as possible.[650]

Such objectifying livestock analogies—*breed, meat, market*—epitomize the fiercely contested position of the free labor market in postbellum working-class discourse. As Amy Dru Stanley has shown, organized labor characterized the free labor market as little better than the market for sex, animals, or slaves. Female labor commodification was understood as the principal reason that male workers were no longer able to support a family, that working-class women were pushed out of the protected sphere of the home, and, ultimately, that female wage workers earned so little that they were forced to sell not only their labor, but also their bodies.[651] This logic clearly resonated with the nascent movement of German-American workers, a movement that eventually took shape in the formation of the Social Democratic Party of North America. Founded in 1874 with a predominantly Lassallean outlook, the New York City-centered SDPNA fiercely opposed the unregulated commodification of women's work. Its house organ stressed that the new party would struggle for the universal introduction of an eight-hour normal working day in various trades, but also promote the "restriction of female labor and its prohibition in places where men work."[652] This was precisely the course that the Eisenachers had taken in Berlin. In New York, however, the demand to restrict female labor provoked angry opposition by some working-class feminists. During a public social-democratic lecture, Pauline Lilienthal argued that the ban on female labor was a "barbarity." If ever signed into law, the social-democratic proposal would deprive all women of the potential for autonomy. Instead of banning female labor, a certain Mr. Jonas proposed to replace the current paragraph with the demand of "equal

650 "Die Arbeiterbewegung und die Frauen," *Der Volksstaat*, 25 July 1873, 1; "Die Arbeiterbewegung und die Frauen," *Arbeiter-Zeitung*, 4 October 1873, 3.

651 See, in particular, Stanley, *From Bondage to Contract*, 218–263.

652 "Programm der Social-Demokratischen Arbeiterpartei von Nord-Amerika," *Social-Demokrat* (New York), 28 November 1874, 1. ("[…] Beschränkung der Frauenarbeit und Verbot derselben in Räumen, wo Männer arbeiten.")

pay for equal work." This would end both the terrible exploitation of women and at the same time suspend the wage competition that working men feared.[653] Against this minority position, the émigré Gustav Lyser formulated the majority view that no decent society could tolerate unregulated female labor, especially not in dangerous, arduous, and dirty professions. In the eyes of the popular German social democrat, it was a dreadful idea

> to conceive of women, half-drunk with brandy, hurry the streets like furies after the end of the work day, blackened and dressed in wretched rags. It would be a degeneration below beasts.[654]

Directly addressing Lilienthal, who had condemned unilateral labor restrictions as a "barbarity," New York's *Social-Demokrat* declared that

> Women shall participate equally in all the pleasures this rich and beautiful earth provides; they shall ennoble us. But the industrial battle, the difficult and partly dangerous work, "we barbarians" reserve for ourselves.[655]

Frustrated with the German-American workers' demand to restrict female labor, the aforementioned Mr. Jonas argued at the same convention that no native-born worker in New York would ever accept such a discriminatory proposal. After all, he claimed, the American worker was much more supportive of women's quest for equal rights. At first sight, this judgment seems accurate. In official statements and declarations, native-born workers in New York and postbellum America in general did not oppose the increase in female employment. When the member unions of the NLU convened in New York City in 1868, they passed a resolution that wholeheartedly endorsed the struggle of working women. According to official NLU rhetoric, women enjoyed the right to offer their labor power under the same working conditions as men.[656] Unlike the large majority of German immigrants, native-born workmen in New York had apparently internalized a universalist

---

653 "Correspondenzen: New York, den 11. Januar," *Social-Demokrat* (New York), 17 January 1875, 2.

654 Ibid. ("[…] wenn man nach Feierabend die in elende Lumpen gehüllten, über und über schwarzen und vom Branntwein halb trunkenen Weiber gleich Furien an sich vorbeieilen sähe. Es wäre eine Entartung bis unter's Vieh.")

655 Ibid. ("Die Frauen sollen an allen Genüssen dieser reichen, schönen Erde gleichen Antheil haben, sie sollen auf uns veredelnd einwirken, aber der Kampf auf dem Gebiete der Industrie, die schweren und zum Theil gefährlichen Arbeiten behalten 'wir Barbaren' uns vor.")

656 "National Labor Congress: Third Annual Session," *The Workingman's Advocate*, 4 September 1869, 2.

concept of industrial conflict. Protective legislation had to apply equally to all laborers irrespective of their sex. Though trade unions did not usually allow mixed memberships, they promised to do what they could to support the organization of female branches.

At the same time as American workers thus opened to the "Woman Question," the American feminist movement turned its attention to the "Social Question." In the pages of their newly founded feminist weekly, Susan B. Anthony and Elizabeth Cady Stanton declared that women's struggle for political equality was intertwined with labor's struggle for participation.[657] Following a short-lived flirt with the Democratic Party, the New York City based *Revolution* adopted the main principles of the NLU and embraced the latter's view that labor was the sole source of value, a precious source that needed to be protected from capital.[658] By the end of 1868, *The Revolution* had successfully merged prominent working-class ideas with the women's struggle. Its editors were certain that with "the right of suffrage to all comes an end to the dynasty of capital over labor, the most terrible from of slavery that now curses the earth."[659] Feminists in New York and elsewhere rejoiced over the prospect of a new and independent labor party that would struggle for the equality and participation of all. Yet as they soon found out, many in the labor movement did not welcome their support.

Late in 1867, the male typesetters of New York City had called a strike against one of the leading newspapers in the city, the *New York World*, which offered training and employment for female workers. When Local 6 of the Typographical Union and the *World* finally settled their dispute in the autumn of 1868, the former required that all female typesetters be laid off. This caused an outcry among the female workers involved, but also from the city's leading suffragists, who defended the right of female labor in the pages of *The Revolution*. Thanks to the suffragists' initiative, the Working Women's Association (WWA) was established at the office of *The Revolution*, just in time to provide Anthony and Mary Kellogg Putnam with the labor credentials necessary to attend the NLU congress of 1868.[660] In the course of its

657 Burrows and Wallace, *Gotham*, 982. The new paper soon dropped its subtitle "Organ of the National Party of New America."

658 Ibid., 989. See also DuBois, *Feminism and Suffrage*, 105–110.

659 J.C.C. Whaley, William H. Sylvis, and William J. Jessup, "Capital and Labor," *The Revolution*, 4 June 1868, 264.

660 While the proceedings of the National Labor Congress list Anthony and Putnam as delegates of the older Workingwomen's Protective Association, in fact they represented the recently established Working Wom[e][a]n's Association; see Commons et al. (eds.), *A*

brief existence, the WWA served as a training ground for New York City's female typesetters in particular, among whom Anna Tobbitt, Susie Johns, Augusta Lewis, and Emily Peers quickly rose to local prominence. While the *bourgeois* feminists disagreed with the female workers on the proper role of the suffrage demand, they agreed that the objective of the association was not to lead women back to their supposedly natural place at home, but to improve the situation of wage-working women in all trades. What the association thus demanded was that women receive the respect they deserved, that they earn the same wage for the same work, and that they work neither longer nor shorter hours than their male colleagues. In order to promote these demands in the printing trade, the female typesetters established their very own Women's Typographical Union (WTU). While the latter was designed as a union and producers' co-operative for female typesetters, the WWA remained open to all women irrespective of their trade, as the presence of seamstresses indicates.[661] Over the course of the following months, the women's new union won the support of the International Typographical Union. As Robert Lewis, representative of the city's Local 6 and husband to female typesetter Augusta, promised in a meeting of the association in September, 1868, the male typesetters of New York would assist the women in building their female union. Co-operation between female and male typesetters was paralleled by a growing disaffection between the working women and local suffragists. The female typesetters of New York City increasingly saw themselves drawn to the camp of organized labor and away from the struggle for political equality. The Typographical Union eventually welcomed the WTU as the first female chapter in its history.[662]

The male typesetters' support does not mean, however, that they had abandoned their hostile position towards the expansion of female labor into their trade. The NLU congress of 1869 brought this conflict into the open. Shortly after the congress had begun and paid its respects to the recently deceased former NLU president, William H. Sylvis, delegate Mike Walsh of

Documentary History of American Industrial Society, vol. 9, 195; "Workingwomen's Association," *The Revolution*, 24 September 1868, 181–182; "Eine Versammlung von Frauen," *Die Arbeiter-Union*, 26 September 1868, 7. See also Burrows and Wallace, *Gotham*, 990; DuBois, *Feminism and Suffrage*, 126–134.

661 Ibid., 133–142; Janiewski, *Making Common Cause*, 784–786.

662 DuBois, *Feminism and Suffrage*, 142–143, 153–154.

the Typographical Union No. 6 of New York City took the floor and challenged Anthony's credentials.[663] According to Walsh, the WWA, which Anthony represented, was not a labor organization as required by the NLU platform. Even worse, Anthony had revealed her utter disrespect for working-class solidarity when she promoted the training of girls and women who then replaced striking male typesetters. As Walsh put it, the prominent suffragist had thus actively "striven to procure situations for girls from which the men had been discharged, at lower wages than they had received."[664] There was no way Walsh or the two thousand typesetters he claimed to represent would accept Anthony's presence as a delegate. He thus urged the congress to unseat Anthony.[665] Over the lengthy and heated debate that followed Walsh's motion the following day, it became obvious that the issue of Anthony's seating was not, as Walsh took pains to stress, merely a dispute of whether her organization qualified as a *bona fide* labor organization. Walsh did indeed go out of his way to emphasize that Anthony was a *bourgeois* reformer who imposed her "peculiar" ideas of political equality and middle-class reformism upon the working-class female membership of the association. In order to support his charge, Walsh read out a letter he had received from Augusta Lewis of the female typesetters of New York. In it, Lewis stated that the "wealthy ladies of the Working Women's Association" had driven all working-class members out of the association. The message Walsh wanted to convey was clear. The organization had become a *bourgeois* vehicle for suffrage and charity rather than an association of proletarian struggle.[666]

Strictly speaking, this was not far from the truth, as Ellen Carol DuBois has shown in her detailed account of the conflict. At the end of 1869, the membership of the association was exclusively middle-class, and it focused on ideas of self-help rather than female class conflict.[667] Often, Anthony and other middle-class reformers lacked even a basic understanding of industrial contestation. At a public meeting of the WWA, for instance, Anthony lectured the attending girls and women that they should struggle for a certain

663 Not to be confused with New York City's antebellum labor activist and prominent congressman Michael Walsh; see Wilentz, *Chants Democratic*, 327–329.

664 "National Labor Congress: Third Annual Session," *The Workingman's Advocate*, September 4, 1869, 1; DuBois, *Feminism and Suffrage*, 157.

665 "Der nationale Arbeiter-Congreß in Philadelphia," *Die Arbeiter-Union*, 18 August 1869, 2. For a discussion of this conflict, see also Messer-Kruse, *The Yankee International*, 86–88.

666 "Der nationale Arbeiter-Congreß in Philadelphia," *Die Arbeiter-Union*, 18 August 1869, 2.

667 DuBois, *Feminism and Suffrage*, 147–153.

wage, but if they were unable to enforce it, they should settle for less.[668] Since in her eyes this suggestion simply meant that women had to take any chance to secure employment, Anthony did not hesitate to publish it in *The Revolution.* To the trade-union movement, however, this highly uncommon public announcement was the best way to assure employers that women would accept lower wages even before collective bargaining had begun. It thereby seriously undermined the bargaining position of female workers. In addition, Anthony's suggestion convinced organized male workers that she was preparing women to undersell men by accepting lower wages. But *bourgeois* feminists not only seemed to lack insight into strategies of industrial struggle, they also revealed a naïve understanding of the daily realities of working women. In the pages of their feminist paper, the colorful activists and editors Victoria Woodhull and Tennessee Celeste Claflin expressed the hope that "all our girls and women will soon be educated up to the standard of preferring the glorious freedom of self-support, even as washerwomen or ragpickers [...]."[669] Yet the female washerwomen of New York surely wondered which glorious freedom the paper referred to. After all, what sort of education did the ragpicking trade actually require, and what sort of independence or self-support did it yield? Similarly, Anthony urged working women not to work merely for subsistence, but for independence, to make their work a trade for life in which to excel and become wealthy.[670] Yet the tens of thousands of seamstresses and washing women of New York knew that no matter how much they struggled, there was no getting rich in their trades. As a consequence of this lack of understanding, middle-class feminists regularly failed to appreciate why the nascent trade-union movement insisted on its independent working-class character.

All these examples demonstrate that Walsh was not so far from the truth when he dismissed the leadership of the WWA as ignorant of working-class realities. This does not mean, however, that Walsh or the male unionists he represented qualify as disinterested defenders of the female typesetters of New York City. Rather, his dismissal of Anthony's credentials drew upon a broader uneasiness with female labor in general. Despite Walsh's assurance that he welcomed any working-class delegate irrespective of his or her sex as long as he or she respected the rights of labor, he suggested that there was

668 "Working Women's Association No. 1," *The Revolution*, 8 October 1868, 214.
669 "Woman's Ability to Earn Money," *Woodhull and Claflin's Weekly*, 17 September 1870, 11.
670 "Working Women's Association No. 1," *The Revolution*, 8 October 1868, 214.

in fact another reason that he was opposed to Anthony. The typesetter from New York City was profoundly upset by the fact that the

> lady goes in for taking women away from the wash tub; and in the name of heaven who is going there if they don't? I believe in a woman doing her work, and men marrying them and supporting them.[671]

What disturbed men like Walsh was the feminist attack on the concept of the male-provided family wage. Walsh's ideas about the proper sphere of women were in fact not so different from those espoused by workers in Berlin. Following a short controversy over whether she had a right to address the convention or not, Anthony was finally allowed to speak. She understood that what was really at stake here was the question of whether organized labor would grant women the right to have new areas of employment open to them and become equal partners and co-workers with men, wherever men worked. To thousands of girls and women in New York City, the protection that marriage entailed was not available. These women needed employment to support themselves and it was, Anthony concluded, their right to secure it. For the time being, only free access to wage labor, or, put differently, the unrestricted commodification of female labor power, guaranteed women a decent living and independence from male domination. And this was exactly what she had hoped to promote by training New York's women in typesetting. In no way was this meant to undersell male labor or undermine ongoing strike efforts. Speaking on behalf of his union, Walsh rejected Anthony's demand to open his trade to women. It was one thing to organize female workers who were already in the trade. Yet it was highly naïve to ask a trade union to promote its trade and teach its skills to girls and women who did not already work as typesetters. "You might as well ask," Walsh declared, "why we don't send for the colored men or the Chinese to learn the trade. There are too many in it now [...]."[672] Walsh argued that unions protected their trade against any competition that the organized men deemed illegitimate. They had no interest in seeing the supply of labor rise.

With no solution in sight, Andrew Cameron, the widely respected editor and labor leader from Chicago, eventually offered to withdraw Anthony's name from the list of delegates so as to spare the congress the disgrace, as

671 "National Labor Congress: Third Annual Session," *The Workingman's Advocate*, 4 September 1869, 1; DuBois, *Feminism and Suffrage*, 159.

672 "National Labor Congress: Third Annual Session," *The Workingman's Advocate*, 4 September 1869, 4.

Anthony put it, of a vote rejecting the feminist. But determined to make an example of their working-class commitment, Anthony's adversaries dismissed Cameron's offer. By a small margin, Anthony was seated. Interestingly, many of the minority group of naysayers came from New York City, including prominent representatives of the GGWA like Sigfrid Meyer, our expat from Berlin. Yet this was not the end of the debate. The next day, delegate Walsh presented a telegram to the convention that he had received from William Stirk, president of the Typographical Union No. 6 in New York City. The short text read:

> If Miss Anthony is admitted you are directed to withdraw from the convention, informing them that it is an insult to Union No. 6, and we will remember it. We are opposed to humbugs.[673]

This settled Anthony's fate. The convention would rather lose a prominent suffragist than one of its most active local memberships. As a delegate put it rather straightforwardly, the thousands of typesetters of New York were more important that the voice of a single woman who had no legitimate mandate.[674] Anthony was ejected by a landslide. The male typesetters of New York City had won.[675]

The clash at the NLU congress once more epitomized the deeper conflict between organized labor and the women's movement. The NLU convention did adopt a resolution on female labor that emphasized equal rights for working women, but the typesetters' opposition demonstrated that such resolutions had little effect. Although prominent labor representatives like Jessup and trade unionists like Walsh disagreed on the question of whether and under what condition female labor associations were to be welcomed, they still agreed, as DuBois stresses, on the general position of women in society. Even the late Sylvis, who had expressed his wholehearted support for any female organization willing to back organized labor, believed "that once relations between capital and labor had been revolutionized, women would leave wage labor and return to their 'natural' place in the home."[676] Despite its reputation for greater openness towards women's demands, the native-born scene of organized labor in New York espoused similar ideas

673 Ibid., 2.

674 "Specialberichte der 'Arbeiter-Union,'" *Die Arbeiter-Union*, 19 August 1869, 2.

675 "Der nationale Arbeiter-Congreß," *Die Arbeiter-Union*, 20 August 1869, 2; Burrows and Wallace, *Gotham*, 990–991; Commons et al. (eds.), *A Documentary History of American Industrial Society*, vol. 9, 231; DuBois, *Feminism and Suffrage*, 157–160.

676 Ibid., 120.

about women and wage work as their German-speaking comrades. They, too, largely shared the vision of a working-class family in which female members would derive "their social worth from their households, and where both their labor and their sexual conduct would be subject to the authority of husbands and fathers."[677] This was the reason that, of all forms of women's work, it was indoor wage labor outside of the proletarian home that provoked the fiercest criticism among organized workers.[678] Yet, contrary to Berlin, this did not result in demands for special hour legislation addressing women only. Instead, resistance to the commodification of female labor legitimized struggles to push women out of formal indoor wage work and into the much more informal world of outwork and domestic service. In so doing, the local workers' movement effectively excluded female workers in New York from the very protection it was fighting for for itself. The centralization of workers in closely monitored production facilities together with a proto-managerial documentation of work performance and a general accessibility for public authorities made indoor workshops not only a prime target for normal workday legislation, but also a central stage for accommodations with employers who expected that shorter hours would increase productivity. Therefore, indoor wage workers were far more likely to benefit from hour reductions than domestic servants or home producers. Elizabeth Cady Stanton saw this very clearly. In an article that appeared in 1868 in the pages of *The Revolution*, she argued that the "eight-hour strikers totally ignored women in their aspirations to reduced hours of labor."[679] Opposing the commodification of female wage labor, male workers struggled to keep women in the supposedly non-commodified sphere of the home. Whether in contracted outwork, poorly documented domestic service, or undocumented (and unwaged) housework, the exclusion from formal wage work deprived women of the very concessions that labor was wresting from capital. As a case in point, trade-union hostility towards full female equality translated into women's exclusion from universal eight-hour protection. Stanton's co-editor at the office of *The Revolution* thus concluded that while

---

677 Stansell, *City of Women*, 127. The notion of a male-provided family wage became an important element in working-class discussions of the mid-1850s, and it remained so among organized labor in general for the coming decades; see Burrows and Wallace, *Gotham*, 800–802.

678 For a characteristic illustration of this aspect, see the in-depth discussion in "Die Frauenarbeit in den Fabriken und die Auflösung der Familie," *Social-Politische Blätter*, 9 April 1873, 75–79.

679 "Workingwomen's Association," *The Revolution*, 24 September 1868, 182.

men might soon be able to enjoy their eight-hour day, "it will be found still true that 'Woman's work is never done.'"[680]

6.3. Chapter Conclusion

This chapter has shown that working-class Berlin and New York adopted two very different approaches towards female wage labor and the length of the workday, neither of which benefited working women. While working women in Berlin experienced discrimination through *inclusion* in a protective framework designed explicitly for them, working women in New York City experienced discrimination as a result of the factual *exclusion* from particular sectors and forms of employment that promised both material and non-material improvements. Berlin's social democrats fought for the protection of women through gendered labor legislation. Such legislative protection was motivated by widespread opposition to the commodification of female labor. According to dominant working-class discourse, women required protection from free markets not because the latter jeopardized their status as citizens, as producers of value, or as equal human beings. Rather, working women were seen as in need of protection from the laws of supply and demand because these very laws undermined working-class notions of both manhood and womanhood.[681] On the one hand, women were characterized as especially vulnerable to market exploitation. Due to their supposedly frail nature, they were regarded as utterly defenseless against the pressures of commodification. The free market thus threatened the physical and mental well-being of working women. Even worse, it also jeopardized their moral integrity. In the eyes of organized workers, it was but a short distance from the commodification of female labor power to the commodification of the female body. Prostitution was thereby only the most visible and obnoxious excess of the commodification of female labor. Yet at its heart, organized workers concluded, the female labor market was no different from the female sex market. On the other hand, working men in Berlin also feared the free market's threat to dominant notions of manhood. Unrestricted female wage labor resulted in wage competition and the increasing inability of men to control the labor and life of daughters and wives. At the same time, the

680 P.[arker]P.[illsbury], "Largest Store in the World," *The Revolution*, 3 September 1868, 137.
681 See also Braun, *Gewerbeordnung und Geschlechtertrennung*, 60.

commodified labor of women (or, for that matter, of convicts or children) undermined the pride and dignity that working men derived from their work. Women were believed unable to compete with men in skill or strength, even while the spread of commodified female labor increasingly eroded the plausibility of this tenet.[682] Berlin's organized workers therefore struggled to push women into the supposedly non-commodified sphere of the home.[683]

Workers in New York City also equated the unregulated commodification of female labor and female sexuality. Amy Dru Stanley's discussion of female prostitution in postbellum America shows that the nexus of commodification, women's work, and female sexuality made working-class discourse compatible with broader discussions about the moral boundaries of the free market. Especially in urban places like New York City, the commodification of sex reflected the ambiguities of wage labor. The prostitute, Stanley argues, "was the quintessential commodity, and she was thoroughly metropolitan."[684] Here, too, anxieties about the commodification of female sexuality fueled widespread opposition to the commodification of female labor. At first sight, protective struggles for labor legislation seem to have been fought more inclusively in New York. But despite the integrative rhetoric of American working-class organizations, New York's trade unionists struggled actively to keep women out of their trades. In so doing, they contributed to the concentration of working women in the very sectors that were excluded from the protection organized labor was fighting for.

At the annual meeting of New York State's Workingmen's Assembly in 1870, delegates adopted an amendment that was sent to the legislature in order to replace the existing eight-hour law. As the assembly's president William J. Jessup proudly announced the following year, the draft had passed both houses and been signed into law by Governor Hoffman.[685] The amendment underscored that eight hours constituted a normal workday for all laborers in New York, but it retained the paragraph that the law should not

682 See also Losseff-Tillmanns, *Frauenemanzipation und Gewerkschaften*, 54.

683 When an independent social-democratic women's movement finally took shape towards the end of the century, it was confronted with the same opposition that male workers had formulated a generation earlier; see Schmitt, *Der Arbeiterinnenschutz im deutschen Kaiserreich*, 43–62. Organized women eventually accepted gendered legislation as a compromise between the liberal movement's demand for an unrestricted commodification of female labor on the one hand and the early labor movement's initial struggle against all women's work on the other; see ibid., 62–79.

684 Stanley, *From Bondage to Contract*, 222.

685 *Proceedings of the Seventh Annual Session of the Workingmen's Assembly*, 5.

"alter the present hours of farm labor or domestic labor."[686] Of the roughly 50,000 domestic laborers whom the ninth census of 1870 counted for New York City, about 42,000 were women.[687] The working men of New York would rather exclude female servants from protection than jeopardize their bill. Male resistance to female competition thus played into the hands of an expanding domestic-service sector and the growth of an urban outwork economy. Christine Stansell argues persuasively that the fact that outwork quickly gave way to more centralized forms of production in some regions and sectors of the industrializing US does not mean that the putting-out system can generally be seen as a quickly fading interlude in the development from artisanal to industrial production. Especially in urban contexts like that of New York City, the putting-out system constituted a central element in stratifying the nascent labor force and translating gendered forms of subordination from the family to the labor market. Whereas employers in other places in the US used out-work only "until they overcame cultural resistance to women working outside the home, New York employers capitalized upon and strengthened that resistance."[688]

Whether women were singled out as addressees of labor legislation (as in Berlin) or virtually excluded from indoor wage labor (as in New York), both strategies were framed as protective measures that allowed women to withdraw to their home, the last safe haven in a world fully determined by market exchange. Yet outside of this market, women were deprived not only of their right to economic participation and self-determination, but also of the concessions and improvements that male workers struggled for. Whether in domestic service, home production, or reproductive labor, the isolated sphere of the home seriously hampered women's ability to organize collectively and enforce better wages or working conditions. Male movements for labor protection in Berlin and New York thus resulted in severe discrimination and the marginalization of working women. From the perspective of the latter, free access to the labor market—or, put differently, the commodification of female labor power—could serve as a remedy for social and familial forms of domination. Then again, the free labor market jeopardized the material well-being of women. Poorly documented, hardly regulated, and stripped of legal protection—or, put differently, largely *dis-embedded*—the urban labor market was characterized by extremely long hours at disastrously

686 *Proceedings of the Sixth Annual Session of the Workingmen's Assembly*, 59.
687 "Selected Occupations, with Age and Sex, and Nativity."
688 Stansell, *City of Women*, 107.

low wages. Working women in mid-nineteenth-century Berlin and New York were thus caught in a contradictory dynamic that seemed to offer either an exit from domination through the exploitative reality of free wage labor or a shield against unprotected commodification through culturally charged forms of domination.[689] Therewith, working women faced, as Nancy Fraser puts it, a twofold movement of marketization and protection, both of which undermined female emancipation.[690]

In an approach that she describes as neo-Polanyian, Fraser criticizes Polanyi for portraying nineteenth- and early twentieth-century social contestation as a double movement of free market vs. social protection forces. According to Fraser, this dichotomy fails to acknowledge the inextricable third element in the process, that is, emancipation. The commodification of society not only provoked responses by movements for social protection; it also gave rise to new claims to justice and recognition. Such demands were not necessarily congruent with those for social protection or the free market. Rather, they built a movement in its own right, at times pairing with social protection against the market, at times joining the market against social protection's second face, that is, domination, at times striving against both. Though movements for emancipation struggle against a wide array of injutices, they are united, Fraser suggests, in their desire to "remove obstacles that prevent some people from participating fully, or on par with others, in social life."[691] This definition points to Fraser's idea of participatory parity, which in turn rests on her notion of recognition.[692] Unlike Charles Taylor or Axel Honneth, Fraser does not understand recognition primarily as an act of self-realization, but as a question of justice. In her eyes, it is first and foremost

> unjust that some individuals and groups are denied the status of full partners in social interaction simply as a consequence of institutionalized patterns of interpretation and evaluation in whose construction they have not equally participated and that dis-

689 This dilemma re-emerged in second-wave feminist debates; see Notz, "Mehr Zeit zum Schaffen, Träumen, Kämpfen."

690 Fraser, "Marketization, Social Protection, Emancipation."

691 Ibid., 149.

692 This builds on a theoretical distinction that Fraser has developed over the past two decades; see Fraser and Gordon, "Contract Versus Charity;" Fraser, "From Redistribution to Recognition;" Fraser, "Social Justice in the Age of Identity Politics."

parage their distinctive characteristics or the distinctive characteristics assigned to them.[693]

Movements for emancipation are thus struggles for justice through recognition as equal partners. Yet movements for protection regularly invoke notions of justice as well. Interpreting equality as a material prerequisite for any meaningful notion of justice, such movements strive to redistribute unevenly accumulated wealth and thereby level existing inequalities. While redistribution generally addresses processes of socio-economic exploitation rooted in the political economy, recognition confronts various forms of misrepresentation and domination based on cultural valuation. The former thus intends to reform or replace the economic cause of unequal distribution, whereas the latter is primarily concerned with the removal of stigmatizing or otherwise dominantly ascribed attributions. It follows that redistribution and recognition are expressions of distinct dimensions of justice based on economic and cultural equality, respectively.[694] Yet while maintaining the theoretical distinctiveness of the two spheres of justice, Fraser nevertheless develops a *unifying* framework. Injuries inflicted on groups in society do not necessarily sit neatly at one or the other end of the protection-emancipation spectrum. Rather, groups might be victims of economic exploitation and cultural domination at the same time. Fraser calls such collectivities "bi-valent." Women, for example, experience injustice due to systemic exploitation as un- or underpaid care workers, and they also suffer injustice stemming from androcentrist modes of cultural domination and status hierarchization. The two dimensions of injustice are hence intertwined.

Fraser argues that Polanyi remained blind to the fundamental distinction between emancipation and protection because he disregarded what Fraser calls the "ethical substance," the "normative stuff," or "*Sittlichkeit*" that legitimized any form of embedding and protection.[695] Societies did not react as homogenous entities to threats triggered by marketization. Instead, nation states institutionalized only certain protective provisions that were signified and substantiated by societal actors—from churches to trade unions to workers' movements. Such selective protection helped establish social hier-

693 Ibid., 3.

694 This distinction is rejected by Axel Honneth who argues that, ultimately, demands for equal distribution also originate from a desire for social recognition. Redistribution in Honneth's account is an expression of the struggle for recognition that marks all aspects of social life; see Fraser and Honneth, *Redistribution or Recognition.*

695 Fraser, "Marketization, Social Protection, Emancipation," 147.

archies rather than promote the equal protection of all members of society. Polanyi was by no means unaware of such contradictions, but he was unable to integrate them analytically into his narrow model of a double movement.

Applied to the movement for shorter hours in Berlin and New York City in the 1860s and early 1870s, Fraser's critique reveals a major short-coming in Polanyian thought. As this study has shown, the mere idea that women's work was transformed into a commodity triggered opposition from the nascent workers' movement. Protesting the reign of the free market for female labor in Berlin and New York, Polanyi's protective movement posed a two-fold threat to working-class women. Both the *inclusion* of women in a *non-gender-neutral* protective framework (in Berlin) and their *exclusion* from a *gender-neutral* protective framework (in New York) undermined women's claims to equality and emancipation. The distinct rationalities underlying shorter-hour demands for men and women show that social democrats and trade unionists did not struggle against the commodification of female labor and in favor of shorter-hour legislation for women as independent producers of value who deserved the omnipresent "full fruits of their labor." Rather, they demanded shorter-hour legislation for women because it promised to ease wage competition for men and reinforce patriarchal hierarchies in the economy as well as the family. Women were thus not seen as self-governing agents, but as helpless wards in need of special protection. The "normative stuff" that Fraser finds missing in Polanyi featured here as a central argument in defense of a de-commodified domestic sphere and the alleged need for labor legislation that applied to female workers only. In nineteenth-century working-class discourse, women's supposedly threatened *Sittlichkeit* was thereby used to negate female subjectivity.[696]

696 Braun, *Gewerbeordnung und Geschlechtertrennung*, 78.

7. Conclusion: The Past and Present of Commodification

"Winning two hours a day will make us better citizens, better men, and better workers."[697]
Arbeiter-Union, 1869

In many ways, the workers' movements of nineteenth-century Berlin and New York were worlds apart. While ethnic diversity played a major role in stratifying New York's labor force, working-class Berlin was extremely homogenous. While workers in New York City flocked to the emerging trade unions rather than political parties, social-democratic parties in Berlin dominated the young trade-union movement. While organized labor was able to operate relatively unhampered in the American metropolis, it faced serious forms of surveillance and repression in Berlin. Yet despite all these differences, working-class Berlin and New York developed a strikingly similar rationale when making demands. As this book has shown, close personal and intellectual exchange was a crucial element in fostering similarity.

Towards the late 1860s prominent members of Berlin's young socialist movement like Edward Grosse, Sigfrid Meyer, and August Vogt left their home town for New York City, where they helped build one of the most vibrant movements in the nation. Activists from Berlin became influential supporters of the German-speaking sections of the First International in New York. Others, like the Berliner A. Mundt, presided over the New York City branch of the ADAV, which had been established by Lassallean immigrants in 1866. These activists from Berlin were accompanied by ordinary workers who populated Manhattan's Little Germany, from where they sent home correspondence informing relatives and friends about how they were faring in the American metropolis. Such letters were often published by a very lively working-class press. Local papers in Berlin covered eight-hour strikes and other working-class events in New York City. German-language

697 "Unsere Widerlegung," *Die Arbeiter-Union*, 17 December 1869, 2. ("Zwei Stunden Arbeitszeit täglich gewonnen [...machen...] jeden Arbeiter bedeutend tüchtiger als Mensch, Bürger und Fachmann.")

papers in New York City translated and published key labor documents in the US, such as statements or declarations by the National Labor Union. Often an article that had appeared in a Berlin-based paper was published several weeks later by the working-class press of New York City. Some labor papers such as New York's *Toiler* even appeared in bilingual editions. All this testifies to the enormous significance of early working-class media for the trans-Atlantic spread of ideas.

Not least thanks to their media, organized workers in Berlin and New York City were able to establish a shared understanding of "what qualified as work and who qualified as worker."[698] Nowhere was this more salient than in the ideas that legitimized the struggle for shorter hours. In the eyes of urban workers on both sides of the Atlantic, shorter workdays promised to make them, as one of their papers put it in the quotation above, better *citizens*, better *men*, and better *workers*. These hopes largely correspond to the spheres of the *polity*, *society*, and *economy* discussed in the previous chapters. This study has revealed that whether in Berlin or New York, shorter-hour rhetoric was heavily influenced by resistance to the commodification of labor—a central yet widely neglected element in mid-nineteenth-century working-class discourse.

On both sides of the Atlantic, the early labor movement yearned for a mythical past of producerist autonomy. In the eyes of shorter-hour activists, the unrestricted exchange of labor threatened their status as independent producers. By forcing them under the "yoke of wage slavery," the detested free labor market undermined working-class notions of selfhood. In so doing, it jeopardized their rights as free and equal citizens. As the analysis of the political rationale for shorter hours has demonstrated, organized workers saw workday legislation as a crucial remedy to the phenomenon of commodification and the accompanying attack on their civic rights. In addition, socialist intellectuals and party officials were particularly opposed to the uncontrolled exchange of labor power as an alienating act of dehumanization. Comparing the realities of wage labor to animals and machinery, social-democratic discourse highlighted the vicious brutality and impersonal coldness of market-mediated labor relations. For these intellectuals and party officials, the shorter-hour demand represented a de-commodifying struggle for the protection of society from the power of unfettered markets. At the same

698 "Was ist Arbeit und wer ist Arbeiter," *Arbeiter-Zeitung*, 1 March 1873, 1; "Wer ist Arbeiter," *Die Arbeiter-Union*, 21 November 1868, 1, 4; "Work and Wages," *Woodhull and Claflin's Weekly*, 14 May 1870, 10.

time, they saw the demand to shorten the workday as a crucial tool in the struggle against the hegemony of *laissez-faire* economics.

The analysis of the economic rationale underlying the shorter-hour demand has shown, however, that leading trades in the urban economies of Berlin and New York increasingly refrained from opposing the commodification of labor towards the early 1870s. Whether shorter-hour activists accepted the mechanisms of the market—including the selling and buying of labor power—depended very much upon their respective occupational background and their role within the movement. While many craftsmen and party officials continued to draw upon resistance to commodification as a reservoir for shorter-hour demands, organized construction workers increasingly accepted the commodification of labor power as a precondition for successful struggles to shorten the workday. Often, the same activist could openly endorse the logic of commodification when speaking as trade unionist but fiercely oppose it when speaking as reformer or social democrat. Berlin's prominent bricklayer and future leader of immigrant workers in the American Midwest, Paul Grottkau, personifies this tension very vividly. When discussing the political role of the social-democratic party in a letter to Germany's organized bricklayers, Grottkau depicted the commodifying pressure of the free labor market as the main culprit for the dehumanization and destitution of an entire class. The party, Grottkau argued, had the duty to end the commodification of labor. Yet when discussing the trade-union movement in the same letter, Grottkau accepted the notion of commodified labor power, explaining that a reduction of daily hours would reduce the supply of working hands, which would inevitably increase wages.[699] Depending on whether he spoke as social democrat or trade unionist, Grottkau opposed the commodification of labor power or urged workers to use it to their advantage. The analysis of economic shorter-hour arguments has thus revealed that some urban trades had given up resistance to commodification by the early 1870s. The more the everyday life of urban workers was determined by the realities of wage labor, the less these workers opposed the resulting commodification of their labor power. This shift helped wage workers present their struggle as beneficial for employees and employers alike. The latter had long opposed any infringement upon what they saw as their right to use the labor power they had bought for as long as they wished. But employers increasingly understood that a shorter workday could also mean

699 Paeplow, *Zur Geschichte der deutschen Bauarbeiterbewegung*, 689–694.

a more efficient utilization of labor power.[700] By the turn of the century, more and more employers saw the normal workday as a means to boost productivity and preserve their employees' capacity to work for as long as possible. Instead of further struggling against commodification, workers began accepting the category of commodified work as a weapon in the conflict over who would determine the conditions for the selling and usage of labor, including the question of time. It was no coincidence that these perceptions changed first in the construction trades. Rather than mechanization, here it was the growing separation from former masters, the proliferation of wage work, and the further institutionalization of collective bargaining that proved decisive for this paradigm shift in urban places like Berlin and New York.

As the nineteenth century faded and the twentieth matured, the industrial realities of Fordism, together with the political experiences of the early welfare state, pushed concerns about the commodification of labor further to the side. For the first time, effective labor legislation allowed for a modest degree of de-commodification, while changes in the regime of accumulation—such as relatively stable employment and the rise of mass consumption—rendered arguments opposing the commodification of labor power increasingly meaningless. Demands for de-commodification began to re-emerge at the very moment that the Fordist system came to an end, starting in the 1970s. The less that welfare-state benefits, full employment, large-scale industrial production, and relatively stable and high wages cushioned the pressure of the labor market, the more that arguments opposing the commodification of labor power resurfaced. The current revival of the concept of commodification in social-movement discourse directly responds to the dramatic re-commodification of labor.[701] This is no wonder given that, despite the significant differences between them, there exist clear parallels between the post-Fordist urban labor of today and the pre-Fordist urban labor of the 1860s.[702]

A female graphic designer in present-day Berlin or New York, for instance, shares important features with a seamstress in either of the two cities one and a half centuries earlier. Following years of flexibilization and outsourcing, this graphic designer is very likely to work in some form of fictitious self-employment that lacks the benefits of formal employment. As a consequence of two decades of welfare-state reform, she is deprived of many

700 Reulecke, "Vom Blauen Montag zum Arbeiterurlaub," 215.

701 Burawoy, "Facing an Unequal World," 12–16.

702 See also Hermann, "Kampf um die Arbeitszeit," 83–102.

of the de-commodifying concessions that full-blown welfare states once provided. Due to a heavily gendered employment structure, chances are high that she works part-time for less pay than her male counterparts. At the same time, her wage is further diminished by the parallel re-commodification of urban housing and the subsequent increase in rents in inner-city neighborhoods. And, finally, she faces a dominant ideology of austerity, which impedes any form of social protection. *Laissez-faire* economics, rising rents in the city, fictitious self-employment in outwork, and a lack of welfare-state provisions—all these aspects also characterized female labor in mid-nineteenth-century Berlin and New York. Now as then, the lives of many workers are determined by the largely unfettered commodification of labor power in an intellectual, legal, and political-economic climate that is dominated by a paradigm of non-intervention. Today, following decades of disembedded markets and social protection, the "Polanyian Pendulum" has fully swung back.[703] Yet while this testifies to the fruitfulness of Polanyi's concept of commodification for the study of both past and present contestation, this book has also buttressed the view that his framework requires critical re-evaluation in at least two respects.

First, this study has illustrated what Nancy Fraser and others criticize as Polanyi's blindness towards the ambiguity of protection. Although the nineteenth-century shorter-hour movement might have had, as David R. Roediger argues, "a capacity to unify workers across the lines of craft, race, sex, skill, age and ethnicity," it also had the capacity to disunite them along these very lines.[704] Focusing on the "gender line," this study has revealed that the struggle for shorter hours in fact contributed to the marginalization of working women. Organized male workers in Berlin and New York generally opposed the unregulated workday and its underlying logic of commodification as a threat to their understanding of masculinity, material participation, producerist autonomy, human dignity, and civic rights. They thus interpreted the shorter-hour demand as a struggle for autonomy and selfhood. When demanding the regulation of the female workday, however, the same workers drew upon a very different rationale. According to dominant working-class discourse, women were in need of protective labor legislation, but not because the free market undermined women's rights to political self-determination, social participation, and redistribution. Rather, female labor had to be regulated because unchecked commodification disturbed patriarchal

703 See Silver, *Forces of Labor*, 16–20.

704 Roediger, *The Movement for a Shorter Working Day*, 5.

concepts of social and economic control in both the family and society at large.[705] While shorter-hour arguments for men thus drew upon an emancipatory rhetoric of equality and freedom, arguments for shorter hours for women rested on an essentializing logic of reproductive duty, moral vulnerability, economic competition, and sexual integrity—a set of arguments that was later expanded by the imperialist-racist concern for the health of "the mothers of the race."[706] Such argumentation deprived women of the very subjectivity that organized male workers were fighting for for themselves.

It was no coincidence that the skilled trades stood at the forefront of organized labor's struggle against a free market for working women. On both sides of the Atlantic, the paradigm of commodified labor won acceptance among workers by clearly demarcating the social sphere that would be exempt or protected from the dominion of the market. As Amy Dru Stanley has shown in her compelling analysis of commodification in the age of slave emancipation, this sphere was the working-class home. Mid-nineteenth-century liberal economics suggested that it was a home free from market incursion that distinguished the families of free wage workers from families in slavery.[707] The promise that the domestic sphere would be protected from unfettered commodification proved crucial in bringing organized labor into line. Put differently, the fact that the paradigm of commodification won acceptance among the skilled workers in places like Berlin and New York presupposed the de-commodification of the domestic realm. The experience of mid-nineteenth-century female workers thus confirmed what Fraser suggests on a more abstract level. Working women in the 1860s and early 1870s faced a powerful struggle between forces pushing for the commodification of female labor power and forces that strived for its de-commodification. While the former promised to free working-class women from domination, the exploitative reality of mid-nineteenth-century labor markets clearly jeopardized women's understanding of social justice and economic participation. And while social protection promised to shield working women from this very exploitative reality, it undermined their autonomy and independence. In New York City, organized labor struggled to keep women out of the skilled trades, which resulted in women's concentration in those sectors and trades in which, due to their informal and "domestic" nature, labor power

705 See also Wecker, "Normalarbeitstag, Gesundheitsschutz und Nachtarbeitsverbot."

706 Braun, *Gewerbeordnung und Geschlechtertrennung*, 68; Jansz, "Women or Workers;" Kessler-Harris, *Out of Work*, 191, 202–203.

707 Stanley, *From Bondage to Contract*, 170.

was less directly commodified. In Berlin, the juxtaposition of the free market and the home underscored protective measures that addressed women only. Social-democratic and conservative voices here agreed that women required special protection from the commodifying pressures of the free market. German social democrats actively pushed for shorter-hour legislation that applied specifically to female workers rather than to all workers irrespective of their sex. Both in Berlin and New York, the logic of female de-commodification pushed women back into the sphere of un- or under-waged reproductive and home work. Whether they were singled out as addressees of protective labor legislation (as in Berlin) or excluded from the skilled trades that actually promised effective protection (as in New York City), working women did not benefit from Polanyi's counter-movement.

The critique of Polanyi's blindness towards the ambiguity of protection points, secondly, to his strikingly underdeveloped conception of state and society. Polanyi argues that the commodification of money, land, and human labor is fictitious and, as a result, disturbingly "unnatural."[708] Throughout *The Great Transformation*, he displays a deeply organic understanding of society. According to Polanyi, society will always defend its basic interest against any threat to its integrity. But what is the common interest of society—and, for that matter, what is society? As Michael Burawoy has argued, Polanyi simply equates state and society, thereby neglecting the complicated and often intertwined layers of contestation that characterize modern nation states and liberal market societies.[709] Discussing Burawoy's thoughtful juxtaposition of Gramscian and Polanyian notions of hegemony and social interest, Ronaldo Munck infers that, for Polanyi, counter-hegemony was not a subaltern movement or proletarian consciousness directed against the hegemony of the capitalist class, as Gramsci had it.[710] Rather,

> it was a social reaction to the market that would spur a counter-hegemonic movement. Not only the subaltern classes but also powerful capitalist interests would be threatened by the anarchy of the market and would thus react.[711]

The comparison with Gramsci is particularly telling because for Gramsci, social interests were expressions of class antagonisms. *What the ruling class does when it rules* is, in Gramscian terms, not simply an act of domination, but

708 Polanyi, *The Great Transformation*, 257.

709 Burawoy, "From Polanyi to Pollyanna," 302–304.

710 Burawoy, "For a Sociological Marxism."

711 Munck, "Globalization and Contestation," 181.

a constant process of renegotiating power relations within society.[712] This complex process of renegotiation allowed the ruling class to maintain its hegemonic position in society by portraying its own interests as the commonsensical interest of all. Any opposition to the allegedly shared interest could thus be depicted as counterproductive or outright absurd.[713] Polanyi, in contrast, lacks a notion of class as a central agent in historical contestation. He thus replaces Gramsci's rigid class perspective with a shallow concept of society in which the only coalitions of interests conceivable are those that defend or oppose the self-regulating market. To put it differently, Polanyi maintains that the self-regulating market inevitably triggers alliances across society because the commodification of life threatens society as a whole. With his insistence that it is society *per se* rather than a particular class that struggles for protection, Polanyi's analysis of social conflict becomes rather vague. Pace Munck, one does not have to be an adherent of the "neoliberal" or "post-modernist" creeds, according to which "there is no such thing as society," to find Polanyi's idealization of the organic fabric of society unsettling.[714] Polanyi's notion of a supposedly universal social interest points to an epistemological obscurity that runs like a thread through his work. Polanyi asserted that market societies inevitably fight commodification because the latter threatens the social foundations, because it is inorganic, inhumane, somehow unnatural. But, to put it provocatively, who says that humans are not produced for the market? Is it nature itself that forbids this? Is it an ethical underpinning derived from the belief in a supernatural order that determines what humans are, and what they are not? Is it a question of historical experience or of rights and entitlements? Because Polanyi fails to define his normative social theory explicitly, the alternative he provides remains diffuse. This has been illustrated by the historical movement analyzed in this study.

Shorter-hour activists in Berlin and New York regularly dismissed the commodification of labor as a threat to their notion of political liberty and social status. Often, states accepted this logic of de-commodification, yet instead of applying it equally to all, they referred to the supposedly organic and natural state of society, which required the exclusive protection of some selected groups rather than others. The alleged right of women to be protected from commodification—a right that was widely acknowledged by male

712 Therborn, *What Does the Ruling Class Do When It Rules.*

713 See Morton, *Unravelling Gramsci*, 76–108.

714 Munck, "Globalization and Contestation," 184.

workers, employers, clergymen, and legislators alike—fueled the eventual passage of shorter-hour laws that exclusively addressed female workers towards the end of century. Rather than promoting a universal right to market protection, Polanyi's counter-movement fostered the hierachization of working classes along the lines of gender, but also along other lines such as race and age. After all, the gendered ambiguity of shorter-hour discourse discussed in this study is but one of the many examples of how selective forms of protection from commodification reinforced existing inequalities. The history of social protection from market demands reveals that protection was regularly bought at the expense of the exclusion of, discrimination against, and domination over others: Laboring men seeking protection from female competition, skilled artisans demanding privileges over the unskilled masses, employed workers despising the support of their unemployed fellows, one dominant ethnic group insisting on the exclusion of their racialized colleagues, whole regimes of protection based on the exploitation of a colonized workforce abroad. The shortcomings discussed here are not meant to imply that we should dismiss the Polanyian perspective altogether, but that we ought to employ it with caution. The concepts of commodification and protection constitute important analytical categories for the study of past and present contestation, but they must be embedded in a critical theory of social and political power.

Abbreviations

ADAV	Allgemeiner Deutscher Arbeiterverein (General German Workers' Association)
ADF	Allgemeiner Deutscher Frauenverein (General German Women's Association)
AFL	American Federation of Labor
BAV	Berliner Arbeiterverein (Workers' Association of Berlin)
CMIU	Cigar Makers' International Union
GGWA	General German Workingmen's Association (Allgemeiner Deutscher Arbeiter-Verein, NY)
IWA	International Workingmen's Association
LADAV	Lassallscher Allgemeiner Deutscher Arbeiterverein (Lassallean ADAV)
NLU	National Labor Union
SAP	Sozialistische Arbeiterpartei Deutschlands (Socialist Workers' Party of Germany)
SED	Sozialistische Einheitspartei Deutschlands (Socialist Unity Party of Germany)
SDAP	Sozialdemokratische Arbeiterpartei (Social Democratic Workers' Party)
SDPNA	Social Democratic Party of North America
SLP	Socialist Labor Party
SPD	Sozialdemokratische Partei Deutschlands (Social Democratic Party of Germany)
VDAV	Vereinstag Deutscher Arbeitervereine (Congress of German Workers' Associations)
WWA	Working Women's Association
WTU	Women's Typographical Union

Bibliography

Primary Sources

Archives

Geheimes Staatsarchiv Preußischer Kulturbesitz, I. HA Rep. 90 A, Nr. 2257: "Regelung des Vereins- und Versammlungsrechts," Bd. 1, 1794–1893.

Geheimes Staatsarchiv Preußischer Kulturbesitz, I. HA Rep. 120 A, I, 1, Nr. 56: "Die beim Reichstage des Norddeutschen Bundes eingegangenen Petitionen," 1867–1873.

Geheimes Staatsarchiv Preußischer Kulturbesitz, I. HA Rep. 120 BB VII, 3, Nr. 2, Bd. 1, 1872–1876: "Sechzehnter Bericht der Kommission für Petitionen, Deutscher Reichstag, 1. Legislaturperiode, III. Session 1872."

New York Public Library, ZL-352: "New York City Typographical Union No. 6, Regular Meetings Minutes," 1870–1917.

Wisconsin Historical Society, U.S. Mss 9 A, Box 2, Folder 1: "Ira Steward Papers," 1876–1883.

Newspapers and Journals

Agitator: Organ des Allgemeinen Deutschen Arbeitervereins (Berlin)

Arbeiter-Zeitung (New York)

Cigar Makers' Official Journal: Issued by the Cigar Makers International Union of America (New York)

Demokratische Zeitung (Berlin)

Der Botschafter: Organ der Deutschen Cigarrenarbeiter (Leipzig)

Der Social-Demokrat: Organ des Allgemeinen Deutschen Arbeiter-Vereins/ Organ der Social-Demokratischen Partei (Berlin)

Der Social-Demokrat: Organ und Eigenthum der Sozial-Demokratischen Arbeiterpartei von Nord-Amerika (New York)

Der Volksstaat (Leipzig)

Der Wahre Jacob (Hamburg/Stuttgart/Berlin)

Die Arbeiter-Union: Volkswirthschaftliches und sociales Organ der Arbeiter (New York)

Die Zukunft: Demokratische Zeitung (Berlin)
Gleichheit: Organ der Sozialdemokratischen Arbeiterpartei in Oesterreich (Vienna)
Königlich Privilegirte Berlinische Zeitung (Berlin)
Labor Standard: Organ of the Wage Workers of the United States (New York/Boston)
Neue Bahnen: Organ des Allgemeinen Deutschen Frauenvereins (Leipzig)
Neuer Social-Demokrat: Organ der Socialistischen Arbeiter-Partei Deutschlands (Berlin)
New Yorker Arbeiter-Zeitung: Wochenschau für Unterhaltung und Belehrung (New York)
New York Tribune (New York)
Oesterreichische Revue: Organ für Assekuranz und Volkswirtschaft (Vienna)
Pionier: Central-Organ der Gewerkschaften Deutschlands und der eingeschriebenen Hülfs-Cassen (Mannheim; Hamburg)
Social-Politische Blätter zur Unterhaltung und Belehrung für die deutschen Arbeiter: Eigentum der Lassalleaner (Berlin)
The National Workman (New York)
The New York Times (New York)
The Revolution (New York)
The Socialist: An Organizer of the Working Classes (New York)
The Toiler: Organ of the Labor Interest (New York)
The Workingman's Advocate (Chicago)
Vorwärts: Central-Organ der Sozialdemokratie Deutschlands/Zentralorgan der Sozialdemokratischen Partei Deutschlands (Leipzig/Berlin)
Woodhull and Claflin's Weekly (New York)

Other Primary Material

Allgemeine Preußische Gewerbe-Ordnung nebst dem Entschädigungs-Gesetz vom 17. Januar (1845). Elberfeld: Julius Bädeker.

"August Vogt und Wilhelm Liebknecht an Julius Vahlteich" (1973). In Georg Eckart (ed.), *Wilhelm Liebknecht: Briefwechsel mit deutschen Sozialdemokraten*, Quellen und Untersuchungen zur Geschichte der deutschen und österreichischen Arbeiterbewegung, vol. 1 (1862–1878), 3–5. Assen: Van Gorcum.

Baader, Ottilie (2013). *Ein Steiniger Weg: Lebenserinnerungen einer Sozialistin*. Michael Holzinger (ed.), Berliner Ausgabe, http://www.zeno.org/Kulturgeschichte/M/Baader,+Ottilie/Ein+steiniger+Weg.+Lebenserinnerungen+einer+Sozialistin (accessed 8 May 2016).

Berger, Adeline (1889). *Die zwanzigjährige Arbeiterinnen-Bewegung Berlins und ihr Ergebnis, beleuchtet von einer Arbeiterin*. Quellenedition zur Geschichte der deutschen Arbeiterbewegung, Projekt 2: Proletarische Frauenbewegung. Berlin: Selbstverlag.

"Carl August Schramm an Wilhelm Liebknecht" (1973). In Georg Eckart (ed.), *Wilhelm Liebknecht: Briefwechsel mit deutschen Sozialdemokraten*, Quellen und Untersuchungen zur Geschichte der deutschen und österreichischen Arbeiterbewegung, vol. 1 (1862–1878), 783–784. Assen: Van Gorcum.

Census of the State of New York for 1865 (1867). Compiled by Franklin B. Hough. New York State, Secretary's Office. Albany: C. van Benthuysen & Sons.

Census of the State of New York for 1875 (1877). Compiled by C.W. Seaton. New York State, Secretary's Office. Albany: Weed, Parsons and Company.

Daul, Anthony (1867). *Die Frauen-Arbeit oder der Kreis ihrer Erwerbsfähigkeit: Nach dem Amerikanischen der Mrs. Virginia Penny in mehr als 600 Erwerbs- und Berufsarten praktisch nachgewiesen*, vol. 1. Altona: Hammerich.

Deutsches Weber-Central-Comitee (ed.) (1871). *Ausführlicher Bericht über die Verhandlungen des ersten Deutschen Webertags abgehalten zu Glauchau in Sachsen vom 28. bis 30. Mai 1871*. Quellenedition zur Geschichte der deutschen Arbeiterbewegung, Projekt 2: Proletarische Frauenbewegung. Crimmtschau: Junghahn, Stolle & Comp.

Dieterici, Carl Friedrich Wilhelm (1857). *Über die Zunahme der Bevölkerung im Preussischen Staate in Bezug auf Vertheilung derselben nach Stadt und Land.* Berlin: Duemmler.

Engel, Ernst (n.d.). "Die Industrie der großen Städte: Eine sozial-statistische Betrachtung." In *Berlin und seine Entwickelung: Gemeinde-Kalender und städtisches Jahrbuch für 1868*, vol. 2, 134–164. Berlin: J. Guttentag.

– (1878). *Die industrielle Enquete und die Gewerbezählung im Deutschen Reiche und im Preussischen Staate am Ende des Jahres 1875: Ein Vortrag gehalten in der Volkswirthschaftlichen Gesellschaft zu Berlin am 9. Februar 1878*. Berlin: Simion.

Engels, Friedrich (1971). "Die Englische Zehnstundenbill." In Institut für Marxismus-Leninismus beim ZK der SED (ed.), *Marx-Engels-Werke*, vol. 7, 233–243. Berlin (East): Dietz.

– (1971). "Die Zehnstundenfrage." In Institut für Marxismus-Leninismus beim ZK der SED (ed.), *Marx-Engels-Werke*, vol. 7, 226–232. Berlin (East): Dietz.

"F. A. Sorge an Wilhelm Liebknecht" (1973). In Georg Eckart (ed.), *Wilhelm Liebknecht: Briefwechsel mit deutschen Sozialdemokraten*, Quellen und Untersuchungen zur Geschichte der deutschen und österreichischen Arbeiterbewegung, vol. 1 (1862–1878),422–423. Assen: Van Gorcum.

"F. A. Sorge an Wilhelm Liebknecht" (1973). In Georg Eckart (ed.), *Wilhelm Liebknecht: Briefwechsel mit deutschen Sozialdemokraten*, Quellen und Untersuchungen zur Geschichte der deutschen und österreichischen Arbeiterbewegung, vol. 1 (1862–1878), 416–417. Assen: Van Gorcum.

"F. A. Sorge an Wilhelm Liebknecht" (1973). In Georg Eckart (ed.), *Wilhelm Liebknecht: Briefwechsel mit deutschen Sozialdemokraten*, Quellen und Untersuchungen zur Geschichte der deutschen und österreichischen Arbeiterbewegung, vol. 1 (1862–1878), 342. Assen: Van Gorcum.

Fitzhugh, George (1960). *Cannibals All! Or Slaves without Masters.* The John Harvard Library. Cambridge, Mass.: Belknap Press of Harvard University.

– (1965). *Sociology for the South or The Failure of Free Society.* Reprint. Burt Franklin Research and Source Works Series 102. New York: Franklin.

Gunton, George (1887). *Wealth and Progress: A Critical Examination of the Labor Problem; the Natural Basis for Industrial Reform; or How to Increase Wages without Reducing Profits or Lowering Rents: The Economic Philosophy of the Eight Hour Movement.* New York: D. Appleton.

Heinzen, Karl P. (1848). *Die Helden des teutschen Kommunismus.* Bern: Jenni/Sohn.

International Workingmen's Association (ed.) (1868). *Resolutions of the Congress of Geneva, 1866, and the Congress of Brussels, 1868.* London: Westminster Printing.

Kletke, G.M. (ed.) (1873). *Die Verfassungs-Urkunde für den Preußischen Staat vom 31. Januar 1850.* Brandenburg a.d.H.: Müller.

Lassalle, Ferdinand (1864). *Herr Bastiat-Schulze von Delitzsch, der ökonomische Julian oder: Capital und Arbeit.* Berlin: Reinhold Schlingmann.

– (1868). *An die Arbeiter Berlins: Eine Ansprache im Namen der Arbeiter des Allgemeinen Deutschen Arbeitervereins.* Leipzig: Verlag des Lassalle'schen Allgemeinen Deutschen Arbeitervereins.

Magistrat der Stadt Berlin (ed.) (1879). *Bericht über die Gemeinde-Verwaltung der Stadt Berlin in den Jahren 1861 bis 1876*, vol. 1. Berlin: Julius Sittenfeld.

Manufactures of the United States in 1860, Compiled from the Original Returns of the Eight Census, under the Direction of the Secretary of the Interior (1865). Washington, D.C.: Government Printing Office.

Marx, Karl (1923). *Two Speeches by Karl Marx: Address to the Communist League, 1850, and The Inaugural Address of the International Workingmen's Association, 1864.* Vancouver: Historical Research Bureau.

– (1973). "Kritik des Gothaer Programms." In *Marx-Engels-Werke*, vol. 19, 4th ed., 13–32. Berlin (East): Dietz.

– (1974). *Capital*, vol. 1. New York and London: Dutton/Dent (Everyman's Library).

– (1975). "Plagiarismus." In *Marx-Engels-Werke*, vol. 16, 6th ed., 221–225. Berlin (East): Dietz.

– (2008). *Das Kapital: Kritik der Politischen Ökonomie*, vol. 1. *Marx-Engels-Werke*, vol. 23, 23rd ed. Berlin: Karl Dietz.

– and Friedrich Engels (1988). *Collected Works*, vol. 43: Letters, 1868–1870. London: Lawrence & Wishart.

McGill, P. M. (1867). *The Wrongs and Rights of Labor Fully and Fairly Shown, and a Remedy Proposed.* Washington: Gibson Brothers.

McNeill, George E. (n.d.) *Argument on the Hours of Labor, Delivered before the Labor Committee of the Massachusetts Legislature.* New York: Labor Standard Publishing Association.

Müller, Moritz (1865). *Vortrag über die Frauenfrage: Gehalten am dritten Arbeitertage in Stuttgart.* Coburg: Streit.

– (1866). *Eine Ansprache über die Arbeitszeit! Den deutschen Arbeitervereinen gewidmet.* Stuttgart: Metzler.

– (1867). *Über die Frauenfrage, respective Frauenarbeit: Ein Gutachten den deutschen Arbeitervereinen gewidmet.* Stuttgart: Metzler.

Otto-Peters, Louise (1866). *Das Recht der Frauen auf Erwerb: Blicke auf das Frauenleben der Gegenwart.* Hamburg: Hoffmann und Campe.

Penny, Virginia (1863). *The Employments of Women: A Cyclopaedia of Woman's Work.* Boston: Walker, Wise & Company.

"Population by County 1790–1870" (1872). In Francis Amasa Walker (ed.), *Ninth Census of the United States*, vol. 1: The Statistics of the Population of the United States, 51. Washington, D.C.: Government Printing Office.

Prince-Smith, John (1877). "Der Markt: Eine Skizze." In Otto Michaelis (ed.), *John Prince-Smith's Gesammelte Schriften*, vol. 1, 1–25. Berlin: F. A. Herbig.

– (1877). "Die sogenannte Arbeiterfrage." In Otto Michaelis (ed.), *John Prince-Smith's Gesammelte Schriften*, vol. 1, 26–42. Berlin: F. A. Herbig.

Proceedings of the Sixth Annual Session of the Workingmen's Assembly (1870). New York: Journeymen Printers' Co-operative Association.

Proceedings of the Seventh Annual Session of the Workingmen's Assembly (1871). New York: Journeymen Printers' Co-operative Association.

Schramm, Carl August (1872). *Mein offener Brief an Dr. Max Hirsch nebst Antwort und Rückantwort.* Berlin: C. Lübeck.

Schwabe, Hermann (ed.) (1869). *Die Resultate der Berliner Volkszählung vom 3. December 1867: Bearbeitet, erläutert und graphisch dargestellt.* Berlin: Kortkampf.

Schweitzer, Johann Baptist von (1868). "Der Schlingel." In Allgemeiner Deutscher Arbeiterverein (ed.), *Aus dem Social-Demokrat: Leitartikel und Aufsätze aus dem Organ der Social-Demokratischen Partei*, 130–148. Berlin: Selbstverlag von W. Grüwel.

"Selected Occupations, with Age and Sex, and Nativity" (1872). In Francis Amasa Walker (ed.), *Ninth Census of the United States*, vol. 1: The Statistics of the Population of the United States, 793. Washington, D.C.: Government Printing Office.

"Sigfrid Meyer an Ernestine Liebknecht" (1973). In Georg Eckart (ed.), *Wilhelm Liebknecht: Briefwechsel mit deutschen Sozialdemokraten*, Quellen und Untersuchungen zur Geschichte der deutschen und österreichischen Arbeiterbewegung, vol. 1 (1862–1878), 190–191. Assen: Van Gorcum.

"Sigfrid Meyer an Wilhelm Liebknecht" (1973). In Georg Eckart (ed.), *Wilhelm Liebknecht: Briefwechsel mit deutschen Sozialdemokraten*, Quellen und Untersuchungen zur Geschichte der deutschen und österreichischen Arbeiterbewegung, vol. 1 (1862–1878), 116–118. Assen: Van Gorcum.

"Sigfrid Meyer an Wilhelm Liebknecht" (1973). In Georg Eckart (ed.), *Wilhelm Liebknecht: Briefwechsel mit deutschen Sozialdemokraten*, Quellen und Untersuchungen zur Geschichte der deutschen und österreichischen Arbeiterbewegung, vol. 1 (1862–1878), 118–120. Assen: Van Gorcum.

"Sigfrid Meyer an Wilhelm Liebknecht" (1973). In Georg Eckart (ed.), *Wilhelm Liebknecht: Briefwechsel mit deutschen Sozialdemokraten*, Quellen und Untersuchungen zur Geschichte der deutschen und österreichischen Arbeiterbewegung, vol. 1 (1862–1878), 142–145. Assen: Van Gorcum.

Smith, Adam (1838). *An Inquiry into the Nature and the Causes of the Wealth of Nations.* Edinburgh: Thomas Nelson.

Steward, Ira (1958). "A Reduction of Hours, an Increase of Wages." In John R. Commons, Ulrich B. Phillips, Eugene A. Gilmore, Helen L. Sumner, and John B. Andrews (eds.), *A Documentary History of American Industrial Society*, vol. 9, 284–301. New York: Russell & Russell.

"Wilhelm Liebknecht an August Geib" (1973). In Georg Eckart (ed.), *Wilhelm Liebknecht: Briefwechsel mit deutschen Sozialdemokraten*, Quellen und Untersuchungen zur Geschichte der deutschen und österreichischen Arbeiterbewegung, vol. 1 (1862–1878), 444–448. Assen: Van Gorcum.

Working Women's Protective Union (ed.) (1877). *About the Working Women of New York*. New York.

Secondary Sources

Abelshauser, Werner (2002). *Die BASF: Eine Unternehmensgeschichte*. Munich: Beck.

Adams, Peter (2005). *The Bowery Boys: Street Corner Radicals and the Politics of Rebellion*. Westport, Conn. et al.: Praeger.

Andrews, John B. (1926). "Nationalisation." In John R. Commons, David J. Saposs, Helen L. Sumner, E.B. Mittelman, H.E. Hoagland, John B. Andrews, and Selig Perlman (eds.), *History of Labour in the United States*, vol. 2, 3–191. New York: Macmillan.

Armytage, W.H.G. (1971). "Owen in America." In Sidney Pollard and John Salt (eds.), *Robert Owen, Prophet of The Poor: Essays in Honour of the Two Hundredth Anniversary of his Birth*, 214–238. Lewisburg: Bucknell University Press.

Baar, Lothar (1986). "Berlin in der Industriellen Revolution: Zu Anstoß und Anlauf, Durchsetzung und Abschluß." In Akademie der Wissenschaften (ed.), *Zur Wirtschafts- und Sozialgeschichte Berlins vom 17. Jahrhundert bis zur Gegenwart*, Jahrbuch für Wirtschaftsgeschichte, Sonderband, 67–84. Berlin (East): Akademie.

Bailey, Brian J. (1998) *The Luddite Rebellion*. New York. New York University Press.

Barreyre, Nicolas (2011). "The Politics of Economic Crisis: The Panic of 1873, the End of Reconstruction, and the Realignment of American Politics." *The Journal of the Gilded Age and Progressive Era* 10 (4): 403–423.

Bates, Harry C. (1955). *Bricklayers' Century of Craftsmanship: A History of the Bricklayers, Masons and Plasterers' International Union of America*. Washington, D.C.: Bricklayers, Masons and Plasterers' International Union of America.

Baumann, Carl-Friedrich (1995). *Von der Stahlhütte zum Verarbeitungskonzern: Thyssen Industrie 1870–1995*. Essen: Thyssen Industrie AG.

Bergmann, Jürgen (1973). *Das Berliner Handwerk in den Frühphasen der Industrialisierung*. Einzelveröffentlichung der Historischen Kommission zu Berlin, vol. 11. Berlin: Colloquium.

Bernstein, Eduard (1907). *Die Geschichte der Berliner Arbeiterbewegung: Ein Kapitel zur Geschichte der deutschen Sozialdemokratie*, vol. 1: Vom Jahre 1848 bis zum Erlaß des Sozialistengesetzes. Berlin: Buchhandlung Vorwärts.

Bernstein, Iver (1990). *The New York City Draft Riots: Their Significance for American Society and Politics in the Age of the Civil War*. New York et al.: Oxford University Press.

Bernstein, Samuel (1965). *The First International in America*. Reprints of Economic Classics. New York: Kelley.

Bezirksleitung Berlin der SED, Kommission zur Erforschung der Geschichte der örtlichen Arbeiterbewegung (ed.) (1987). *Geschichte der revolutionären Berliner Arbeiterbewegung*, vol. 1: Von den Anfängen bis 1917. Berlin (East): Dietz.

Biernacki, Richard (2001). "Labor as an Imagined Commodity." *Politics and Society* 29 (2): 173–206.

– (1997). *The Fabrication of Labor: Germany and Britain, 1640–1914*. Berkeley et al.: University of California Press, 1997.

Blackmar, Elizabeth (1991). *Manhattan for Rent, 1785–1850*. Ithaca: Cornell University Press.

Block, Fred (2003). "Karl Polanyi and the Writing of 'The Great Transformation.'" *Theory and Society* 32 (3): 275–306.

– and Margaret R. Somers (2003). "In the Shadow of Speenhamland: Social Policy and the Old Poor Law." *Politics and Society* 31 (2): 283–323.

– and Margaret R. Somers (2014). *The Power of Market Fundamentalism: Karl Polanyi's Critique*. Cambridge, Mass.: Harvard University Press.

Blos, Wilhelm Joseph (1914). *Denkwürdigkeiten eines Sozialdemokraten*, vol. 1. Munich: G. Birk.

Bodenhorn, Howard (2000). *A History of Banking in Antebellum America: Financial Markets and Economic Development in an Era of Nation-Building*, Studies in Macro-economic History. Cambridge et al.: Cambridge University Press.

Boxer, Marilyn J. (1986). "Protective Legislation and Home Industry: The Marginalization of Women Workers in Late Nineteenth- and Early Twentieth-Century France." *Journal of Social History* 20 (1): 45–65.

Braun, Kathrin (1993). *Gewerbeordnung und Geschlechtertrennung: Klasse, Geschlecht und Staat in der frühen Arbeitsschutzgesetzgebung*, Nomos Universitätsschriften Politik, vol. 45. Baden-Baden: Nomos.

Brexel, Bernadette (2004). *The Knights of Labor and the Haymarket Riot: The Fight for an Eight-Hour Workday*. New York: Rosen Publishing Group.

Bringmann, August (1981). *Geschichte der deutschen Zimmerer-Bewegung*, vol. 1 and 2, Reprints zur Sozialgeschichte. Berlin and Bonn: J.H.W. Dietz Nachf.

Brody, David (1989). "Time and Work during Early American Industrialism." *Labor History* 30 (1): 5–46

– (1993). *In Labor's Cause: Main Themes on the History of the American Worker*. New York and Oxford: Oxford University Press.

– (1993). Review of "The Wages of Whiteness: Race and the Making of the American Working Class" by David R. Roediger. *The Journal of Interdisciplinary History* 24 (2): 378–380.

Bruns, Claudia and Michaela Hampf (eds.) (forthcoming). *Wissen, Transfer, Differenz: Transnationale und interdiskursive Verflechtungen von Rassismus ab 1700*. Göttingen: Wallstein.

Budde, Gunilla, Sebastian Conrad, and Oliver Janz (2006). "Preface." In Gunilla Budde, Sebastian Conrad, and Oliver Janz (eds.), *Transnationale Geschichte: Themen, Tendenzen und Theorien*, 11–14. Göttingen: Vandenhoeck & Ruprecht.

Bugra, Ayse and Kaan Agartan (2007). *Reading Karl Polanyi for the Twenty-First Century: Market Economy as a Political Project.* New York: Palgrave Macmillan.

Burawoy, Michael (2003). "For a Sociological Marxism: The Complementary Convergence of Antonio Gramsci and Karl Polanyi." *Politics and Society* 31 (2): 193–261.

– (2007). "Public Sociology vs. the Market." *Socio-Economic Review* 5, (2): 356–367.

– (2010). "From Polanyi to Pollyanna: The False Optimism of Global Labor Studies." *Global Labour Journal* 1 (2): 301–313.

– (2015). "Facing an Unequal World." *Current Sociology* 63 (1): 5–34.

Burrows, Edwin G. and Mike Wallace (1999). *Gotham: A History of New York City to 1898*. New York et al.: Oxford University Press.

Büsch, Otto (1971). *Industrialisierung und Gewerbe im Raum Berlin/Brandenburg*, vol. 1: 1800–1850, Eine empirische Untersuchung zur gewerblichen Wirtschaft einer hauptstadtgebundenen Wirtschaftsregion in frühindustrieller Zeit, Einzelveröffentlichungen der Historischen Kommission zu Berlin, vol 9. Berlin: Colloquium.

Cahill, Marion C. (1932). *Shorter Hours: A Study of the Movement since the Civil War.* New York: Columbia University Press.

Caporaso, James and Sidney Tarrow (2007). "Polanyi in Brussels: European Institutions and the Embedding of Markets in Society." Prepared for presentation at the Penn/Temple European Studies Colloquium, November 27.

Cashman, Sean Dennis (1993). *America in the Gilded Age: From the Death of Lincoln to the Rise of Theodore Roosevelt*, 3rd ed. New York and London: New York University Press.

Cohen, Deborah and Maura O'Connor (2004). "Introduction: Comparative History, Cross-National History, Transnational History, Definitions." In Deborah Cohen and Maura O'Connor (eds.), *Comparison and History: Europe in Cross-National Perspective*, ix–xxiv. New York and London: Routledge.

Commons, John R., David J. Saposs, Helen L. Sumner, E.B. Mittelman, H.E. Hoagland, John B. Andrews, and Selig Perlman (eds.) (1918). *History of Labour in the United States*, vol. 2. New York: Macmillan.

– and John B. Andrews (1958). "Introduction to Volumes IX and X." In John R. Commons, Ulrich B. Phillips, Eugene A. Gilmore, Helen L. Sumner, and John

B. Andrews (eds.), *A Documentary History of American Industrial Society*, vol. 9, 19–51. New York: Russell & Russell.

Conze, Werner (1972). "Arbeit." In Otto Brunner, Werner Conze, and Reinhart Koselleck (eds.), *Geschichtliche Grundbegriffe*, vol. 1, 154–215. Stuttgart: Klett-Cotta.

Cooper, Patricia A. (1987). *Once a Cigar Maker: Men, Women, and Work Culture in American Cigar Factories, 1900–1919*, The Working Class in American History Series. Urbana et al.: University of Illinois Press.

– (1979). "What Ever Happened to Adolph Strasser?" *Labor History* 20 (3): 414–419.

Corliss, Paul and Samuel Duncan Parnell (2008). *A Legacy: The 8 Hour Day, Labour Day and Time Off.* Christchurch: Purple Grouse Press & Unions Canterbury.

Cross, Gary S (1988). "Worktime and Industrialization: An Introduction." In Gary S. Cross (ed.), *Worktime and Industrialization: An International History*, Labor and Social Change Series, 3–19. Philadelphia: Temple University Press.

– (1989). *The Quest for Time: The Reduction of Work in Britain and France, 1840–1940.* Berkeley et al.: University of California Press.

Dale, Gareth (2010). *Karl Polanyi: The Limits of the Market*, Key Contemporary Thinkers Series. Oxford et al.: Polity Press.

Davis, Lance Edwin and Robert J. Cull (1994). *International Capital Markets and American Economic Growth, 1820–1914.* Cambridge et al.: Cambridge University Press.

Demps, Laurenz (2001). "Die Kaiserstadt: Das Königlich-Preußische Berlin." In Julius H. Schoeps and Bildarchiv Preußischer Kulturbesitz (eds.), *Berlin: Geschichte einer Stadt*, 84–119. Berlin: be.bra.

Deutschmann, Christoph (1985). *Der Weg zum Normalarbeitstag: Die Entwicklung der Arbeitszeiten in der deutschen Industrie bis 1918*, Studienreihe des Instituts für Sozialforschung Frankfurt am Main. Frankfurt et al: Campus.

– and Gisela Dybowski-Johannson (1979). "Wirtschaftliche und soziale Determinanten der Arbeitszeitpolitik." Mitteilungen aus der Arbeitswelt- und Berufsforschung 12 (3): 313–327.

Dietrich, Richard (1981). "Berlins Weg zur Industrie- und Handelsstadt." In Richard Dietrich (ed.), *Berlin: Zehn Kapitel seiner Geschichte*, 2nd ed., 159–198. Berlin and New York: de Gruyter.

Dlubek, Rolf and Evgenija Akimovna Stepanova (1964). *Die I. Internationale in Deutschland (1864–1872): Dokumente und Materialien.* Berlin (East): Dietz.

Douglas, Dorothy W. (1932). "Ira Steward on Consumption and Unemployment." *Journal of Political Economy* 40 (4): 532–543.

Dowe, Dieter (1970). *Aktion und Organisation: Arbeiterbewegung, Sozialistische und Kommunistische Bewegung in der Preußischen Rheinprovinz 1820–1852*, Schriftenreihe des Forschungsinstituts der Friedrich-Ebert-Stiftung, vol. 78. Hannover: Verlag für Literatur und Zeitgeschehen.

– (1978). "Die deutsche Sozialdemokratie von den Anfängen bis zum ersten Weltkrieg." In Karl Josef Rivinius (ed.), *Die soziale Bewegung im Deutschland des neunzehnten Jahrhunderts*, 37–60. Munich: Moos.

– (ed.) (1980). *Berichte über die Verhandlungen der Vereinstage deutscher Arbeitervereine 1863 bis 1869*, Reprints zur Sozialgeschichte. Berlin and Bonn: J.H.W. Dietz Nachf.

DuBois, Ellen Carol (1978). *Feminism and Suffrage: The Emergence of an Independent Women's Movement in America, 1848–1869.* Ithaca and London: Cornell University Press.

Eichengreen, Barry (2008). *Globalizing Capital: A History of the International Monetary System.* Princeton, N.J: Princeton University Press.

Enstad, Nan (1999). *Ladies of Labor, Girls of Adventure: Working Women, Popular Culture, and Labor Politics at the Turn of the Twentieth Century*, Popular Cultures, Everyday Lives Series. New York: Columbia University Press.

Erbe, Michael (1988). "Berlin im Kaiserreich, 1871–1918." In Wolfgang Ribbe (ed.), *Geschichte Berlins*, vol. 2: Von der Märzrevolution bis zur Gegenwart, 691–793. Munich: C.H. Beck.

Ernst, Robert (1965). *Immigrant Life in New York City, 1825–1863.* Port Washington, N.Y.: Ira J. Friedman.

Escher, Felix (1985). *Berlin und sein Umland: Zur Genese der Berliner Stadtlandschaft bis zum Beginn des 20. Jahrhunderts*, Einzelveröffentlichungen der Historischen Kommission zu Berlin, vol. 47. Berlin: Colloquium.

Espagne, Michel (1994). "Sur les limites du comparatisme en histoire culturelle." *Genèses* 17: 112–121.

Esping-Andersen, Gøsta (1990). *The Three Worlds of Welfare Capitalism.* Princeton, N.J.: Princeton University Press.

Evans, Peter (2000). "Fighting Marginalization with Transnational Networks: Counter-Hegemonic Globalization." *Current Sociology* 29: 230–241.

– (2005). "Counter-Hegemonic Globalization: Transnational Social Movements in the Contemporary Global Political Economy." In Thomas Janoski, Alexander M. Hicks, Mildred A. Schwartz, and Robert R. Alford (eds.), *The Handbook of Political Sociology: States, Civil Societies and Globalization*, 655–670. Cambridge, Mass. et al.: Cambridge University Press.

– (2008). "Is an Alternative Globalization Possible?" *Politics and Society* 36 (2): 271 305.

Evans, Richard J. (1979). *The Feminists: Women's Emancipation Movements in Europe, America and Australasia 1840–1920*, paperback ed. London: Croom Helm.

– (1987). *Death in Hamburg: Society and Politics in the Cholera Years, 1830–1910.* Oxford and New York: Clarendon Press and Oxford University Press.

– (1989). *Kneipengespräche im Kaiserreich: die Stimmungsberichte der Hamburger Politischen Polizei 1892–1914.* Reinbek bei Hamburg: Rowohlt.

Federici, Silvia (2012). *Revolution at Point Zero: Housework, Reproduction, and Feminist Struggle.* Brooklyn and Oakland: Common Notions and PM Press.

Feis, Herbert (1924). "The Attempt to Establish the Eight-Hour Day by International Action." *Political Science Quarterly* 39 (3 and 4): 373–413 and 624–649.

Feldenkirchen, Wilfried (1997). *Siemens: Von der Werkstatt zum Weltunternehmen.* Munich et al.: Piper.

Fine, Sidney (1953). "The Eight-Hour Day Movement in the United States, 1888–1891." *The Mississippi Valley Historical Review* 40 (3): 441–462.

Foner, Eric (1984). "Why Is There No Socialism in the United States?" *History Workshop* 17: 57–80

– (1995). *Free Soil, Free Labor, Free Men: The Ideology of the Republican Party Before the Civil War.* New York: Oxford University Press.

Foner, Philip S. (1947). *History of the Labor Movement in the United States*, vol. 1: From Colonial Times to the Founding of the American Federation of Labor. New York: International Publishers.

– and Brewster Chamberlin (eds.) (1977). *Friedrich A Sorge's Labor Movement in the United States: A History of the American Working Class from Colonial Times to 1890.* Westport, Conn. and London: Greenwood.

Fraser, Nancy (1995). "From Redistribution to Recognition? Dilemmas of Justice in a 'Postsocialist' Age." *New Left Review* 212: 68–93

– (1998). *Social Justice in the Age of Identity Politics: Redistribution, Recognition, Participation.* WZB Discussion Paper, No. FS I 98-108.

– (2009). "Feminism, Capitalism and the Cunning of History." *New Left Review* 56: 97–117.

– (2011). "Marketization, Social Protection, Emancipation: Toward a Neo-Polanyian Conception of Capitalist Crisis." In Craig Calhoun and Georgi Derluguian (eds.), *Business as Usual: The Roots of the Global Financial Meltdown*, Possible Futures Series, 137–157. New York and London: New York University Press.

– and Axel Honneth (2003). *Redistribution or Recognition? A Politcal-Philosophical Exchange*, trans. by Joel Golb, James Imgram, and Christiane Wilke. London and New York: Verso.

– and Linda Gordon (1992). "Contract versus Charity: Why Is There no Social Citizenship in the United States?" *Socialist Review* 22: 45–68.

Fricke, Dieter (1987). *Handbuch zur Geschichte der deutschen Arbeiterbewegung 1869 bis 1917*, vol. 1. Berlin (East): Dietz.

Galenson, Walter (1983). *The United Brotherhood of Carpenters: The First Hundred Years.* Cambridge, Mass.: Harvard University Press.

Gemkow, Heinrich (1959). "Zur Tätigkeit der Berliner Sektion der I. Internationale." *Beiträge zur Geschichte der deutschen Arbeiterbewegung* 3: 515–531.

Glasner, David (1997). "Crisis of 1873." In David Glasner and Thomas F. Cooley (eds.), *Business Cycles and Depressions: An Encyclopedia*, 132–134. New York: Garland.

Glickstein, Jonathan A. (1979). "'Poverty Is Not Slavery:' American Abolitionists and the Competitive Labor Market." In Lewis Perry and Michael Fellman, *Antislavery Reconsidered: New Perspectives on the Abolitionists*, 195–218. Baton Rouge: Louisiana State University Press.

Goff, Jacques Le (1984). *Für ein anderes Mittelalter: Zeit, Arbeit und Kultur im Europa des 5.–15. Jahrhunderts*. Frankfurt et al.: Ullstein.

Grebing, Helga (2007). *Geschichte der deutschen Arbeiterbewegung: Von der Revolution 1848 bis ins 21. Jahrhundert*. Berlin: vorwärts.

Green, Nancy L. (2004). "Forms of Comparison." In Deborah Cohen and Maura O'Connor (eds.), *Comparison and History: Europe in Cross-National Perspective*, 41–56. New York and London: Routledge.

Groyens, Tom (2007). *Beer and Revolution: The German Anarchist Movement in New York City, 1880–1914*. Urbana et al.: University of Illinois Press.

Gutman, Herbert G. and Ira Berlin (1987). "Class Composition and the Development of the American Working Class, 1840–1890." In Herbert G. Gutman (ed.), *Power and Culture: Essays on the American Working Class*, 380–394. New York: Pantheon Books.

Hachtmann, Rüdiger (1997). *Berlin 1848: Eine Politik- und Gesellschaftsgeschichte der Revolution*, Veröffentlichungen des Instituts für Sozialgeschichte e.V. Bonn: J.H.W. Dietz Nachf.

Halbert, Debora (2005). "Resistance Is Fertile: The Commodification of Life and Environmental Protest in the 21st Century." Paper presented at the 4th Annual Conference on Environmental Justice and Global Citizenship, Mansfield College, Oxford, July 5.

Hallgrimsdottir, Helga Kristin and Cecilia Benoit (2007). "From Wage Slaves to Wage Workers: Cultural Opportunity Structures and the Evolution of the Wage Demands of the Knights of Labor and the American Federation of Labor, 1880–1900." *Social Forces* 85 (3): 1393–1411.

Hann, C. M. and Keith Hart (2009). *Market and Society: The Great Transformation Today*. Cambridge and New York: Cambridge University Press.

Harvey, Mark, Ronnie Ramlogan, and Sally Randles (eds.) (2007). *Karl Polanyi: New Perspectives on the Place of the Economy in Society*. Manchester and New York: Manchester University Press.

Haslam, Nick (2006). "Dehumanization: An Integrative Review." *Personality and Social Psychology Review* 10 (3): 252–264.

Haupt, Heinz-Gerhard and Jürgen Kocka (2010). "Comparison and Beyond: Traditions, Scope, and Perspective of Comparative History." In Heinz-Gerhard Haupt and Jürgen Kocka (eds.), *Comparative and Transnational History: Central European Approaches and New Perspectives*, 1–30. New York: Berghahn Books.

Henderson, William O. (1976) *The Life of Friedrich Engels*, vol. 2. London and New York: Routledge.

Hentschel, Volker (1975). *Die deutschen Freihändler und der Volkswirtschaftliche Kongreß 1858 bis 1885*, Industrielle Welt: Schriften des Arbeitskreises für moderne Sozialgeschichte, vol. 16. Stuttgart: Ernst Klett.

Hermann, Christoph (2008). "Kampf um die Arbeitszeit: Ein Überblick." *PROKLA: Zeitschrift Für Kritische Sozialwissenschaft* 38 (1): 83–102.

Herzfeld, Hans (1981). "Berlin auf dem Wege zur Weltstadt." In Richard Dietrich (ed.), *Berlin: Zehn Kapitel seiner Geschichte*, 2nd ed., 239–271. Berlin and New York: de Gruyter.

Hicks, Obadiah (1896). *Life of Richard F. Trevellick, the Labor Orator, or the Harbinger of the Eight-Hour System.* Joliet, Ill.: J.E. Williams.

Hillquit, Morris (1971). *History of Socialism in the United States*, 5th ed. New York: Dover.

Hobsbawm, Eric J. (1952). "The Machine Breakers." *Past and Present* 1: 57–70.

Hoffrogge, Ralf (2011). *Sozialismus und Arbeiterbewegung in Deutschland: Von den Anfängen bis 1914.* Stuttgart: Schmetterling.

Holm, Andrej and Leo Kühberger (eds.) (2014). *Wohnraum ist keine Ware! Sozialer Wohnbau: Geschichte, Kämpfe, Perspektiven.* Vienna: Mandelbaum.

Honneth, Axel (2008). *Reification: A New Look at an Old Idea.* New York et al.: Oxford University Press.

Hornbeck, Stanley K. (1909). "The Eight Hour Day on Public Work in New York." *The American Political Science Review* 3 (2): 214–217.

Jacobi, Otto, Eberhard Schmidt, and Walther Müller-Jentsch (eds.) (1980). *Arbeitskampf um Arbeitszeit: Kritisches Gewerkschaftsjahrbuch 1979/1980.* Berlin: Rotbuch.

Janiewski, Dolores (1976). "Making Common Cause: The Needlewomen of New York, 1831–1869." *Signs* 1 (3): 777–786.

Jansz, Ulla (1995). "Women or Workers? The 1889 Labor Law and the Debate on Protective Legislation in the Netherlands." In Ulla Wikander, Alice Kessler-Harris, and Jane Lewis (eds.), *Protecting Women: Labor Legislation in Europe, the United States, and Australia, 1880–1920*, 188–209. Urbana: University of Illinois Press.

Jenaczek, Friedrich (ed.) (1970). *Ferdinand Lassalle: Reden und Schriften.* Munich: dtv.

Kaelble, Hartmut (2005). "Die Debatte über Vergleich und Transfer und was jetzt?" *H-Soz-U-Kult*, February 8, http://hsozkult.geschichte.hu-berlin.de/forum/id=574&type=artikel (accessed 25 November 2014).

Karsten, Luchien (1990). *De Achturendag: Arbeidstijdverkorting in Historisch Perspectief, 1817–1919*, IISG Studies, vol. 14. Amsterdam: Stiching beheer IISG.

Katznelson, Ira (1986). "Working-Class Formation: Constructing Cases and Comparisons." In Ira Katznelson and Aristide R. Zolberg (eds.), *Working-Class Formation: Nineteenth-Century Patterns in Western Europe and the United States*, 3–42. Princeton: Princeton University Press.

Kelsey, Jan (2000). "Polanyi Revisited: Globalisation and its Contradictions in the New Millennium." In Martin Richardson (ed.), *Globalisation and International Trade Liberalisation: Continuity and Change*, 170–183. Cheltenham and Northampton, MA: Edward Elgar.

Kessler-Harris, Alice (2003). *Out of Work: A History of Wage-Earning Women in the United States.* 20th anniv. ed. New York et al.: Oxford University Press.

Keynes, John Maynard (1935). *The General Theory of Employment Interest and Money.* New York: Harcourt, Brace and Company.

Kimber, Julie and Peter Love (2007). *The Time of Their Lives: The Eight Hour Day and Working Life*. Melbourne: Australian Society for the Study of Labour History.

Kocka, Jürgen (1975). "Von der Manufaktur zur Fabrik: Technik und Werkstattverhältnisse bei Siemens 1847–1873." In Karin Hausen and Reinhard Rürup (eds.), *Moderne Technikgeschichte*, Neue Wissenschaftliche Bibliothek, vol. 81, 267–290. Cologne: Kiepenheuer & Witsch.

– (1990). *Arbeitsverhältnisse und Arbeiterexistenzen: Grundlagen der Klassenbildung im 19. Jahrhundert*, Geschichte der Arbeiter und der Arbeiterbewegung in Deutschland seit dem Ende des 18. Jahrhunderts, vol. 2. Bonn: J.H.W. Dietz Nachf.

– (2003). "Comparison and Beyond." *History and Theory* 42: 39–44.

– and Claus Offe (eds.) (2000). *Geschichte und Zukunft der Arbeit*. Frankfurt a.M.: Campus.

Kosak, Hadassa (2000). *Cultures of Opposition: Jewish Immigrant Workers, New York City, 1881–1905*. Albany: State University of New York Press.

Kuritz, Hyman (1956). "Ira Steward and the Eight Hour Day." *Science and Society* 20 (2): 118–134.

Kutz-Bauer, Helga (1988). *Arbeiterschaft, Arbeiterbewegung und bürgerlicher Staat in der Zeit der Grossen Depression: Eine regional- und sozialgeschichtliche Studie zur Geschichte der Arbeiterbewegung im Grossraum Hamburg, 1873–1890*. Bonn: Neue Gesellschaft.

Lange, Annemarie (1972). *Berlin zur Zeit Bebels und Bismarcks: Zwischen Reichsgründung und Jahrhundertwende*. Berlin (East): Dietz.

Laufenberg, Heinrich (1911). *Geschichte der Arbeiterbewegung in Hamburg, Altona und Umgebung*, vol. 1 and 2. Hamburg: Auer.

Laurie, Bruce (1997). *Artisans into Workers: Labor in Nineteenth-Century America*. Urbana and Chicago: University of Illinois Press.

Lenger, Friedrich (1986). *Zwischen Kleinbürgertum und Proletariat: Studien zur Sozialgeschichte der Düsseldorfer Handwerker 1816–1878*, Kritische Studien zur Geschichtswissenschaft, vol. 71. Göttingen: Vandenhoeck & Ruprecht.

Linebaugh, Peter (2008). *The Magna Carta Manifesto: Liberties and Commons for All*. Berkeley: University of California Press.

Losseff-Tillmanns, Gisela (1978). *Frauenemanzipation und Gewerkschaften*. Wuppertal: Peter Hammer.

Lucas, Erhard (1983). *Vom Scheitern der deutschen Arbeiterbewegung*. Basel and Frankfurt: Stroemfeld/Roter Stern.

Lukács, Georg (1970). *Geschichte und Klassenbewusstsein: Studien über Marxistische Dialektik*, 6th ed., vol. 11. Darmstadt and Neuwied: Luchterhand.

Machtan, Lothar (1984). *Streiks und Aussperrungen im Deutschen Kaiserreich: Eine sozialgeschichtliche Dokumentation für die Jahre 1871 bis 1875*, Historische Kommission zu Berlin, Beihefte zur Internationalen wissenschaftlichen Korrespondenz zur Geschichte der deutschen Arbeiterbewegung, vol 9. Berlin: Colloquium.

Marcuse, Peter (2008). "The Housing Change We Need." *Shelterforce* 156: 26–29.

Mayer, Gustav (1970). *Johann Baptist von Schweitzer und die Sozialdemokratie: Ein Beitrag zur Geschichte der deutschen Arbeiterbewegung*, Reprint. Glashütten im Taunus: Detlev Auvermann.

McRobbie, Kenneth and Kari Polanyi-Levitt (eds.) (2005). *Karl Polanyi in Vienna: The Contemporary Significance of The Great Transformation*, 2nd ed., Critical Perspectives on Historic Issues, vol. 8. Montreal and New York: Black Rose Books.

Mendell, Marjorie (2001). "A Karl Polanyi Revival." *Canadian Dimension* 35 (2): 48–50.

Messer-Kruse, Timothy (1998). *The Yankee International: Marxism and the American Reform Tradition, 1848–1876*. Chapel Hill and London: University of North Carolina Press.

– (2001). "Eight Hours, Greenbacks and 'Chinamen:' Wendell Phillips, Ira Steward, and the Fate of Labor Reform in Massachusetts." *Labor History* 42 (2): 133–158.

Michels, Tony (2005). *A Fire in Their Hearts: Yiddish Socialists in New York*. Cambridge, et al.: Harvard University Press.

Mirola, William A. (1995). *Fighting in the Pews and Fighting in the Streets: Protestantism, Consciousness and the Eight-Hour Movement in Chicago, 1867–1912*. PhD Diss. Indiana University.

– (2003). "Asking for Bread, Receiving a Stone: The Rise and Fall of Religious Ideologies in Chicago's Eight-Hour Movement." *Social Problems* 50 (2): 273–293.

Mizen, Paul (ed.) (2003). *Monetary History, Exchange Rates and Financial Markets: Essays in Honour of Charles Goodhart*, vol. 2. Cheltenham, UK: Edward Elgar.

Molloy, Scott (2004). "Eight-Hour Movement." In Robert E. Weir and James P. Hanlan (eds.), *Historical Encyclopedia of American Labor*, 153. Westport, CT and London: Greenwood Press.

Montgomery, David (1967). *Beyond Equality: Labor and the Radical Republicans, 1862–1872*. New York: Alfred A. Knopf.

– (1987). *The Fall of the House of Labor: The Workplace, the State, and American Labor Activism, 1865–1925*. Cambridge: Cambridge University Press

– (1993). *Citizen Worker: The Experience of Workers in the United States with Democracy and the Free Market during the Nineteenth Century*. Cambridge et al.: Cambridge University Press.

Morton, Adam (2007). *Unravelling Gramsci: Hegemony and Passive Revolution in the Global Economy*. London and Ann Arbor, MI: Pluto Press.

Munck, Ronaldo (2006). "Globalization and Contestation: A Polanyian Problematic." *Globalizations* 3 (2): 175–186.

Murphy, Teresa (1988). "Work, Leisure, and Moral Reform: The Ten-Hour Movement in New England, 1830–1850." In Gary S. Cross (ed.), *Worktime and Industrialization: An International History*, Labor and Social Change Series, 59–76. Philadelphia: Temple University Press.

– (1992). *Ten Hours' Labor: Religion, Reform, and Gender in Early New England*. Ithaca et al.: Cornell University Press.

Na'aman, Shlomo (1969). *Demokratische und soziale Impulse in der Frühgeschichte der deutschen Arbeiterbewegung der Jahre 1862/63*, Institut für europäische Geschichte Mainz. Wiesbaden: F. Steiner.

– (1976). *Von der Arbeiterbewegung zur Arbeiterpartei: Der fünfte Vereinstag der deutschen Arbeitervereine zu Nürnberg im Jahre 1868, Eine Dokumentation*, Historische Kommission zu Berlin, Beiheft zur internationalen wissenschaftlichen Korrespondenz der deutschen Arbeiterbewegung (IWK) 4. Berlin: Colloquium.

– (1980). "Arbeitervereine, Arbeitertage und Arbeiterverband: Drei Etappen auf dem Weg zur Arbeiterpartei." In Dieter Dowe (ed.), *Berichte über die Verhandlungen der Vereinstage deutscher Arbeitervereine 1863 bis 1869*, Reprints zur Sozialgeschichte, ix–li. Berlin and Bonn: J.H.W. Dietz Nachf.

Nadel, Stanley (1990). *Little Germany: Ethnicity, Religion, and Class in New York City, 1845–80*. Urbana: University of Illinois Press.

Negrey, Cynthia L. (2012). *Work Time: Conflict, Control, and Change*. Cambridge et al.: Polity Press.

Newton-Matza, Mitchell (2004). "Eight-Hour Day Movement." In Immanuel Ness (ed.), *Encyclopedia of American Social Movements*, 521. Armonk, NY: Sharpe.

Niland, John (2008). "The Birth of the Movement for an Eight Hour Working Day in New South Wales." *Australian Journal of Politics and History* 14 (1): 75–87.

Nipperdey, Thomas (1993). *Deutsche Geschichte 1866–1918*, vol. 2: Machtstaat vor der Demokratie. Munich: C.H.Beck.

Nolte, Paul (1994). "Der Durchbruch der amerikanischen Marktgesellschaft: Wirtschaft, Politik und Kultur in der frühen Republik (1790–1850)." *Historische Zeitschrift* 259 (3): 695–716.

– (1996). "Amerikanische Sozialgeschichte in der Erweiterung: Tendenzen, Kontroversen und Ergebnisse seit Mitte der 1980er Jahre." *Archiv für Sozialgeschichte* 36: 363–394.

Notz, Gisela (1985). "Mehr Zeit zum Schaffen, Träumen, Kämpfen: Für eine feministische Arbeitszeitpolitik." In Eckart Hildebrandt, Eberhard Schmidt, and Hans Joachim Sperling (eds.), *Arbeit zwischen Gift und Grün, Kritisches Gewerkschaftsjahrbuch 1985*, 127–137. Berlin: Rotbuch.

Obschernitzki, Doris (1987). *"Der Frau ihre Arbeit!" Lette-Verein: zur Geschichte einer Berliner Institution, 1866 bis 1986*, Stätten der Geschichte Berlins, vol. 16. Berlin: Ed. Hentrich.

Offe, Claus (2006). "Staatstheorie und Sozialpolitik: Funktionen und Innovationsprozesse der Sozialpolitik." In Jens Borchert and Stephan Lessenich (eds.), *Strukturprobleme des kapitalistischen Staates: Aufsätze zur politischen Soziologie*, revised ed., 153–180. Frankfurt a.M.: Campus.

Offermann, Toni (2002). *Die erste deutsche Arbeiterpartei: Materialien zur Organisation, Verbreitung und Sozialstruktur von ADAV und LADAV 1863–1871*, Archiv für Sozialgeschichte, vol. 22. Bonn: J.H.W. Dietz Nachf.

Oncken, August (1886). *Die Maxime laissez faire et laissez passer, ihr Ursprung, ihr Werden: Ein Beitrag zur Geschichte der Freihandelslehre*, Berner Beiträge zur Geschichte der Nationalökonomie, vol. 2. Bern: K. J. Wyß.

Otto, Karl A. (1989) *Die Arbeitszeit! Von der vorindustriellen Gesellschaft bis zur "Krise der Arbeitsgesellschaft,"* vol. 2. Pfaffenweiler: Centaurus, 1989.

Paeplow, Fritz (1932). *Zur Geschichte der deutschen Bauarbeiterbewegung: Werden des Deutschen Bauarbeiterbundes*. Berlin: Deutscher Bauhandwerksbund.

Paffhausen, Jürgen (2012). "Fortschreibung des Bevölkerungsbestandes." *Zeitschrift für amtliche Statistik Berlin Brandenburg* 1/2: 88–92.

Paschen, Joachim (1977). *Demokratische Vereine und preußischer Staat: Entwicklung und Unterdrückung der demokratischen Bewegung während der Revolution von 1848/49*, Studien zur Modernen Geschichte, vol. 22. Munich et al.: Oldenbourg.

Pattillo, Mary (2013). "Housing: Commodity versus Right." *Annual Review of Sociology* 39 (1): 509–531.

Peiss, Kathy L. (1986). *Cheap Amusements: Working Women and Leisure in Turn-of-the-Century New York*. Philadelphia: Temple University Press.

Perlman, Selig (1949). *A Theory of the Labor Movement*, Reprint. New York: Augustus M. Kelly.

Piketty, Thomas (2014). "Das Ende des Kapitalismus im 21. Jahrhundert?" *Blätter für deutsche und internationale Politik* 59 (12): 41–52.

Polanyi, Karl (1957). "The Economy as Instituted Process." In Karl Polanyi, Conrad M. Arensberg, and Harry W. Pearson (eds.), *Trade and Market in the Early Empires: Economies in History and Theory*, 243–270. Chicago: Henry Regnery.

– (1971). *Primitive, Archaic, and Modern Economics: Essays of Karl Polanyi*. George Dalton (ed.). Boston: Beacon Press.

– (2001). *The Great Transformation: The Political and Economic Origins of Our Time*, 2nd paperback ed. Boston, Mass.: Beacon Press.

Pollard, Sidney (1963). "Factory Discipline in the Industrial Revolution." *The Economic History Review*, New Series, 16 (2): 254–271.

Postel, Verena (2009). *Arbeit und Willensfreiheit im Mittelalter*, Vierteljahrschrift für Sozial- und Wirtschaftsgeschichte, vol. 207. Stuttgart: Steiner.

Prodnik, Jernej (2012). "A Note on the Ongoing Processes of Commodification: From the Audience Commodity to the Social Factory." *tripleC* 10 (2): 274–301.

Reed, Merl E. (1984). "Strasser, Adolph." In Gary M. Fink (ed.), *Biographical Dictionary of American Labor*, 2nd ed., 532–533. Westport, Conn. and London: Greenwood Press, 1984.

Reick, Philipp (2014). "We are the 99%: Zum Selbstbild der deutschen und amerikanischen Arbeiterbewegung in der Mitte des 19. Jahrhunderts." *Nebulosa: Figuren des Sozialen* 06: 89–98.

Renzsch, Wolfgang (1978). "Einleitung." In Wolfgang Renzsch (ed.), *Agitator*, vol. 1–2, Reprints zur Sozialgeschichte, v–xiv. Berlin and Bonn: J.H.W. Dietz Nachf.

– (1980). *Handwerker und Lohnarbeiter in der frühen Arbeiterbewegung: Zur sozialen Basis von Gewerkschaften und Sozialdemokratie im Reichsgründungsjahrzehnt.* Göttingen: Vandenhoeck & Ruprecht.

Reulecke, Jürgen (1976). "Vom Blauen Montag zum Arbeiterurlaub: Vorgeschichte und Entstehung des Erholungsurlaubs für Arbeiter vor dem Ersten Weltkrieg." *Archiv für Sozialgeschichte* 16: 205–248.

– (1998). "Die Vereinsbewegung für das Wohl der arbeitenden Klassen." In Ottfried Dascher and Everhard Kleinertz (eds.), *Petitionen und Barrikaden: Rheinische Revolutionen 1848/49*, 47–54. Münster: Aschendorff.

Richter, Günter (1987). "Zwischen Revolution und Reichsgründung, 1848–1870." In Wolfgang Ribbe (ed.), *Geschichte Berlins*, vol. 2: Von der Märzrevolution bis zur Gegenwart, 605–687. Munich: C.H. Beck.

Ritter, Gerhard A. and Klaus Tenfelde (1992). *Arbeiter im Deutschen Kaiserreich 1871 bis 1914,* Geschichte der Arbeiter und der Arbeiterbewegung in Deutschland seit dem Ende des 18. Jahrhunderts, vol. 5. Bonn: J.H.W. Dietz Nachf.

Rock, Howard (1988). "Independent Hours: Time and the Artisan in the New Republic." In Gary S. Cross (ed.), *Worktime and Industrialization: An International History*, Labor and Social Change Series, 21–39. Philadelphia: Temple University Press.

Roediger, David R. (1980). *The Movement for a Shorter Working Day in the United States before 1866.* PhD diss., Northwestern University.

– (1986). "Ira Steward and the Anti-Slavery Origins of American Eight-Hour Theory." *Labor History* 27 (3): 410–426.

– (2007). *The Wages of Whiteness: Race and the Making of the American Working Class*, Haymarket Series, revised ed. London and New York: Verso.

– and Philip S. Foner (1989). *Our Own Time: A History of American Labor and the Working Day*, Haymarket Series. London and New York: Verso.

Rosenzweig, Roy (1985). *Eight Hours for What We Will: Workers and Leisure in an Industrial City, 1870–1920.* Cambridge: Cambridge University Press.

Rößler, Johannes (1957). *Zur Lage der Berliner Arbeiter und ihrer sozialistischen Bewegung vom Gründerkrach bis zu den Reichstagswahlen im Jahre 1881.* PhD diss., Hochschule für Ökonomie Berlin.

Scharf, Günter (1987). *Geschichte der Arbeitszeitverkürzung: Der Kampf der deutschen Gewerkschaften um die Verkürzung der täglichen und wöchentlichen Arbeitszeit*, Schriftenreihe der Otto Brenner Stiftung, vol. 40. Cologne: Bund.

Schmiede, Rudi (1980). "Die Entwicklung der Arbeitszeit in Deutschland." In Otto Jacobi, Eberhard Schmidt, and Walther Müller-Jentsch (eds.), *Arbeitskampf um Arbeitszeit*, Kritisches Gewerkschaftsjahrbuch 1979/1980, 71–87. Berlin: Rotbuch.

Schmitt, Sabine (1995). "'All These Forms of Women's Work Which Endanger Public Health and Public Welfare:' Protective Labor Legislation for Women in Germany, 1878–1914." In Ulla Wikander, Alice Kessler-Harris, and Jane Lewis (eds.), *Protecting Women: Labor Legislation in Europe, the United States, and Australia, 1880–1920*, 125–149. Urbana and Chicago: University of Illinois Press, 1995.

– (1995). *Der Arbeiterinnenschutz im deutschen Kaiserreich: Zur Konstruktion der schutzbedürftigen Arbeiterin*, Ergebnisse der Frauenforschung, vol. 37. Stuttgart and Weimar: J.B. Metzler.

Schneider, Dorothee (1994). *Trade Unions and Community: The German Working Class in New York City, 1870–1900*. Urbana: University of Illinois Press.

Schneider, Michael (1984). "Der Kampf um die Arbeitszeitverkürzung von der Industrialisierung bis zur Gegenwart." *Gewerkschaftliche Monatshefte* 35 (2): 77–89.

Schoeps, Julius H. (2001). "Berlin wird Weltstadt: Zwischen Jahrhundertwende und Reichsgründung." In Julius H. Schoeps and Bildarchiv Preußischer Kulturbesitz (eds.), *Berlin: Geschichte einer Stadt*, 54–83. Berlin: be.bra.

Schröder, Wilhelm H. (1978). *Arbeitergeschichte und Arbeiterbewegung: Industriearbeit und Organisierungsverhalten im 19. und frühen 20. Jahrhundert*. Frankfurt and New York: Campus.

Silver, Beverly J. (2008). *Forces of Labor: Workers' Movements and Globalization since 1870*, Cambridge Studies in Comparative Politics. Cambridge et al.: Cambridge University Press.

Smith, Mark M. (1998). *Debating Slavery: Economy and Society in the Antebellum American South*. Cambridge: Cambridge University Press.

Sombart, Werner (1906). *Warum gibt es in den Vereinigten Staaten keinen Sozialismus?* Tübingen: Mohr.

Spehr, Michael (2000). *Maschinensturm: Protest und Widerstand gegen technische Neuerungen am Anfang der Industrialisierung*, Theorie und Geschichte der Bürgerlichen Gesellschaft, vol. 18. Münster: Westfälisches Dampfboot.

Stanley, Amy Dru (1998). *From Bondage to Contract: Wage Labor, Marriage, and the Market in the Age of Slave Emancipation*. Cambridge: Cambridge University Press.

– (2014). "Slave Emancipation and the Sovereign Market: Human Rights in America." Paper presented at the conference Rethinking Capitalist Crisis, Berlin, November 4–5.

Stansell, Christine (1986). *City of Women: Sex and Class in New York, 1789–1860*, Borzoi Book. New York: Alfred A. Knopf.

Steinisch, Irmgard (1986). *Arbeitszeitverkürzung und sozialer Wandel: Der Kampf um die Achtstundenschicht in der deutschen und amerikanischen Eisen- und Stahlindustrie 1880–1929*, Veröffentlichungen der Historischen Kommission zu Berlin, vol. 65. Berlin et al.: de Gruyter, 1986.

Steinmetz, Willibald (2002). *Begegnungen vor Gericht: Eine Sozial- und Kulturgeschichte des englischen Arbeitsrechts, 1850–1925*, Veröffentlichungen des Deutschen Historischen Instituts London, vol. 51. Munich: Oldenbourg.

Stott, Richard B. (1990). *Workers in the Metropolis: Class, Ethnicity, and Youth in Antebellum New York City*. Ithaca et al.: Cornell University Press.

Stöver, Bernd. (2010). *Geschichte Berlins*. Munich: C.H. Beck.

Stowell, Charles J. (1918). *The Journeymen Tailors' Union of America: A Study in Trade Union Policy*, University of Illinois Studies in the Social Sciences, vol. 7 (4). Urbana: The University of Illinois.

Stuhlberger Wjuniski, Bernardo and Ramón G. Fernandez (2010). "Karl Polanyi, Athens and Us: The Contemporary Significance of Polanyi's Thought." *Revista de Economia Política* 30 (3): 420–437.

Sylvers, Malcom (2005). "Marx, Engels und die USA: Ein Forschungsprojekt über ein wenig beachtetes Thema." In *Marx-Engels-Jahrbuch 2004*, 31–53. Berlin: Akademie.

Tenfelde, Klaus (1987). "Die Entstehung der deutschen Gewerkschaftsbewegung vom Vormärz bis zum Ende des Sozialistengesetzes." In Ulrich Borsdorf (ed.), *Geschichte der deutschen Gewerkschaften von den Anfängen bis 1945*, 15–165. Cologne: Bund.

– and Gerhard A. Ritter (eds.) (1981). *Bibliographie zur Geschichte der deutschen Arbeiterschaft und Arbeiterbewegung 1863 bis 1914, Berichtszeitraum 1945 bis 1976*, Archiv für Sozialgeschichte, vol. 8. Bonn: Neue Gesellschaft.

Therborn, Goran (2007). *What Does the Ruling Class Do When It Rules? State Apparatuses and State Power under Feudalism, Capitalism and Socialism*. London: Verso.

Thomasberger, Claus (2005). "Karl Polanyi: Vom Philosophischen Ökonom zum Historiker der Gegenwart." In Jürgen G. Backhaus (ed.), *Historische Schulen*, Wirtschaft: Forschung und Wissenschaft, vol. 11. Münster: LIT.

Thompson, Edward P. (1967). "Time, Work-Discipline, and Industrial Capitalism." *Past and Present* 38: 56–97.

– (1971). "The Moral Economy of the English Crowd in the 18th Century." *Past and Present 50*: 76–136.

– (1991). *The Making of the English Working Class*, Reprint. London et al.: Penguin.

Tracy, George A. (1913). *History of the Typographical Union: Its Beginnings, Progress and Development, Its Beneficial and Educational Features*. Indianapolis: International Typographical Union.

Tsuzuki, Chushichi (1971). "Robert Owen and Revolutionary Politics." In Sidney Pollard and John Salt (eds.), *Robert Owen, Prophet of the Poor: Essays In Honour of The Two Hundredth Anniversary of His Birth*, 13–38. Lewisburg: Bucknell University Press.

Twellmann, Margrit (1993). *Die deutsche Frauenbewegung: Ihre Anfänge und erste Entwicklung 1843–1889*, Athenäums Studienbuch Geschichte. Frankfurt a. M.: Hain.

Ullrich, Volker (1976). *Die Hamburger Arbeiterbewegung vom Vorabend des Ersten Weltkrieges bis zur Revolution 1918/19*. Hamburg: Lüdke.

Weatherford, Doris (1986). *Foreign and Female: Immigrant Women in America, 1840–1930*. New York: Schocken.

Weaver, Stewart (1988). "The Political Ideology of Short Time: England, 1820–1850." In Gary S. Cross (ed.), *Worktime and Industrialization: An International History*, Labor and Social Change Series, 77–102. Philadelphia: Temple University Press.

Wecker, Regina (1997). "Normalarbeitstag, Gesundheitsschutz und Nachtarbeitsverbot: Zwischen Schutz und Konstruktion von Weiblichkeit und Männlichkeit." In Hansjörg Siegenthaler (ed.), *Wissenschaft und Wohlfahrt: Moderne Wissenschaft und ihre Träger in der Formation des Schweizerischen Wohlfahrtsstaates während der zweiten Hälfte des neunzehnten Jahrhunderts*, 217–238. Zurich: Chronos.

Wehler, Hans-Ulrich (2008). *Deutsche Gesellschaftsgeschichte*, vol. 3: Von der "Deutschen Doppelrevolution" bis zum Beginn des Ersten Weltkrieges, 1849–1914. 3rd ed. Munich: C.H. Beck.

Weipert, Axel (2013). *Das Rote Berlin: Eine Geschichte der Berliner Arbeiterbewegung*. Berlin: Berliner Wissenschaftsverlag.

Welskopp, Thomas (1994). *Arbeit und Macht im Hüttenwerk: Arbeits- und industrielle Beziehungen in der deutschen und amerikanischen Eisen- und Stahlindustrie von den 1860er bis zu den 1930er Jahren*, Veröffentlichungen des Instituts für Sozialgeschichte e.V. Bonn: J.H.W. Dietz Nachf.

– (2000). *Das Banner der Brüderlichkeit: Die deutsche Sozialdemokratie vom Vormärz bis zum Sozialistengesetz*, Politik- und Gesellschaftsgeschichte, vol. 54. Bonn: J.H.W. Dietz Nachf.

– (2005). "Markt und Klasse in der deutschen Sozialdemokratie, 1848–1878." In *Marx-Engels-Jahrbuch* 2004, 9–30. Berlin: Akademie.

– (2005). Review of "Die erste deutsche Arbeiterpartei: Organisation, Verbreitung und Sozialstruktur von ADAV und LADAV 1863–1871" by Toni Offermann. *Vierteljahrschrift für Sozial- und Wirtschaftsgeschichte* 92 (3): 357–359.

– (2009). "Birds of a Feather: A Comparative History of German and US Labor in the Nineteenth and Twentieth Centuries." In Jürgen Kocka and Heinz-Gerhard Haupt (eds.), *Comparative and Transnational History: Central European Approaches and New Perspectives*, 149–177. New York and Oxford: Berghahn Books.

Werner, Michael and Bénédicte Zimmermann (2002). "Vergleich, Transfer, Verflechtung: Der Ansatz der Histoire Croisée und die Herausforderung des Transnationalen." *Geschichte und Gesellschaft 28* (4): 607–636

– (2006). "Beyond Comparison: Histoire Croisée and the Challenge of Reflexivity." *History and Theory* 45: 30–50.

Whaples, Robert (2001). "Hours of Work in US History." *EH.net Encyclopedia*, Economic History Association, http://eh.net/encyclopedia/hours-of-work-in-u-s-history/ (accessed 7 August 2015).

Wiedfeldt, Otto (1898). *Statistische Studien zur Entwicklungsgeschichte der Berliner Industrie von 1720 bis 1890*, Staats- und sozialwissenschaftliche Forschungen, vol. 69. Leipzig: Duncker & Humblot.

Wilentz, Sean (1997). "Society, Politics, and the Market Revolution, 1815–1848." In Eric Foner (ed.), *The New American History*, 61–84. Philadelphia: Temple University Press.

– (2004). *Chants Democratic: New York City and the Rise of the American Working Class, 1788–1850*. 20th anniv. ed. New York et al.: Oxford University Press.

Willke, Gerhard (2002). *John Maynard Keynes*. Frankfurt a. M.: Campus.

Wolff, Wilhelm (1926). *Der 8-Stunden-Tag: Seine Geschichte und die Erfahrungen mit seiner gesetzlichen Einführung in Deutschland.* Berlin: Verlagsgesellschaft des Allgemeinen Deutschen Gewerkschaftsbundes.

Yellowitz, Irwin (1978). "Eight Hours and the Bricklayers' Strike of 1868 in New York City." In Irwin Yellowitz (ed.), *Essays in the History of New York City: A Memorial to Sidney Pomerantz*, Interdisciplinary Urban Series, 78–100. Port Washington, N.Y. and London: Kennikat Press.

Zetkin, Clara (1906). *Die Anfänge der proletarischen Frauenbewegung in Deutschland*, Quellenedition zur Geschichte der deutschen Arbeiterbewegung, Projekt 2: Proletarische Frauenbewegung, Der Neue Welt-Kalender, 64–70.

– (1984). *Zur Geschichte der proletarischen Frauenbewegung Deutschlands.* 3rd ed. Frankfurt a. M.: Marxistische Blätter.

Zinn, Howard (2003). *A People's History of the United States.* 5th ed., Modern Classics. New York et al.: Harper Collins.

Index of Subjects

Index of Persons